THE ADMINISTRATION OF THE COLONIES

A Da Capo Press Reprint Series

THE ERA OF THE AMERICAN REVOLUTION

GENERAL EDITOR: LEONARD W. LEVY

Claremont Graduate School

THE ADMINISTRATION OF THE COLONIES

Wherein Their Rights and Constitution are Discussed and Stated

By Thomas Pownall

DA CAPO PRESS · NEW YORK · 1971

51917

A Da Capo Press Reprint Edition

This Da Capo Press edition of
The Administration of the Colonies
is an unabridged republication of the fourth
edition published in London in 1768.

Library of Congress Catalog Card Number 79-146155
SBN 306-70123-5

Published by Da Capo Press
A Division of Plenum Publishing Corporation
227 West 17th Street, New York, N.Y. 10011
All Rights Reserved

Manufactured in the United States of America

THE ADMINISTRATION OF THE COLONIES

THE
ADMINISTRATION
OF THE
COLONIES.

(THE FOURTH EDITION.)

WHEREIN THEIR

RIGHTS AND CONSTITUTION

Are difcuffed and ftated,

By THOMAS POWNALL,

Late Governor and Commander in Chief of his
his Majefty's Provinces, Maffachufetts-Bay and
South-Carolina, and Lieutenant-Governor of
New-Jerfey.

---

*Pulchrum eft benefacere Reipublicæ, etiam bene-
dicere haud abfurdum eft.* SALLUSTIUS.

LONDON:

Printed for J. WALTER, at Homer's Head,
Charing-Crofs. MDCCLXVIII.

TO THE RIGHT HONOURABLE

GEORGE GRENVILLE, Efq;

SIR,

WHEN I firſt publiſhed my opinions upon the adminiſtration of the Colonies, I addreſſed the book to you. You was then miniſter in this country, and had taken an active and leading part in the adminiſtration of thoſe affairs. I did not by that addreſs dedicate, as is the uſual phraſe, my opinions to the miniſter, for our opinions differed on ſeveral points: But as diſputes upon a queſtion, pregnant with the moſt dangerous conſequences, began to be agitated between the miniſter of this country and the Coloniſts, which I ſaw muſt ſoon extend themſelves in contentions

A 3   with

with-parliament itself: As I saw a spirit of suspicion and alarm arising, a temper of ill blood infusing itself into the minds of men; I endeavoured to obviate these mischiefs, by marking in that address, that, as there were neither arbitrary intentions on one hand against the liberties of the Colonies, nor rebellious designs on the other against the just imperium of government; so there was a certain good temper and right spirit, which, if observed on all sides, might bring these matters of dispute to such a settlement as political truth and liberty are best established upon.

You had conceived, that government hath a right to avail itself in its finances, of the revenues of all its dominions, and that the imposing taxes, by parliament, for the said purpose, was the constitutional mode of doing this. The Colonists who were not represented in parliament by knights and burgesses of their own election, " did appre-
" hend, they had reason to fear some dan-
" ger of arbitrary rule over them, when
" the supreme power of the nation had
" thought

" thought proper to impofe taxes on his
" Majefty's American fubjects, with the
" fole and exprefs purpofe of raifing a re-
" venue, and without their confent."

Parliament had, by a folemn act, declared
that it hath a right to make laws, which
fhall be binding upon the people of the
Colonies, fubjects of Great Britain, in *all
cafes whatfoever*,—while the Colonifts fay,
in *all cafes which can confift with the fundamental rules of the conftitution*; by which
limitation, they except the cafe of taxation,
where there is not reprefentation. Hence
the Colonifts have, by many, been deemed
factious, undutiful and difloyal, and even
chargeable with treafon itfelf.———

I had been fufficiently converfant in thefe
affairs, although neither employed nor con-
fulted in them, fince I left America, to
know that thefe alternate charges were falfe
and groundlefs; that there were neither
arbitrary intentions on one hand, nor fedi-
tious views on the other. As therefore, by
my addrefs, I meant to do juftice to your
principles, which I knew to be thofe of

A 4

peace

peace and government eftablifhed on political liberty,—fo I took that occafion, as I will ever efteem it a duty to do, to bear my teftimony to the affection which the Colonifts ever bore to the mother country, to their zeal for its welfare, to their fenfe of government and their loyalty to their fovereign, as alfo how much they have merited from this country, and how much they deferve to be confidered by it, in order to put thefe matters of difpute on a footing of reconciliation, fair difcuffion and equitable fettlement.——

It is great pity that queftions of this nature were ever raifed, * " for, it is a very " unfafe thing in fettled governments, to " argue the reafon of the fundamental con-" ftitutions."—But when contrary propofitions are alternately brought forward by the reprefentatives of two people, as the avowed principles of their refpective conftituents ; when an inferior government, which invariably acknowledges its dependence on a fupe-

* Comm. Journal 16$\frac{3}{7}$2.

rior

rior and fupream government, thinks it hath a right to call into queftion fome particular exertions of power in that government, by rules which limit the extent of that power, it is abfolutely neceffary to decide fuch queftion, or to give fuch explanations of the matter, that it may ceafe to be a queftion ;— for fo long as it continues in doubt, the parties will alternately charge each other with arbitrary principles, and a fpirit of fedition, with tyranny and rebellion ;——and frequent injurious acts of violence, which numberlefs events will ever give occafion to, muft neceffarily be animated with a fpirit too nearly allied to the one and to the other. —The matter is in that ftate that it ought to come before parliament, it muft, it will,— it is neceffary to the fupport of government that it fhould ;—it is neceffary to the fecurity of the nation and its intereft ;—it is neceffary to the peace, liberties, and conftitution of the Colonies; it is neceffary to the fafety of minifters.

Many matters therefore, the publication of which I had fufpended, while I thought
that

that this queſtion might be waved, or ſome way compromiſed, I now publiſh in this edition. I continue my addreſs, Sir, to you, now you are no longer miniſter, nor perhaps ever likely to be. I addreſs myſelf to the private country gentleman, who will alway have a great ſhare in the buſineſs of his country;—to Mr. George Grenville, as to one who hath, and alway will have great intereſt, lead and authority in parliament, from an opinion really and deeply grounded in the minds of the moſt ſerious of his countrymen, that, while for the ſake of the peace and liberties of the whole, he means to ſupport the conſtitutional powers of government in the crown ; ſo is he equally, by principle, determined, as by abilities able, to guard the civil rights of the ſubjects with a peculiar regard to, and management of, their intereſts in their property.

This American queſtion, in which liberty and the rights of property are ſo deeply engaged, muſt now come forward. From the part which you have already taken, you muſt ſtill bear a conſiderable part in the debates

bates and confultations which will be held upon it. I therefore addrefs, to your moft ferious confideration, that ftate of this bufinefs which the following book contains; nor will I defpair of your affent to what fo firmly eftablifhes the rights of property, on the foundations of liberty, by an equal extenfion and communication of government, to wherefoever the people and dominions, having thefe rights, do extend. In the matters which I propofe, I fpeak my own fentiments, not yours. I addrefs them to your ferious confideration, as I do to every man of bufinefs in the nation, with an hope that from conviction of the juftice, policy and neceffity of the meafure, they may become the general fentiments of the government, and of the people of Great Britain. From the fame fentiments, and with the fame view of general peace and liberty, I could wifh to recommend the fame propofitions to the Americans. Nor would I defpair of their affent to things, were there no jealoufies of, no prejudices againft men. I am convinced that thefe maxims are true in theory, and do fincerely believe, that they are the only

prin-

principles, by which the peace, the civil liberty, and commercial profperity of the Britifh dominions can be maintained and fupported. I am no Partizan. I do not palliate the errors of Great Britain. I do not flatter the paffions of America. My zeal and many fervices towards the one, have appeared in the effect of thofe fervices; and my affection to the other, if it be not already known, will be feen, as, under the accident of a certain event, I mean to end my days there in a private character.

I have, in this prefent edition, gone into the difcuffion of this matter, *as it lies in fact,* and as it hath, at the firft fettlement of the Colonies, and in the different periods of their progrefs, *exifted in right,* eftablifhed on fuch fact. I have ftated the fact, and the right, in hopes to point out what is the true and conftitutional relation between Great Britain and the American Colonies, what is the precife ground on which this dangerous queftion ought to be fettled: How far they are to be governed by the vigour of external principles, by the fupreme fuperintending power of the mother country: How far, by by the vigour of the internal principles of their own peculiar body politic: And what ought to be the mode of adminiftration, by which they are to be governed in their legiflative, executive, judicial and commercial departments, in the conduct of their money and revenues in their power of making peace or war.——

Analyfing by the experience of fact, this inquiry,——I mark the falfe policy which derives by neceffary confequence from ftating the Colonies, as fubject only to the King in his feignoral capacity.——I fhow alfo that no precedents can be drawn from that period, when the two houfes of parliament affumed the exercife of the fovereignty, and confidered the Colonies *as their fubjects.*—I fhow how the Colonies ought to be confidered as parts of the realm, and by fhowing the perplexities in reafoning, and the dangerous confequences in practice, which attend the ftating of the Colonies as without, and no part of the realm, at the fame time that they are ftated as fubjects of the King, Lords and Commons collectively taken as fovereign. I mark the falfe ground and fuperftructure of that pofition.

In

In the courfe of this reafoning, while I
ftate the rights of the Colonifts, as thofe
of Englifhmen, to all intents and purpofes;
while I ftate *how* the Colonies have been
adminiftered, as diftinct, free communities,
and *how* they ought ftill to be adminiftered,
if they are not united to the realm.——I
fhow that the Colonies, although without
the limits of the realm, are yet in fact, of
the realm; are *annexed*, if not yet *united*
parts of the realm; are precifely in the
predicament of the counties Palatine of Durham and Chefter; and therefore ought, in
the fame manner, to be *united* to the realm,
in a full and abfolute communication and
communion of all rights, franchifes and
liberties, which any other part of the realm
hath, or doth enjoy, or ought to have and
to enjoy: in communication of the fame
burthens, offices, and emoluments, in communion of the fame foedoral and commercial rights, in the fame exercife of judicial
and executive powers,—in the fame participation of council.—And that therefore,
in the courfe and procedure of our government with the Colonies, there muft arife a
duty

duty in government to give, a right in the Colonies to claim, a ſhare in the legiſlature of Great-Britain, by having Knights and Burgeſſes of their own election, repreſenting them in parliament.

It makes no difference in the matter of the truth, whether the government of England ſhould be averſe to the extending of this privilege to the Colonies, or whether the Colonies ſhould be averſe to the receiving of it:—Whether we, from pride and jealouſy, or they, from fears and doubts, ſhould be repugnant to this union. For, whether we reaſon from *experience* and the authority of *example:* Or whether we conſider the policy, juſtice, and neceſſity of the meaſure, the concluſion is unavoidably the ſame; the propoſition invariably *true.* That *the Britiſh iſles, with our poſſeſſions in the Atlantic and in America, are in* FACT, UNITED INTO A ONE GRAND MARINE DOMINION: *And ought therefore, by policy, to be united into a one Imperium, in a one center, where the ſeat of government is.* And ought to be governed from thence, by

an

an adminiſtration founded on the baſis of the whole, and adequate and efficient to the whole.

I have not ſtated the neceſſity of this meaſure, for reaſons which cannot but be obvious to any prudent man; but I have ventured to affirm, that ſuch is the actual ſtate of the ſyſtem of the Britiſh dominions, that neither the power of government, over theſe various parts, can long continue under the preſent mode of adminiſtration; nor the great intereſt of commerce, extended throughout the whole, long ſubſiſt under the preſent ſyſtem of the laws of trade.

As I do, from my beſt judgment, ſin-cerely believe, that a general and intire union of the Britiſh dominions, is the only meaſure by which Great Britain can be continued in its political liberty, and com-mercial proſperity, perhaps in its exiſtence: So I make no ſcruple to averr, that if this meaſure be not adopted in *policy*, as it really exiſts in *fact*, it will ſoon become the duty of the ſeveral diſunited parts, to look nar-rowly

rowly to, and ftand firm in, the mainte-
nance of their undoubted rights in that ftate
and relation, in which the adminiftration
of government fhall hold them. As I have
pointed out the mode, how government
may purfue its duty, confiftent with the
fundamentals of the conftitution; fo have
I fuggefted, through every ftep, how the
American may fortify himfelf in thefe rights,
confiftent with his alliance.

When I had firft an opportunity of con-
verfing with, and knowing the fentiments
of, the * commiffioners of the feveral provinces in North America, convened at
Albany; of learning from their experience
and judgment, the actual ftate of the American bufinefs and intereft; of hearing
amongft them, the grounds and reafons of
that *American union* which they then had
under deliberation, and tranfmitted the plan
of to England: I then firft conceived the
idea, and faw the neceffity of a general

* Appointed by their refpective provinces, to attend
a congrefs at Albany, in 1754, to which they were
called by the crown.

Britifh

Britifh union. I then firft mentioned my
fentiments on this fubject to feveral of thofe
commiffioners,—and at that time, firft
propofed my confiderations on a general
plan of union,——I had the fatisfaction to
find many of the meafures, which I did
then propofe, adopted; and the much
greater fatisfaction of feeing the good effect
of them: But this particular meafure was
at that time, I dare fay, confidered as
theory and vifion, and perhaps may, at
this time, be thought fo ftill: but every
event that hath fince arifen, every meafure
which hath fince been taken, through every
period of bufinefs in which I have been
concerned, or of which I have been cogni-
fant, hath confirmed me in my idea of the
ftate of things, and of the truth of the meafure: At this period, every man of bufinefs
in Britain, as well as in America, fees the
effect of this ftate of things, and may, in
future, fee the neceffity of this meafure.
The whole train of events, the whole courfe
of bufinefs, muft perpetually bring forward
into practice, and neceffarily in the end,
into eftablifhment—*either an American or a
Britifh union.*—There is no other alternative,
the

the only confideration which remains to every good man, who loves the peace and liberties of mankind, is whether the one or the other fhall be forced into exiftence, by the violence of parties, and at the hazard of events; or whether by the deliberate legiflative advice of the reprefentative of all who are concerned.——

May both the Briton and the American take this confideration to heart: and, whatever be the fate of parties and factions, of patriots or minifters, may the true government of laws prevail, and the rights of men be eftablifhed in political liberty.

With the higheft efteem and regard, I have the honour to be,

Sir,

Your moft obedient humble fervant,

T. POWNALL.

ADVERTISEMENT.

THAT I may obviate thofe prejudices by which many people might be led to think, that the doctrines and reafonings contained in the following book are novel, and theories of imagination : That I may at leaft crave a fufpenfion of thofe opinions, from whence many people pronounce, that the application made by th Colonies, to deprecate the levying of taxes, when impofed by parliament, is unconftitutional and unprecedented : I have here inferted, as publifhed by Daniel King in 1656, the record of a like application from the county palatine of Chefter in the like cafe. With the King's anfwer, and ordinance made out in form. Wherein not only fimilar reafonings are exhibited, but a precedent alfo is holden forth. By which, government, on one

hand,

hand, may fee, that this county Palatine was exempted from taxes laien by parliament, while the faid county had not Knights and Burgeffes of their own election, to reprefent them in parliament: and wherein the Colonies may fee on the other hand, by purfuing the precedents relative to this county, that when it was thought proper and advifeable to fubject it to taxes impofed by parliament, the privilege of fending Knights and Burgeffes to parliament was the proper and conftitutional remedy fought and obtained.

Copy

Copy of a Supplication, exhibited to King Henry VI. by the inhabitants of the County Palatine of Chefter.

To the KING, our Sovereign Lord. Anno D. 1450.

MOST Chriftian Benigne, and Gracious King; We your humble fubjects, and true obaifant liege people, the Abbots, Priors, and all the clergy; your Barons, Knights, and Efquires; and all the Commonalty of your County Palatine of Chefter, meekly prayen and befeechen your Highnefs: Where the faid county is, and hath been a county palatine, as well before the conqueft of England, as continually fince, diftinct and feparate from the crown of England: within which county, you, and

a 4　　　　　　all

all your noble progenitors fithen it came into your hands, and all rulers of the fame,
before that time, have had your high courts
of parliment to hold at your wills, your chancery, your exchequer, your juftice to hold
pleas, as well of the crown, as of common
pleas. And by authority of which parliament, to make or to admit laws within the
fame, fuch as be thought expedient and
behovefull for the weal of you, of the
inheritors, and inheritance of the faid county.
And no inheritors or poffeffioners within the
faid county, be not chargeable, lyable, nor
have not been bounden, charged nor hurt,
of their bodies, liberties, franchifes, land,
goods, nor poffeffions, within the fame
county, [*_but by fuch laws as they_] have agreed
unto. And for the more proof and plain
evidence of the faid franchifes, immunities,

* The above is a literal tranfcript of the Record
as publifhed by Daniel King. I have not the means
of confulting the original, there is certainly fome
omiffion or default in the copy. I have inferted the
words, _but by fuch laws as they_, printed between hooks.
I fee no other way of making fenfe of it. I have alfo
in the fame manner between hooks inferted the words
be wrong.

and

and freedoms; The most victorious King
William the conqueror your most noble
progenitor, gave the same county to Hugh
Loup his nephew, to hold as freely to him
and to his heirs *by the sword*; as the same
King should hold all England *by the crown*.
Experience of which grant, to be so in all
appeals and records, out of the same; where,
at your common-law it is written, contra
coronam et dignitatem vestram: It is written
in your time, and your noble progenitors,
sinth the said Earldome came into your hands,
and in all Earls times afore. Contra dignitatem gladii cestriæ. And also they have
no Knights, Citizens, ne Burgesses ne ever
had, of the said county, to any parliament
holden *out of the said* county; whereby they
might, in any way of reason be bounden,
And also ye and your noble progenitors, and
all Earles, whose estate ye have in the said
Earledome; as Earles of Chester, sith the
conquest of England have had within the
same; regalem, potestátum, jura regalia, præ-
rogativa regia. Which franchises notwithstanding, there be your commissions directed
out to several commissioners of the same
county, for the levy of subsidy, granted by

the commons of your land, in your parliament, late begun at Weftminfter, and ended at Leicefter, to make levy thereof within the faid county, after the form of their grant thereof, contrary to the liberties, freedoms, and franchifes, of the faid county, and inheritance of the fame, at all times, before this time ufed, that pleafe your noble grace, of your bleffed favour, the premifes gracioufly to confider: and alfo, how that we your befeechers, have been as ready of our true hearts, with our goods, at times of need, as other parts of your lands; and alfo ready to obey your laws and ordinances, made, ordained, and admitted within the faid county, and if any thing amongft us [*be wrong*,] ready to be reformed by your Highnefs, by the advice of your councel, within the faid county; and hereupon to difcharge all fuch commiffioners of levy of the faid fubfidy within the faid county, and of your fpecial meer grace, ever, to fee that there be never act in this parliment, nor in any parliment hereafter, holden out of the faid county, made to the hurt of any of the inheritors, or inheritance of the faid county,

3   of

of their bodies, liberties, franchifes, goods, lands, tenements, or poffeffions, being within the faid county. For if any fuch act fhould be made, it were clean contrary, to the liberties, freedoms, immunities, and franchifes of the faid county. And as to the refigning of fuch poffeffions, as it hath liked your Highnefs, to grant unto any of your fubjects: all fuch as have ought of grant within the faid county, will be ready to fur-render their letters pattents, which they have of your grant, for the more honourable keeping of your eftate; as any other perfon or perfons within any other part of your land; or elfe they fhall be avoided by us, under your authority committed unto us, within your faid county. And furthermore, confidering that your befeechers are, and ever have been true, dreading, obaifant, and loving unto you, and of you, as unto you; and of our moft dowted Sovereign Lord, our Earle and natural Lord: We the faid Barons, Knights, Efquires, and Commons, are ready to live and die with you, againft all earthly creatures; and by your licence, to fhew unto your Highnefs, for the gra-cious expedition of this our moft behoveful

peti-

petition. And we the said Abbots, Priors, and clergy, continually to pray to God for your moſt hounerable eſtate, proſperity, and felicity, which we all beſeek God to continue, with as long life to reign, as ever did prince upon people; with iſſue coming of your moſt gracious body, perpetually to raign upon us for all our moſt ſingular joy and comfort.

The Kings will is, to the ſubſidy in this bill contained: Foraſmuch as he is learned, that the beſeechers in the ſame, their predeceſſors, nor anceſtors, have not been charged afore this time, by authority of any parliament holden out of the ſaide county, of any quindiſme, or ſubſidy, granted unto him or any of his progenitors, in any ſuch parliament; That the beſeechers, and each of them be diſcharged of the paying and levy of the ſaid ſubſidy. And furthermore, the King willeth, that the ſaid beſeechers, their ſucceſſors and heirs, have and enjoy all their liberties, freedoms, and franchiſes, as freely and entirely as ever they, their predeceſſors or anceſtors in his time, or in time of his progenitors, had and enjoyed it.——

Pro-

Profecuta fuit ista Billa ad Dominum
Regem per Johannem Manwaring
Militem, Radulphum Egerton,
Robertum Foulshurst, Robertum
Leigh de Adlington, et Johannem
Needham Anno. R. R. H. 6.
post conquestum Anglie vicessimo
nono.

By the King.

TRUSTY and wellbeloved in God,
and trusty and well beloved we greet
you well. And forasmuch as we have
understanding, by a supplication presented
unto us, on the behalf of all our liege people
within our county palatine of Chester: How
their

their predeceſſors nor anceſtors, have not been charged before this time, with any fifteenth or ſubſidy granted unto us, or any of our progenitors, by authority of any parliament, holden out of our ſaid county, for which cauſe, we have charged our chamberlain of our ſaid county, to make our writs, directed to all our commiſſioners, ordained for the aſſeſſing and levy of the ſubſidy laſt granted unto us: Charging them to ſurceaſe of any execution of our letters of commiſſion, made unto them, in that parties. Wherefore, according to our commandment late given by us, unto our ſaid Chamberlain: We will that ye in our behalf, open and declare unto all our ſaid liege-people: How it is our full will and intent, that they be not charged with any ſuch grant, otherwiſe than they, their predeceſſors and anceſtors have been charged afore time. And that they have and hold, poſſide, and enjoy, all their liberties, freedoms, and franchiſes, in as ample and large form, as ever they had in our, or any of our ſaid progenitors days. And that ye fail

fail not thereof, as we truft you, and as you deem to pleafe us.

Given under our fignet of the Eagle, at our pallace of Weftminfter the eighth day of March, Anno. R. R. H. 6. Viceffimo Nono.

To our trufty and wellbeloved in God, the Abbot of our monaftry of Chefter; and to our trufty and wellbeloved Knights Sir Thomas Stanley, our Juftices of Chefter, Sir John Manwaring, and to every of them.

THE

ADMINISTRATION

OF, THE

C O L O N I E S.

THE feveral changes of territories, which at the laſt Peace took place in the Colonies of the European world, have given riſe to a new fyſtem of intereſts, have opened a new channel of buſineſs, and brought into operation a new concatenation of powers, both commercial and political.—This fyſtem of things ought, at this criſis, to be actuated by a fyſtem of politics, adequate and proportionate to its powers and operations : But while we find not any one comprehenſive or preciſe idea of the criſis now ariſing, we ſee that all which is propoſed as meaſures, is by parts, without connection to any whole, by temporary ex-

pedients,

pedients, and shiftings off of prefent dangers, without any reference to that eventual state of things, which muft be the confequence of fuch meafures, and fuch expedients; much lefs by reference to that eventual state of things, by which the true fyftem ought to be framed, and actuated.

This state of the bufinefs has tempted me to hazard my fentiments on the fubject. My particular fituation in time paft gave me early opportunity of feeing and obferving the ftate of things, which have been long leading to this crifis. I have feen and mark'd, where it was my duty, this nafcent crifis at the beginning of the late war, and may affirm, have forefeen and foretold the events that now form it. My prefent fituation by which I ftand unconnected with the politics of miniftry, or of the colonies, opens the faireft occafion to me of giving to the public, whom it concerns, fuch an impartial uninfluenced opinion of what I think to be the right of things, as I am convinced the following sheets contain. I know what effect this conduct will have, what it has had, on this work and on myfelf. I may be thought neither by the miniftry nor the Colonifts to underftand this fubject, the one may call this work the vifion of a theorift, the other will reprefent the doctrine which it contains, as
the

the prejudices of power and ambition. The one may think me an advocate for the politicks of the colonies, the other will imagine me to be an evil counfellor againſt the colonies to the miniſtry : But as I know that my aim is, without any prudential view of pleaſing others, or of my own intereſt, to point out and to endeavour to eſtabliſh an idea of the true intereſt of the colonies, and of the mother country as related to the colonies, I ſhall equally diſregard what varies from this on the one hand, and equally rejeᴄt what deviates from it on the other.

In the firſt uncultur'd ages of Europe, when men fought nothing but to poſſefs, and to fecure poſſeffion, the power of the *ſword* was the predominant ſpirit of the world ; it was that, which formed the Roman empire ; and it was the fame, which, in the declenſion of that empire, divided again the nations into the ſeveral governments formed upon the ruins of it.

When men afterward, from leiſure, began to exerciſe the powers of their minds in (what is called) learning ; religion, the only learning at that time, led them to a concern for their ſpiritual intereſts, and conſequently led them under their ſpiritual guides. The power of *religion* would hence as naturally

pre-

predominate and rule, and did actually become the ruling fpirit of the policy of Europe. It was this fpirit, which, for many ages formed, and gave away kingdoms; this which created the anointed Lords over them, or again excommunicated and execrated thefe fovereigns; this that united and allied the various nations, or plung'd them into war and bloodfhed; this, that formed the ballance of the power of the whole, and actuated the fecond grand fcene of Europe's hiftory.

But fince the people of Europe have formed their communication with the commerce of Afia; have been, for fome ages paft, fettling on all fides of the Atlantic Ocean, and in America, have been poffeffing every feat and channel of commerce, and have planted and raifed that to an intereft which has taken root;---fince they now feel the powers which derive from this, and are extending it to, and combining it with others; the fpirit of *commerce* will become that predominant power, which will form the general policy, and rule the powers of Europe: and hence a grand commercial intereft, the bafis of a great commercial dominion, under the prefent fcite and circumftances of the world, will be formed and arife. The rife and forming of this commercial intereft is what precifely conftitutes the prefent crifis.

The

The European poffeffions and interefts in the Atlantic and in America lye under various forms, in plantations of fugar, tobacco, rice, and indigo, in farms of tillage and pafture, in fifheries, Indian hunts, forefts, naval ftores, and mines; each different fcite produces fome fpecial matter of fupply neceffary to one part of that food and raiment become requifite to the prefent ftate of the world; but is, as to it's own local power of produce, totally deftitute of fome other equally neceffary branch of fupply. The various nature of the lands and feas lying in every degree and afpect of climate, and the fpecial produce and vegetation that is peculiar to each, forms this local limited capacity of produce. At the fame time that nature has thus confined and limited the produce of each individual fcite to one, or at moft to few branches of fupply, at the fame time hath fhe extended the neceffities of each to many branches beyond what its own produce can fupply. The Weft India iflands produce fugar, meloffes, cotton, &c. they want the materials for building and mechanics, and many the neceffaries of food and raiment: The lumber, hides, the fifh, flour, provifions, live-ftock, and horfes, produced in the northern colonies on the continent, muft fupply the iflands with thefe requifites. On the cther hand, the fugar and meloffes of the

fugar

fugar iflands is become a neceffary interme-
diate branch of the North American trade
and fifheries. The produce of the Britifh
fugar iflands cannot fupply bo:h Great Britain
and North America with the neceffary quantity ; this makes the melloffes of the foreign
fugar iflands alfo neceffary to the prefent ftate
of the North American trade. Without Spanifh filver, become neceffary to the circulation of the Britifh American trade, and even
to their internal courfe of fale and purchafe,
not only great part of that circulation muft
ceafe to flow, but the means of purchafing
the manufactures of Great Britain would be
equally circumfcribed : Without the Britifh
fupplies, the Spanifh fettlements would be
fcarce able to carry on their culture, and would
be in great diftrefs. The ordinary courfe of
the labour and generation of the negroes in
the Weft India iflands makes a conftant external fupply of thefe fubjects neceffary, and
this connects the trade of Africa with the Weft
Indies ; the furr and Indian trade, and the
European goods neceffary to the Indian, are
what form the Indian connection.----I do not
enter into a particular detail of all the reci-
procations of thofe wants and fupplies, nor
into a proof of the neceffary interconnections
arifing from thence ; I only mark out the general *traites* of thefe, in order to explain what
I mean when I fay, that by the limitation
of

of the capacities and extent of the neceffities of each, all are interwoven into a neceffary intercourfe of fupplies, and 'all indiffolubly bound in an union and communion of *one general compofite intereft* of the whole of the Spanifh, French, Dutch, Danifh, and Britifh fettlements. This is the *natural ftate* of the European poffeffions in the Atlantic and in America; this general communion is that natural intereft under which, and by which, they muft fubfift. On the contrary, the fpirit of policy, by which the mother countries fend out and on which they eftablifh colonies, being to confine the trade of their refpective colonies folely to their own fpecial intercourfe, and to hold them incommunicable of all other intercourfe or commerce, the *artificial or political ftate* of thefe colonies becomes diftinct from that which is above defcribed as their natural ftate.---The political ftate is that which policy labours to eftablifh by a principle of repulfion; the natural one is that ftate under which they actually exift and move by a general, common, and mutual principle of attraction. This one general intereft thus diftinct muft have fome one general tendency or direction diftinct alfo, and peculiar to its own fyftem. There muft be fome center of thefe compofite movements, fome lead that will predominate and govern in this general intereft---

That

That particular branch of bufinefs and its connections in this general commercial intereft, which is moft extenfive, neceffary, and permanent, fettles and commands the market; and thofe merchants who actuate this branch muft acquire an afcendency, and will take the lead of this intereft. This lead will predominate throughout the general intercourfe, will diffolve the effect of all artificial connections which government would create, and form the natural connections under which thefe interefts actually exift,—will fuperfede all particular laws and cuftoms, and operate by thofe which the nature and actual circumftances of the feveral interefts require. This lead is the foundation of a commercial dominion, which, whether we attend to it or not, will be formed : whether this idea may be thought real or vifionary is of no confequence as to the exiftence and proceffion of this power, for the intereft, which is the bafis of it, is already formed;—yet it would become the wifdom, and is the duty of thofe who govern us, to profit of, to poffefs, and to take the lead of it already formed and arifing faft into dominion; it is our duty fo to interweave thofe nafcent powers into, and to combine their influence with, the fame interefts which actuate our own government; fo to connect and combine the operations of our trade with this intereft, as to partake of

its

its influence and to build on its power. Although this interest may be, as above described, different and even distinct from the peculiar interests of the mother countries, yet it cannot become independent, it must, and will fall under the dominion of *some* of the potentates of Europe. The great question at this crisis is, and the great struggle will be, which of the states of Europe shall be in those circumstances, and will have the vigour and wisdom so to profit of those circumstances, as to take this interest under its dominion, and to unite it to its government. This lead seemed at the beginning of the late war to oscillate between the English and French, and it was in this war that the dominion also hath been disputed. The lead is now in our hands, we have such connection in its influence, that, whenever it becomes the foundation of a dominion, that dominion must be ours.

It is therefore the duty of those who govern us, to carry forward this state of things to the weaving of this lead into our system, that Great Britain may be no more considered *as the kingdom of this Isle only, with many appendages of provinces, colonies, settlements, and other extraneous parts,* but as A GRAND MARINE DOMINION CONSISTING OF OUR POSSESSIONS IN THE ATLANTIC AND

IN

IN AMERICA UNITED INTO A ONE EMPIRE,
IN A ONE CENTER, WHERE THE SEAT OF
GOVERNMENT IS.

As the rising of this crisis above described,
forms precisely the *object* on which government should be employed; so the taking
leading measures towards the forming all
those Atlantic and American possessions into
one Empire of which Great Britain should
be the commercial and political center, is the
precise duty of government at this crisis.

The great minister, whose good fortune shall
have placed him at this crisis, in the administration of these great and important interests—will certainly adopt the system which
thus lies in nature, and which by natural
means alone, if not perverted, must lead to
a general dominion, founded in the general
interest and prosperity of the commercial
world, must build up this country to an extent of power, to a degree of glory and prosperity, beyond the example of any age that
has yet passed;—* *id est viri et ducis non
deesse fortunæ præbenti se, et oblata casu
flectere ad concilium.*

The forming some general system of administration, some plan which should be

* Liv. l. 28. § 44.

(whatever

(whatever may be the changes of the miniftry at home, or in the governors and officers employed abroad) uniformly and per-
manently purfued by meafures founded on
the actual ftate of things as they arife, leading to this great end, *is, at this crifis, the
precife duty of government*. This is an object which ought not to be overlooked or
miftaken. It ought not to be a ftate myftery, nor can be a fecret. If the Spanifh,
French, and Dutch governments can op-
pofe it, they will; but if it be founded in
nature, fuch oppofition will only haften its
completion, becaufe any meafures of policy
which they can take to obftruct it, muft either deftroy the trade of their own colonies, or
break off their connection. If they attempt
to do this by force, they muft firft form an
alliance, and fettle the union of their mutual interefts, and the eventual partition of
the effect of it; but this will prove a matter
of more difficulty, than can eafily be com-
paffed, and under the difadvantages created
thereby, there will be much hazard of the
utmoft effort of their united forces.

To enable the Britifh nation to profit of
thefe prefent circumftances, or of the future
events, as they fhall fucceffively arife in the
natural proceffion of effects, it is neceffary,
that the adminiftration form itfelf into fuch
eftablifhments

eftablifhments for the direction of thefe interefts and powers, as may keep them in their natural channel, as may maintain their due connections with the government, and lead them to the utmoft effect they are capable of producing towards this grand point.

The firft fpring of this direction, the bafis of this government, is the adminiftration at home. If that department of adminiftration, which fhould have the direction of thefe matters, be not wifely and firmly bottomed, be not fo built, as to be a *practical*—be not fo really fupported by the powers of government, as to be an *efficient adminiftration*, all meafures for the adminiftration of thefe interefts, all plans for the government of thefe powers are vain and felf-delufive; even thofe meafures that would regulate the movements and unite the interefts under a practical and efficient adminiftration, become mifchievous meddling impertinencies where that is not, and muft either ruin the interefts of thefe powers, or render a breach of duty neceffary to the colonies that they may avoid that ruin.

That part of government, which fhould adminifter this great and important branch of bufinefs, ought, in the firft place, to be the center of all information and application

from

from all the interefts and powers which form
it; and ought from this center, to be able,
fully, uniformly, and efficiently, to diftri-
bute its directions and orders. Wherever
the wifdom of ftate fhall determine that this
center of information fhall be fixed; from
whatever department all appointments, orders, and executive adminiftration fhall iffue,
it ought fomewhere to be fixed, known,
of record, and undivided; that it may not
be partial, it ought to extend to all times,
and all cafes. All application, all communication, all information fhould center immediately and folely in this department: this
fhould be the fpring of all nominations, inftructions, and orders.——It is of little confequence where this power of adminiftration
is placed, fo that the department be fuch, as
hath the means of the knowledge of its bufinefs—is fpecially appropriated to the attention
neceffary to it—and officially fo formed as to
be in a capacity of executing it. Whether
this be a Secretary of State, or the Board of
Trade and Plantations, is of no confequence;
but it ought to be entirely in either the one
or the other. Where the power for the direction is lodged, there ought all the knowledge of the department to center; therefore
all officers, civil or military, all fervants of
the government, and all other bodies or private perfons ought to correfpond immediately

ly with this department, whether it be the
Secretary of State or the Board of Trade.
While the military correfpond with the Secretary of State, the civil in one part of their
office with the Secretary of State, in another
with the Board of Trade; while the navy
correfpond in matters not merely naval with
the Admiralty, while the engineers correfpond with the Board of Ordnance, officers of the revenue with the feveral boards
of that branch, and have no communication
with the department which has, or ought
to have, the general direction and adminiftration of this great Atlantic and American,
this great commercial intereft, who is to collect? who does, or ever did collect, into a
one view, all thefe matters of information
and knowledge? What department ever
had, or could have, fuch general direction
of it, as to difcufs, compare, rectify and
regulate it to an official real ufe? In the
firft place, there never was yet any one department form'd for this purpofe; and in
the next, if there was, let any one acquainted with bufinefs dare to fay, how any
attempt of fuch department would operate
on the jealoufies of the others. Whenever, therefore, it is thought proper (as
moft certainly it will, fome time or other,
tho' perhaps too late) to form fuch department, it muft (if I may fo exprefs myfelf)

be

be fovereign and fupreme, as to every thing relating to it; or to fpeak plainly out, *muſt be a ſecretary of ſtate's office in itſelf.* When ſuch is form'd, although the military, naval, ordnance, and revenue officers, ſhould correſpond, in the matters of their reſpective duties, with the departments of government to which they are more immediately ſubordinate and reſponſible, yet, in general matters of information, or points which are matters of government, and the department of this ſtate office, they ſhould be inſtructed to correſpond and communicate with this miniſter. Suppoſe that ſome ſuch miniſter or office now exiſted, is it not of conſequence that he ſhould be acquainted with the Geography of our new acquiſitions? If, therefore, there have been any actual ſurveys made of them, ſhould not ſuch, or copies of ſuch, be ſent to this miniſter or office? If a due and official information of any particular conduct in our colonies, as to their trade, might lead to proper regulations therein, or might point out the neceſſity of a reviſion of the old laws, or the making further proviſion by new ones, would it not be proper that the cuſtom-houſe officers ſettled there ſhould be directed to correſpond and communicate with this miniſter, or office, on theſe points? Would it interfere with their due ſubordination, as officers of

the

the ~~revenue, to the~~ commiffioners of the cuftoms?—If there were any events arifing, or any circumftances exifting, that might affect the ftate of war or peace, wherein the immediate application of military operations were not neceffary or proper, fhould not the military and naval officers be directed to communicate on thefe matters with this mi-nifter, or office? Should not, I fay, all thefe matters of information come officially before this minifter, if any fuch ftate mini-fter, or office, was eftablifhed?

As of information and knowledge centering in a one office, fo alfo of power of execut-ing, it fhould fpring from one undivided department. Where the power of nomi-nating and difmiffing, together with other powers, is feparated from the power of di-recting, the firft muft be a mere privilege or perquifite of office, ufelefs as to the king's bufinefs or the intereft of his colonies, and the latter muft be inefficient. That office, which neither has the means of information, nor can have leifure to attend to the official knowledge produced thereby, nor will be at the trouble to give any official directions, as to the ordinary courfe of the adminiftra-tion of the American matters, muft certainly be always, as it is, embarraffed with the power of nomination, and fetter'd with the

8

chain

chain of applications, which that power drags after it. On the other hand, what effect will any instructions, orders or directions, have from that board, which has not interest to make or dismiss one of the meanest of its own officers : this, which is at present the only official channel, will be despised ; the governors, nay, every the meanest of the officers in the plantations, looking up solely to the *giving power*, will scarce correspond with the *directing*—nay, may perhaps contrive to make their court to the one, by passing by the other. And in any case of improper conduct of these officers, of any neglect of duty, or even of misdemeanour ; what can this directing power do, but complain to the minister who nominates, against the officers appointed by him? If there be no jealousies, no interfering of interests, no competitions of interfering friends, to divide and oppose these two offices to each other : if the minister is not influenced to continue, upon the same motives upon which he first appointed ; if he does not see these complaints in a light of opposition to his nomination and interest ; some redress may, after a due hearing between the party and the office, be had ;—the authority of the board may be supported, and a sort of remedy applied to the special business, but a remedy worse than the disease—a remedy that

C   dishonours

difhonours that board, and holds it forth to the contempt of thofe whom it ought to govern.

It is not only from the natural impracticability of conducting this administration under a divided State of power and direction, that the neceffity of forming a fome one ftate office, or minifter of ftate, for the executing it arifes: but the very nature of the bufinefs of this department, makes the officer who is to adminifter it a ftate officer, a minifter for that department, and who ought to have immediate accefs to the clofet. I muft here repeat, that I am no partizan of the Secretary of State's office, or for the Board of Trade: I have ceafed to have any connection of bufinefs with either, and have not the leaft degree of communication with the one or the other. Without reference, therefore, to either, but with all deference to both, I aim to point out, that the department of the adminiftration of Trade and plantations, be it lodged where it may, fhould be a State office, and have a minifter of ftate. That office, or officer, in a commercial nation like this, who has the cognizance and direction (fo far as government can interfere) of the general trade of the kingdom—whofe duty it is to be the depofitory and reporter of the ftate and condition of it; of every thing
which

which may advance or obftruct it, of the
ftate of manufactures, of the fifheries, of the
employment of the poor, of the promoting
the labour and riches of the country, by ftu-
dying and advifing every advantage, that can
be made of every event which arifes in commercial politics, every remedy, which can
remove any defect or obftruction;—who is
officially to prepare every provifion or revifion neceffary in the laws of trade, for the
confideration of parliament; and to be the
conductor of fuch thro' the neceffary meafures—is certainly an officer of ftate, if the
Secretary of State, fo call'd, is. That office,
or officer, who has cognizance and direction of the plantations in every point of
government, in every matter judicial or commercial; who is to direct the fettlements of
colonies, and to fuperintend thofe already
fettled; who is to watch the plantations in
all thefe points, fo far as they ftand related
to the government, laws, courts and trade
of the mother country——is certainly an
officer of ftate, if the Secretary of State, fo
called, is. That office or officer, who is to
report to his Majefty in council on all thefe
points; whofe official *fiat*, or negative, will
be his Majefty's information in council, as
to the legiflature in the colonies—is certainly
an officer of ftate. That office, or officer,
who is to hear and determine on all matters

of

of complaint, and mal-adminiftration, of the crown officers and others, in the plantations; and can examine witneffes on oath ---is furely an officer of ftate. That office, or officer, who is to correfpond with all the fervants of the crown on thefe points, and to be the iffuer of his Majefty's orders and inftructions to his fervants, on thefe many, great, and important points of ftate—is certainly his Majefty's fecretary, and certainly a fecretary of ftate.

But if it be confidered further, who the perfons are, that are of this very great and extenfive commiffion of the Board of Trade and Plantations; namely, all the great officers of ftate for the time being, with the bifhop of London, the fecretaries of ftate for the time being, and thofe more efpecially called the commiffioners of trade, it will be feen, that it is no longer a doubt or a queftion, as to its being an office of ftate: it is actually fo; and has, as an office, as a board, immediate accefs to his Majefty in council, even to the reporting and recommending of officers. This was the plan whereon it was originally founded, at its firft inftitution, by Lord Sommers.

That great ftatefman and patriot faw that all the powers of government, and feveral departments

departments of adminiftration difunited,
were interfering with, and obftruding each
other on this fubject, and not they only here
in England, but that the refpective officers
of thefe feveral departments carried all this
diftraction into the detail of their bufinefs in
the colonies, which I am afraid is too much
the cafe even at this day : he faw that this
adminiftration could not be conducted but
by an intire union of all the powers of government, and on that idea formed the
board of trade and plantations, where, and
where alone, thefe powers were *united in a
one office.* In which office, and in which
alone, all the bufinefs of the colonies ought
therefore to be adminiftred; for if fuch union
be neceffary, here alone is that *official union.*
Unhappily for the true intereft of government, partly from an intire neglect of this
adminiftration in time paft, and partly from
the defective partial exercife of it, fince fome
idea of thefe matters began again to revive,
this great and wife plan hath been long
difufed ; but it is fortunate for the public in
this important crifis, that fuch is the temper of particulars, fuch the zeal of all for
his Majefty's fervice, fuch the union of his
fervants, that the fpirit of fervice predomi-
nates over thefe natural defects : fo that all
who wifh well to the intereft of this country,
in its trade and colonies, may hope to fee

C 3

that

that union, at prefent only minifterial, become *official* in this bufinefs, and revive again that great, wife and conftitutional plan of office, actuated under the real fpirit of it.

The only queftion at prefent is, who fhall be the executive officer of this department of ftate; whether the fecretary of ftate, properly fo called; or the firft lord, and other commiffioners, properly called *the board of trade*; or whether it fhall remain divided, as it is, between the feveral great departments of adminiftration; *or whether fome more official and practical divifion of this adminiftration may not be made.*

Suppofe now, it fhould be thought proper, that this adminiftration be placed in the fecretary of ftate's office, all the adminiftration of the plantations may be given to the fouthern department: yet the great object of the general trade of Great Britain muft be divided between the fouthern and the northern, as the matters of confideration happen to lie in the one or in the other department; and how will the fouthern department act, when any matter of commerce arifes in the plantations, that has fpecial connections or interferings with the Dutch, Hamborough, Danifh or Ruffian trade?

It

It cannot lie in the board of trade, properly fo called, until it be found proper, and becomes a meafure of government to erect that board into a fecretary of ftate's office for this department, which, firft or laft, it moft certainly will do. That, therefore, the great bufinefs of trade and plantations may not run into confufion, or be at a ftand;—that it may be carried to the effect propofed, held forth, and defired by government, and neceffary to it; all that can be done at prefent is, to put the whole executive adminiftration, the nomination, correfpondence, iffuing of inftructions, orders, &c. under the fecretary of ftate, if he has leifure to attend to it, and can undertake it; and to make the board of trade a mere committee of reference and report; inftead of reporting to the king in council, to report to the fecretary of ftate, who fhall lay the matters before his Majefty, and receive and iffue his orders;—who fhall refer all matters to this committee, for their confideration, and fhall conduct through the legiflature all meafures neceffary to be determined thereby. If this be not practicable, there is no other alternative, than to do directly what ought to be done, and what, fome time or other, muft be done; the making the officer who conducts this department a minifter for that department, with all the powers neceffary thereto. For

C 4

until

until a practical and efficient adminiftration
be formed, whatever the people of this
country may think, the people of the colonies, who know their bufinefs much better
than we do, will never believe government
is in earneft about them, or their intereft,
or even about governing them; and will,
not merely from that reafoning, but from
neceffity of their circumftances, act accordingly.

Until an effective adminiftration for Colony affairs be eftablifhed by government,
all plans for the governing of thofe countries under any regular fyftem of policy,
will be only matter of fpeculation, and become mere ufelefs opprobrious theory. All
official information given and tranfmitted by
thofe whofe duty it is to give it, will, as
accident fhall decide, or as the connexions
of parties fhall run, be received or not; nay,
it may fo happen, that thofe officers who
fhould duly report to government the ftate
of thefe matters, will, as they find themfelves confcientioufly or politically difpofed,
direct that information to thofe who are in,
or to thofe who are out of adminiftration.
Every leader of every little flying fquadron
will have his runner, his own proper channel of information; and will hold forth his
own importance in public, by bringing *his*
plan

plan for American affairs before it. All true and regular knowledge of thefe affairs being difperfed, will be evaporated; every adminiftration, even Parliament itfelf, will be diftracted in its councils by a thoufand odds and ends of propofals, by a thoufand pieces and parcels of plans, while thofe furely, who are fo deeply concerned as the Americans themfelves are, will not be excluded from having their plan alfo; they will have their plan alfo, for however peaceably they may fubmit to the direction of the powers of government, derived through a regular eftablifhed permanent mode of adminiftration, they will by any means that they can juftify, refufe to have their interefts directed and difpofed of by every whim that every temporary empiric can force into execution. If therefore we mean to govern the Colonies, we muft previoufly form at home fome practical and efficient adminiftration for Colony affairs.

Before the erection of the Board of Trade as a particular office, the bufinefs of the Colonies was adminiftered with efficiency; the king himfelf in council adminiftered the government of his Colonies; the ftate officer, each in his proper department was no otherwife Minifter than as minifterially executing the orders which he received, or
officially

officially reporting from his refpective department, the information which he had to lay before the king in council. Since the eftablifhment of that office called the Board of Trade, the adminiftration of the Colonies has either laid dormant, or been overlaid; or, if taken up, become an occafion of jealoufy and ftruggle for power between that Board and every ftate officer who hath been deemed the Minifter for the time being. From this jealoufy and this ftruggle, this Board hath been fuppofed to interfere at different times with every other office, while at one time it hath had the powers and held the port of a minifter's office, and at another hath become a mere committee, inefficient as to execution, unattended to as reporting. The Colonies, and the officers of the Colonies, have one while been taught to look up to this Board as the Minifter for their affairs, and at another, have learned to hold it in that contempt which inefficiency gives; which contempt, however, hath not always ftopped there.

To prevent, on this critical occafion, all fuch appearances on one hand, from mifleading thofe who are to be governed, and to put an end on the other, to all interfering amongft thofe who are to govern in this line of bufinefs---The Board of Trade fhould

either

either be made what it never was intended to be, a Secretary of State's office for the Plantations, or be confined to what it really is, a committee of reference for examination and report, for ftating and preparing bufinefs, while the affairs of the Colonies are adminiftred folely by the King in council, really acting as an efficient board for that purpofe. Somewhere there ought to be an efficiency, and in this fupreme board is the proper refidence of it. To place it here would be really and in fact the eftablifhing of an adminiftration for colony affairs.

The firft ftep that fuch adminiftration would take to fix the bafis of an eftablifhed, permanent and effective fyftem of government for the mother country and the Colonies, muft be made by fome *leading meafure*, which fhall, on real fact, and by actual reprefentation of the parties concerned, examine into the various interefts which have arifen, the various claims which are derived from thofe interefts, and the various rights that may, or may not, be admitted, as founded on thefe, and as confiftent with the general government and intereft of the whole.

To obtain this with truth and certainty, and to engage the colonifts to co-operate in this view with that confidence which a free

people

people muſt have, if they co-operate at all---, government would ſend out to America, *ſome very conſiderable perſon*, under commiſ-ſion and inſtructions, to hear and examine on the ſpot, the ſtate of things there, and by ſuch proper repreſentations and aſſiſtance as can no where be had but upon the ſpot, and from the people themſelves, to form ſuch authentic matter of information for the king in council, as may become the ſolid baſis of real government, eſtabliſhed by the principles of real liberty.

To ſuch conſiderable perſon, and to ſuch commiſſion, only, would the coloniſts give their confidence; they would know that *there* there was no ſpirit of party or faction, that there could be no jobb---They would be convinced that government was in earneſt, and meant to act fairly and honourably with them. They would meet ſuch perſon in the abundance of their loyalty, with diſ-poſitions of real buſineſs in their temper, and with the ſpirit of real union in their hearts.

What commiſſion could be more honour-able and glorious, even to the higheſt cha-racter, than that of acting for the rights and liberties of a whole people, ſo as to be the means of eſtabliſhing thoſe rights and

liberties

liberties, by an adequate fyftem of freedom and government, extended to the whole? What can be more fuited to the moft elevated character, than to be the *great reconciler* between the mother country and her colonies, mif-reprefented to, and mif-informed of each other?

I am almoft certain that this meafure will not be adopted, that it will be, as it has been already, rejected---that there never will be any fyftematical union of government between the mother country and the colonies---that the opportunity when fuch might be eftablifhed on true principles will be neglected---and that the courfe of bufinefs will, on this occafion, be, as the hiftory of mankind informs us it always has been, that thofe errors which might be rectified by the fpirit of policy, will be permitted to go on piling up one mifchief over another, until nothing but power can interpofe, which will then interpofe when the fpirit of policy is no more.

The mother country and her colonies will continue to live on in perpetual jealoufies, jarrings and difputes. The colonies will for fome time *belong to fome faction here*, and be the tool of it, until they become powerful enough to hold a party for themfelves, and

make

make *fome faction their tool.* The latter
ftage of this miferable connection will be
one continued ftruggle, whether Great Britain fhall adminifter the rights and interefts
of the colonies, or whether the intereft and
power of the colonies fhall take a lead in that
adminiftration which fhall govern Great Britain. This convulfion may agitate for a
while, until fome event fhall happen that
will totally break all union between us, and
will end in the ruin of the one or the other,
juft as the accident of the die fhall turn.

Although I am convinced that this will
be the ftate of things, yet, as I know that
what I have here recommended, is founded
on precedents of better and wifer times than
the prefent, is not founded barely on my
own experience, but in that of men who
have long had the lead of bufinefs in thofe
countries, is what every true friend of the
colonies, who lives and has his property
there, would recommend---what every man
of bufinefs here, who wifhes well to the
government of Great Britain, muft approve.
I now propofe it to the public as a meafure,
of which if adminiftration fhould neglect
or refufe to take the lead, the colonies may
profit by thofe means of communication
with one another, and by thofe powers which
their conftitutions and eftablifhments give
them

them for the prefervation of their civil and
commercial interefts; yet, taking it up, as a
meafure, which, for the fake of Great Britain, I wifh adminiftration to adopt, I fay,
government fhould fend out fome confiderable perfon, with a council to affift him,
under a commiffion and inftructions, to call
a congrefs of commiffioners from the feveral colonies.---He fhould have power and
be inftructed to call to his aid and affiftance,
the governors, or any other his Majefty's
fervants, as occafion fhould require.

By the reprefentations and affiftance of
this congrefs and thefe perfons, he fhould inquire into the *actual* ftate of the crown's
authority, as capable of being executed by
the King, and by his governor, and other
the immediate executors of the power of the
crown.

He fhould inquire into the extent of the
exercife and claim of the legiflative powers,
and examine difpaffionately and without
prejudice, on what grounds of neceffity or
expediency any precedents which ftretch beyond perhaps the ftrict line of the commiffions or charters, are founded.

He fhould inquire into the ftate of their
laws, as to their conformity to the laws of
Great Britain, and examine the real ftate of

3   the

the facts or bufinefs which may have made
any deviation neceffary or not.

He fhould examine into the powers and
practice of their courts of judicature, whether, on one hand, they have not extended
their authority beyond their due powers; or
whether, on the other hand, they have not
been reftrained by inftructions, or by the
acts of the colony legiflatures, within bounds
too narrowly circumfcribed to anfwer the
ends for which fuch courts are erected.

He fhould, which can only be known
upon the fpot, inquire into and examine the
actual ftate of their commerce, that where
it deviates unneceffarily from the laws of
trade, it may be reftrained by proper regu-
lations---or where the laws of trade are
found to be inconfiftent with the intereft of
a commercial country having colonies which
have arifen from, and depend upon trade, a
revifion may be made of thofe laws, fo as
that the fyftem of our laws may be made
conform to the fyftem of our commerce,
and not deftructive of it.

Under all thefe various heads, he may
hear all the grievances which the officers of
the crown, or the people, complain of, in
order

order to form a juft and actual reprefentation for the King in council.

He fhould inquire into the ftate of the
King's revenues, his lands, his naval ftores;
and he fhould review the ftate of the military
fervice, the forts, garrifons and forces.---
With the affiftance of proper commiffioners
from the provinces and colonies concerned,
he fhould fettle the feveral difputes of the
colonies amongft themfelves, particularly as
to their boundary lines. He fhould alfo inquire into all fraudulent grants.

All thefe matters duly examined and in-
quired into, a report of the whole bufinefs,
fhould be drawn up, and being authen-
ticated by the original documents, fhould
be laid before the King in council: Thofe
points which were of the fpecial department of any of the boards or offices
under government, would be refered from
thence to thofe refpective offices, for them
to report their opinion upon the matter.
---And when the whole, both of matter
and of opinion, was by the moft authentic
reprefentations, and by the beft advice, thus
drawn together, the King in council would
be enabled to form, and by and with the
advice and authority of Parliament to eftablifh, the only fyftem of government and

D commercial

commercial laws, which would form Great
Britain and her colonies into a one united
commercial dominion.

If this meafure be adopted, a general bill
of rights, and an act for the eftablifhment
of government and commerce on a great
plan of union, will be brought forward;
the colonies will be confidered as fo many
corporations, not without, but united to,
the realm; they will be left in all the free
and full poffeffion of their feveral rights and
liberties, as by grant, charter, or commiffions given; yet, for every power which
they exercife or poffefs, they will depend
upon the government of the whole, and
upon Great Britain as the center. Great
Britain, as the center of this fyftem, of
which the colonies by actual union fhall
become organized, not annexed parts, muft
be the center of attraction to which thefe
colonies, in the adminiftration of every power
of their government, in the exercife of their
judicial powers, in the execution of their
laws, and in every operation of their trade,
muft tend. They will remain under the
conftant influence of the attraction of this
center; and cannot move, but that every
direction of fuch movement will converge
to the fame. And as it is not more neceffary to preferve the feveral governments
fubordinate

fubordinate in their refpective orbs, than it is effential to the prefervation of the whole empire to keep them difconnected and independent of each other, *they muft be guarded by this union againft having or forming any principle of coherence with each other, above that whereby they cohere to this center, this firft mover.* They fhould alway remain incapable of any coherence, or of fo confpiring amongft themfelves, as to create any other equal force which might recoil back on this firft mover. Policy acting upon a fyftem of civil union, may eafily and conftitutionally provide againft all this. The colonies and provinces, as they ftand at prefent, are under the beft form as to this point, which they can be under. They are under the beft frame and difpofition for the government of the general and fupreme power (duly applied) to take place, having at prefent no other principle of civil union between each other, than that by which they naturally are, and in policy fhould be, in communion with Great Britain, as the common center of all. The different manner in which they are fettled; the different modes under which they live; the different forms of charters, grants, and frames of government they poffefs; the various principles of repulfion that thefe create; the different interefts which they actuate; the

different

different religious interefts by which they are actuated; the rivalfhip and jealoufies which arife from hence; and the impracticability of reconciling and accommodating thefe incompatable ideas and claims, will keep them for ever fo, fo long as the fpirit of civil policy remains, and is exerted to the forming and maintaining of this fyftem of union.

However vifionary this may feem to thofe who judge by parts, and act by temporary expedients, thofe truly great minifters who fhall ever take up the adminiftration of the colonies as a fyftem, and fhall have a general practical and adequate knowledge of that fyftem, as interwoven in that of the mother country, will, on the contrary, find this meafure prudential if not a neceffary one, as leading to that great and abfolutely neceffary meafure of uniting the Colonies to Great Britain as parts of the realm, in every degree and mode of communication of its rights and powers. And until fome fteps are taken which may lead and approach to this fyftem of union, as the intereft and power of the Colonies approach to the bearing of a proportion with that of Great Britain, the real intereft of Great Britain and her Colonies will continue to be very inadequately and very unhappily adminiftred, while the bufinefs of the Colonies fhall

in

in the mean time become a faction inftead of a conftitutional part of the adminiftration.

The center of power, inftead of remaining fixed as it now is in Great Britain, will, as the magnitude of the power and intereft of the Colonies increafes, be drawn out from the ifland, by the fame laws of nature analogous in all cafes, by which the center of gravity in the folar fyftem, now near the furface of the fun, would, by an encreafe of the quantity of matter in the planets, be drawn out beyond that furface. Knowing therefore the laws of nature, fhall we like true philofophers follow, where that fyftem leads, to form one general fyftem of dominion by an union of Great Britain and her Colonies, fixing, while it may be fo fixed, the common center in Great Britain, or fhall we without ever feeing that fuch center muft be formed by an inter-communion of the powers of all the territories as parts of the dominions of Great Britain, like true modern politicians, and from our own narrow temporary ideas of a local center, labour to keep that center in Great Britain by force againft encreafing powers, which will, finally, by an overbalance heave that center itfelf out of its place? Such meafures would be almoft as wife as his who ftanding in a fcale fhould thruft his ftick up againft the beam

to

to prevent it from defcending, while his own weight brought it the fafter down. That policy which fhall ever attempt to connect the Colonies to Great Britain *by power*, will in that very inftant connect them *to one another in policy.*

Before we enter into thefe matters, I do not think it would be impertinent juft to mark the idea of colonies, and their fpecial circumftances, which makes it a meafure in commercial governments, to eftablifh, cultivate, and maintain them.

The view of trade in general, as well as of manufactures in particular, terminates in fecuring an extenfive and permanent vent; or to fpeak more precifely, (in the fame manner as fhop-keeping does) in having many and good cuftomers: the wifdom, therefore, of a trading nation, is to gain, and to create, as many as poffible. Thofe whom we gain in foreign trade, we poffefs under reftrictions and difficulties, and may lofe in the rivalfhip of commerce: thofe that a trading nation can create within itfelf, it deals with under its own regulations, and makes its own, and cannot lofe. In the eftablifhing colonies, a nation creates people whofe labour, being applied to new objects of produce and manufacture, opens

new

new channels of commerce, by which they
not only live in eafe and affluence within
themfelves, but, while they are labouring
under and for the mother country, (for
there all their external profits center) become an increafing nation, of appropriated
and good cuftomers to the mother country.
Thefe not only increafe our manufactures,
increafe our exports, but extend our commerce; and if duly adminiftered, extend
the nation, its powers, and its dominions,
to wherever thefe people extend their fettlements. This is, therefore, an intereft which
is, and ought to be dear to the mother
country: this is an object that deferves the
beft care and attention of government: and
the people, who through various hardfhips,
difafters and difappointments; through various difficulties and almoft ruinous expences, have wrought up this intereft to
fuch an important object, merit every protection, grace, encouragement, and privilege, that are in the power of the mother
country to grant.---It is on this *valuable confideration,* (as Mr. Dummer, in his fpirited
defence of the colonies, fays) that they have
a right to the grants, charters, privileges and
protection which they receive; and alfo on
the other hand, it is from thefe grants, charters, privileges and protection given to them,
that the mother country has an exclufive

right

right to the external profits of their labour, and to their cuſtom. As it is the right, ſo it becomes the duty of the mother country to cultivate, to protect and govern the colonies: which nurture and government ſhould preciſely direct its care to two eſſential points. 1ſt, That all the profits of the produce and manufactures of theſe colonies center finally in the mother country: and 2dly, That the colonies continue to be the ſole and proper cuſtomers of the mother country.---To theſe two points, collateral with the intereſts, rights and welfare of the colonies, every meaſure of adminiſtration, every law of trade ſhould tend: I ſay collateral, becauſe, rightly underſtood, theſe two points are mutually coincident with the intereſts, rights and welfare of the colonies.

It has been often ſuggeſted, that care ſhould be taken in the adminiſtration of the plantations; left, in ſome future time, theſe colonies ſhould become independent of the mother country. But perhaps it may be proper on this occaſion, nay, it is juſtice to ſay it, that if, by becoming independent, is meant a revolt, nothing is further from their nature, their intereſt, their thoughts. If a defection from the alliance of the mother country be ſuggeſted, it ought to be, and can be truly ſaid, that their ſpirit

rit abhors the fenfe of fuch ; their attachment to the proteftant fucceffion in the
houfe of Hanover will ever ftand unfhaken ;
and nothing can eradicate from their hearts
their natural, almoft mechanical, affection
to Great Britain, which they conceive under
no other fenfe, nor call by any other name,
than that of *home*. Befides, the merchants
are, and muft ever be, in great meafure
allied with thofe of Great Britain ; their very
fupport confifts in this alliance, and nothing
but falfe po icy *here* can break it. If the
trade of the colonies be protected and directed from hence, with the true fpirit of
the act of navigation, that fpirit under which
it has rifen, no circumftances of trade could
tempt the Colonifts to certain ruin under any
oth r connections. The liberty and religion
of the B itifh colonies are incompatible with
either French or Spanifh government; and
they know full well, that they could hope for
neither liberty nor protection under a Dutch
one. Any fuch fuggeftion, therefore, is a
falfe and unjuft afperfion on their principles
and affections, and can arife from nothing
but an intire ignorance of their circumftances. Yet again, on the other hand,
while they remain under the fupport and
protection of the government of the mother
country ; while they profit of the beneficial
part of its trade ; while their attachment to
the

the present royal family ſtands firm, and
their alliance with the mother country is
inviolate, it may be worth while to inquire,
whether they may not become and act in
ſome caſes independent of the *government
and laws* of the mother country :—and if
any ſuch ſymptoms ſhould be found, either
in their government, courts, or trade, perhaps it may be thought high time, even
now, to inquire how far theſe colonies are
or are not arrived, at this time, in theſe caſes,
at an independency of the government of
the mother country :—and if any meaſure
of ſuch independency, formed upon precedents unknown to the government of the
mother country at the time they were formed, ſhould be inſiſted on, when the government of the mother country was found to
be ſo weak or diſtracted at home, or ſo deeply
engaged abroad in Europe, as not to be able
to attend to, and aſſert its right in America,
with its own people,—perhaps it may be
thought, that no time ſhould be loſt to remedy or redreſs theſe deviations—if any
ſuch be found ; or to remove all jealouſies
ariſing from the idea of them, if none ſuch
really exiſt.

But the true and effectual way to remove
all jealouſies and interfering between the ſeveral powers of the government of the mother

ther country, and the feveral powers of the
governments of the colonies, in the due
and conftitutional order of their fubordination, is to inquire and examine what the
colonies and provinces really are; what their
conftitution of government is; what the relation between them and the mother country;
and in confequence of the truth and principles eftablifhed on fuch examination—to
maintain firmly, both in claim and exercife,
the rights and power of the fupreme government of the mother country, with all acknowledgement of the rights, liberties, privileges, immunities and franchifes of the
Colonifts, both perfonal and political, treating them really as what they are.—Until
this be done, there can be no government
properly fo called; the various opinions,
connections and interefts of Britains, both in
this ifland, and in America, will divide them
into parties—the fpirit of mutual animofity
and oppofition, will take advantage of the
total want of eftablifhed and fixed principles
on this fubject, to work thefe parties into
faction; and then the predominancy of the
one faction, or the other, acting under the
mafk of the forms of government, will alternately be called government.

In the former editions of this book, I had
marked out what points of colony government

ment had fallen, in the courſe of adminiſtration, into diſpute; what the different
apprehenſions were, which had given riſe
to the different meaſures purſued on thoſe
points—I had ſtated the nature of each
queſtion—what was the true iſſue to which
the diſpute ought to be brought; and at
the ſame time that I ſtated the effect of theſe
diſputes in matters of adminiſtration, I
ſhewed how neceſſary it was that they ſhould
be ſome way or other decided. I did not
proceed to give any opinion or deciſion—I
thought the firſt ſufficient, and thought it
was all that was neceſſary. But yet as that
was neceſſary, and as I ſaw an attention to
American affairs ariſing in the minds of moſt
men of buſineſs, I was in hopes that theſe
points might have been diſpaſſionately conſidered, and prudently ſettled; that they
might be fixed on ſuch legal and conſtitutional grounds; that that true ſyſtem of efficient government founded in political liberty
(which all ſeemed to profeſs here) might be
eſtabliſhed in the colonies: I was ſure,
from the ſpirit and genius of the people, it
would be nouriſhed and maintained there,
ſo as to become in ſome future, and perhaps not very diſtant age, an aſylum to that
liberty of mankind, which, as it hath been
driven by the corruption and the conſequent
tyranny of government, *hath been conſtantly*
retiring

retiring weſtward—but from the moment that American affairs became an object of politics, they became the tools and inſtruments of faction. Such hath been their fate, that as on one hand they have given real occaſion to thoſe who mean well to the peace and liberty of mankind; ſo on the other have they ſupplied ſpecious pretences to thoſe who mean only to profit of the force of parties—to diſpute the ſtate and application of every caſe in politics relative to the colonies, by recurring back to the principles on which they appear to have been ſettled, eſtabliſhed, and afterwards governed; and theſe principles, from the variableneſs and fluctuation of the opinion and ſpirit of government, have been ſo often changed, that propoſitions the very reverſe of each other, may ſtrictly be deduced from the conduct of the crown and ſtate towards the colonies. Hence it is, that at this day the conſtitution and rights of the colonies, in the actual exerciſe of them, are unſettled; the relation in which they ſtand connected with the realm and with the King, are diſputed; and Parliament, as well as miniſters, are balancing in opinion what is the true, legal, and conſtitutional mode of adminiſtration by which thoſe colonies are to be governed. Whether the colonies be demeſnes of the crown, without the realm, or parts and parcels of the realm ;

realm; whether thefe foreign dominions of the King be as yet annexed to the realm of England; whether the colonifts be fubjects of the King in his foreign dominions, or whether they be fubjects of, and owe allegiance to the realm; has been at various times, and is at this day called into difpute. This queftion is now no longer of curiofity and theory; it is brought actually into iffue. It is now by deeds and overt acts difcuffed, and muft be decided. To do this truly and juftly, it muft be thoroughly confidered, what were the circumftances of their migration; under what political conftitutions they were eftablifhed and chartered; and by what mode of adminiftration their affairs have been conducted and governed by the King, and by the government of England.

When the lands of America were firft difcovered, the fovereign of that fubject, in each particular cafe, who difcovered them, either from a power given by the Pope, or from fome felf-derived claim, affumed the right of poffeffion in them. If thefe lands were really derelict, preoccupancy might have created a right of poffeffion: yet even in this cafe, fome further circumftances of interconnection with that land, fuch as the mixing labour with it, muft attend that occupancy, or the right would have been very defective.

defective. Where the lands were already occupied by the human species, and in the actual possession of inhabitants, it will be very difficult to show on what true principle or grounds of justice, the Pope, or any other christian prince, assumed the right to seize on, dispose, and grant away, the lands of the Indians in America. Surely, the divine author of our holy religion, who declared that his kingdom was *not of this world*, hath not bequeathed to christians an *exclusive charter*, giving right of possession in the lands of this world, even where the supreme Providence hath already planted inhabitants in the possession of it: and yet, absurd, unjust, and groundless as this claim is, it is the only claim we Europeans can make, the only right we can plead. However, the English title is as good as any other European title, and indisputable against any other European claim.

Let us see the first assumption and exercise of this right in our government, contained in the grant which Henry the Seventh made to Cabot.———Copy of the grant, as it is a curious act, is printed in the appendix. —It contains a grant to Cabot, and his sons, of power, to set up the King's standard in any lands, islands, towns, villages, camps, &c. which he shall discover not in the occu-

8   pancy

pancy of any chriftian power : and that this Cabot, his fons, and their heirs, may feize, conquer, and occupy any fuch lands, iflands, towns, camps, or villages : and as his liege vaffals, governors, locumtenentes, or deputies, may hold dominion over and have exclufive property in the fame.

As the fovereigns of Europe did thus on one hand affume, without right, a predominant claim of poffeffion, againft the Indians in thefe lands ; fo our fovereigns alfo thus at firft affumed againft law an exclufive property in thefe lands, to the preclufion of the jurifdiction of the ftate. They called them their foreign dominions ; their demefne lands in partibus exteris, and held them as their own, the King's poffeffions, not parts or parcels of the realm, ✝ " as not yet annexed " to the crown." So that when the Houfe of Commons, in thofe reiterated attempts which they made by paffing a bill to get a law enacted for eftablifhing a free right of fifhery on the coafts of Virginia, New-England, and Newfoundland, put in the claim of the ftate to this property, and of the parliament to jurifdiction over it ; they were told in the Houfe by the fervants of the crown, ✝ " That it was not fit to make

✝ Journal of the Houfe of Commons, April 25, 1621.

laws

" laws here for thofe countries which are
" not yet annexed to the crown." ‡ " That
" this bill was not proper for this houfe, as
" it concerneth America." Nay, it was
doubted by others, " whether the houfe had
" jurifdiction to meddle with thefe matters."
And when the houfe, in 1624, was about to
proceed upon a petition from the fettlers of
Virginia, to take cognizance of the affairs of
the plantations, " upon § the Speaker's pro-
" ducing and reading to the houfe a letter from
" the king concerning the Virginia petition,
" the petition, by general refolution, was
" withdrawn." And although the bill for a
free fifhery, to the difannulling fome claufes in
the King's charters, paffed the houfe; as
alfo the houfe came to fome very ftrong refolutions upon the nullity of the claufes
in the charters; yet the houfe from this
time took no further cognizance of the plantations till the commencement of the civil
wars. Upon this ground it was the King
confidered the lands as his demefnes, and the
colonifts as his fubjects in thefe his foreign
dominions, not his fubjects of the realm or
ftate.

The plantations were fettled on thefe lands
by his licence and grant; the conftitutions

‡ Ditto, April 29, 1621.
§ Ditto, April 29.

E

and

and powers of government were framed by the King's charters and commiffions; and the colonifts underftanding themfelves as removed out of the realm, confidered themfelves in their executive and legiflative capacity of government, in immediate connection and fubordination to the King, their only fovereign lord.

In the fame manner as this ftate and circumftances of a people migrating from, and fettling in vacate countries, without, or out of the territories of the realm, operated to the eftablifhment of the King's fovereignty there, he having affumed an exclufive right to the property. In the fame manner it muft and did neceffarily operate to the eftablifhment of the people's liberty, both perfonal and political—they had either tacit or exprefs permiffion to migrate from the realm, and to fettle in places out of the realm: thofe who fettled under charters, had, in thofe charters, licence, by an exprefs claufe, to *quit* the realm, and to *fettle* on lands *out of the realm*; as alfo acknowledgement that they and their pofterity were entitled to enjoy all the liberties, franchifes, and immunities, of free denizons and natural fubjects, to all intents and purpofes, as if they had been abiding and born within the realm.

So

So long as they were confidered as natural
born Englifh fubjects *of the realm*, they
muft retain and poffefs in the full enjoyment
and exercife thereof, all the fame rights and
liberties in their perfons, all the fame franchifes and privileges in their property, that
any other Englifh fubject did poffefs.—If
their freehold was part of any manor in any
county of the realm, and that freehold was
worth forty fhillings by the year, fuch freehold undoubtedly gave the poffeffor a vote
for the reprefentative of fuch county ; and
thefe rights muft give this fubject, this freeholder, claim to the fame participation of
council in the legiflative part of government, to the fame communication of power
in the executive part, the fame right to act
and trade, as every other Englifh freeholder
had.

If by migrating from out the realm the
colonifts ceafed to have participation, fuch
legiflative participation in the councils as the
Englifh freeholder hath ; if they ceafed to
have communication in the offices, burthens,
and exercife of government ; if being without the realm they ceafed to be bound by
laws made only for the internal regulation and government of the realm ; if they
ceafed in future to be bound by laws wherein
they were not exprefsly named ; if they

ceafed

ceafed to be under the protection of thofe
laws which were made, and thofe powers
and magiftracies which were created for the
prefervation of the peace within the realm;
if they were (no matter how) feparated from
participation of the benefits of our holy religion, according to the eftablifhed church;
and if the colonies at the fame time were
not parts or parcels of the realm, they undoubtedly ceafed to be fubjects of the realm.
But being by law, both eftablifhed and natural, poffeffed of all the rights, privileges,
franchifes and immunities of a free-born
people—no government lefs free than that
which they had left, could, by any juftifiable
power, be eftablifhed over or amongft them;
and therefore the colonifts were eftablifhed
in a government conformable to the government of England. They had power of
making laws and ordinances, and of laying
impofitions, by a general affembly, or reprefentative legiflature—the power of erecting
courts and creating magiftrates, of the fame
power, and operations, by the fame modes
and proceedings, *mutatis mutandis*, as were
ufed in the government of England; nay,
in fome cafes, by a mode adapted to a de-
mocratic, and even elective, government.
The adminiftrative and executive part had all
the fame checks, and the legiflative all the
fame powers and privileges, only reftrained
from

from not acting contrary to the laws of
England. And upon the fame ground thofe
colonies, of whofe firft fettlement the crown
took no care or cognizance, the colony of
Plymouth, ‖ that of Maffachufetts, Providence
Plantation, and the colony of Connecticut,
eftablifhed among themfelves the like powers
of free government.

And here we may venture to affirm, that
if the colonies were to be deemed without
the realm, not parts or parcels of it, not annexed to the crown of England, though the
demefnes of the King; if the colonifts by
thefe means ceafed to be fubjects of the
realm, and the Parliament had no right or
jurifdiction to make laws about them; if
the government of them refided in the King,
only as *their* fovereign, *dum Rex ei præfit,
ut caput iftius populi, non ut caput alterius
populi,* they were certainly a people *fui juris
---nam imperium quod in rege eft ut in capite,
in populo manet ut in toto, cujus pars eft caput,* * and having an undoubted claim, by the
nature of their liberties, to a participation in
legiflature, had an undoubted right, when

‖ Vide Mr. Prince's New-England Chronology;
and Lt. Gov. Hutchinfon's Hift. of Maffachufetts.
 * *Grotius de B. & P. lib. 2. c. 9. § 8.*

E 3

formed

formed into a ftate of government, to have
a reprefentative legiflature eftablifhed, as
part of their government; and therefore
when fo formed, being a body politic in
fact and name, they had within themfelves,
the King, or his deputy, being part, full
power and authority, to all intents and purpofes, both legiflative and executive, for the
government of all the people,, whether
ftrangers or inhabitants, within their jurifdiction, independent of all external direction
or government, except what might conftitutionally be exercifed by their fovereign lord
the King, or his deputy, and except their
fubordination, not allegiance, to the government of the realm of England *(ut alterius
populi)*. They acknowledged themfelves to
be a government fubordinate to the government of England, fo that they might juftly
be reftrained from doing or becoming any
thing repugnant to the power, rights and intereft of England---but held their allegiance
as due only to their fovereign ; therefore,
thefe premifes admitted, as they did on one
hand truly meafure the duties of this allegiance, by the fame rights and claims as
the King's Englifh fubjects of the realm did ;
fo on the other did they juftly maintain that
in every exercife of their own rights, privileges and powers,--*they were free and independent of all controul, except what was
interwoven

interwoven into their conftitution, fo as to operate in the internal movements of thefe powers, or to. be externally exercifed by the legal powers and negative refiding in the King their fovereign, or in his deputy.

They certainly were not provinces in the fimple idea of Roman provinces governed by laws and power, not deriving from their own rights, and arifing within their own government, but impofed on them by the *imperium alterius populi*, and adminiftered under provincial officers commiffioned from this *imperium*, abfolute as to them. Our colonies and provinces being each a body politic, and having a right to, and enjoying in faĉt, a certain legiflature, indented rather with the cafe of the Grecian colonies, as ftated by Grotius, — *Huc referenda & difceffio quæ ex confenfu fit in colonias, nam fic quoque novus populus fui juris nafcitur.* ἐ γαρ ἰπὶ τῷ Δἕλοι, ἀλλ᾽ ἰπὶ τῷ ὁμοιοι ἕιναι ἰκπέμπονʃαι. *Non enim ut fervi fint fed ut pari jure fint dimituntur.* *—Many inftances may be collеĉted from Thucydides, which would fhew that the dependence of the colonies of Greece on their mother cities, was only the

---

* It fhould be remarked here, though Grotius has omitted to do it, That this is a Pofition of the Locreans, a Colony of Corinth, obviating the Charge of Revolt.   *Thucyd. Lib.* I. *c.* 37.

   connеĉtion

connection of *Fœderates* acknowledging precedence, not the fubordination of fubjects acknowledging allegiance. But having, as above, ftated the circumftances of the migration and firft fettlement of the Englifh colonifts, I fhall confine myfelf to the inftances and facts of the Englifh colonies.

They were bodies corporate, but certainly not corporations in the fenfe of fuch communities *within the realm*. They were erected into provinces, had the *jura regalia*, the patentee as the King's deputy, or the King's governor, as part of their conftitution, whether by commiffion or by charter, was vefted with all the fame royal powers which the King hath in his palace, both executive and legiflative.

Thefe provinces were all, in the true fpirit, intent, and meaning of the thing, COUNTIES PALATINE ; and fome of them were actually and exprefsly created fuch.

The Caribbee Iflands, granted by Charles the firft, in the third year of his reign, to the Earl of Carlifle, were erected into a province or county, by the name of The Province of Carlifle, " with all and every fuch " like and fo large privileges, jurifdictions, " prerogatives, royalties, liberties, freedoms,

" regal

" regal rights and franchifes whatfoever, as
" well by fea as land, within the limits of
" the faid iflands, to have, ufe, exercife,
" and enjoy, as any Bifhop (according to
" the cuftom of Durefme) within the faid
" bifhoprick or county palatine of Durefme,
" in our kingdom of England, ever before
" hath, had, keepeth, ufeth, or enjoyeth,
" or of right could or ought to have, keep,
" ufe, or enjoy."

The grant in 1630, to Sir Robert Heath,
and his heirs, of the lands now called Louifiana, ran in the fame manner.——" We
" erect the fame into a province, and in-
" corporate it by the name of Carolanea,
" or the province Carolanea, with all and
" fingular fuch like, and as ample rights,
" jurifdictions, privileges prerogatives, roy-
" alties, liberties, immunities, and franchi-
" fes, as well by fea as land, within the
" regions, territories, iflands, and limits
" aforefaid, to have, exercife, ufe, and en-
" joy the fame, as any Bifhop of Durefme,
" in the bifhoprick or county palatine of
" Durefme, &c. &c."

In the charter of Maryland is granted as
follows, " We have thought fit to erect the
" fame into a province, with all and fingu-
" lar the like, and as ample rights, jurif-
                                        " dictions,

" dictions, privileges, prerogatives, royal-
" ties, liberties, immunities, royal rights
" and franchifes, of what kind foever, tem-
" poral, as well by fea as by land, within
" the country, ifles, iflets, and limits afore-
" faid, to have, exercife, ufe, and enjoy the
" fame, as amply as any Bifhop of Durham
" within the bifhoprick or county palatine
" of Durham, in our kingdom of England,
" hath any time heretofore had, held, ufed,
" or enjoyed, or of right ought, or might
" have had, held, ufed or enjoyed."

The charter of the 15th of Charles the
firft, to Sir Ferdinando Gorges, erects, creates, and incorporates, all the premifes
granted into a province or county, called
the province or county of Main, granting him
all and fingular, and as large and ample
rights, jurifdictions, privileges, prerogatives,
royalties, liberties, and immunities, franchifes and preheminencies, as well by fea as
land, within the premifes, as the Bifhop of
Durham hath within the county palatine of
Durham.

The charter of Penfylvania *erects the faid*
country into a province or feignory, in the recital of the powers of which all the *regalia*
are granted ; and efpecially the power and
privilege

privilege of not being taxed but by the confent of the freemen, or in parliament.

By the charter of William and Mary,
the provinces of the Maffachufets-bay was
" *erected and incorporated into a real province,*" in the powers of which the Jura
Regalia are defcribed and fully granted.

All thefe provinces have the power of
peace and war, of exercifing law martial, of
life and death, of creating towns, counties,
and other corporations within themfelves;
and the powers of their general affemblies
are very different from, and go beyond the
powers of our common councils within the
realm.

The fact is, that the conftitution of
the government of England, as it ftood at
that time, founded upon, or built up with
the feudal fyftem, could not extend beyond
the realm. There was nothing in the nature of the conftitution providing for fuch
things as colonies, or provinces. Lands without or beyond the limits of the realm, could
not be the property of the realm, unlefs by
being united to the realm. But the people
who fettled upon thefe lands in *partibus exteris,* being the King's liege fubjects, the
King, as fovereign Lord, affumed the right
of

of property, and of government. Yet the people being intitled to the rights, privileges, &c. of freemen, the King established by his commission of government, or charters, these colonies as free states, subordinate according to such precedents or examples as his ministry thought suitable to the present case; and the county palatine of Durham became this precedent, and the model of this constitution as to the *regalia.* This was the actual state of the circumstances of our colonists at their first migration, and of the colonies at their first settlement; and had nothing further intervened, would have been their constitution at this day. Let us examine what has intervened, and mark as precisely as we can, where power has attempted, and where right has effected any change in these circumstances.

Notwithstanding this mode of constitution, acknowleged *de jure*, as well as established *de facto*, we find, that from the moment that these our Kings, and their council, took up the idea of comparing these plantations to the duchies of Gascoigne or Normandy, as we find in the journals of the House of Commons, before referred to. From that moment the constitution of the colonies were treated as being the same with that of Jersey, part of the duchy of Normandy;

and

and the fame mode of adminiftration was adopted for the colonies as had been ufed and accuftomed for the government of that ifland.

Appeals from the provincial law courts were eftablifhed; not to the courts of equity here in England, not to the Houfe of Lords, according to the conftitution and cuftom of England, but as appeals from the courts in Normandy were brought before the King, as Duke in council ; fo here in the plantations, appeals were made to the King in council, according to the ancient cuftom of Normandy. And the fame rules for 'thefe appeals were adopted—" Appeals (fays Mr. Falle in his account of Jerfey) " may be " brought before the council board, in mat- " ters of civil property, * above the value of " 300 livres Tournois, but no appeal is ad- " mitted in matters of lefs value ; nor in " interlocutories, nor in criminal caufes, " which are judged here to be without " appeal."

As the laws of Jerfey may be reduced under thefe three heads : 1. The ancient cuftom of Normandy, as it ftood before the alienation of that duchy, called in the rolls of the itinerant judges *La Somme de Mançel.* This makes what the ftatute law is in England.

* In the fame manner appeals may be brought from the colonies, in matters where the value is £ 300.

2. Muni-

2. Municipal or local usages, which are the unwritten and traditionary law, like the common law in England. 3. Constitutions and ordinances made by the King, or his commissioners royal ; with such regulations and orders, as are from time to time transmitted to Jersey, from the council board.— So Charles the First took up the idea, that the colonies in like manner, his demesnes in his foreign dominions, might be governed by laws, ordinances, and constitutions, made and published with his consent, * by his royal commissioners, established for governing the plantations, together with such further instructions as should be transmitted from the council board ; and that these commissioners, being his council for plantation affairs, might be the dernier court of appeal from the colonies. He left indeed the colonies in some degree in possession of the statute law of England, as it stood before their migration, and allowed them, as far as was consistent with the legislation of this his council, the making and using their municipal and local laws.

Under these Norman ideas of the constitution of our colonies, it was a most fortunate circumstance for them, That the island

* Vide Appendix, for the Commission at length.

of Jerſey had, by its conſtitution, a right to
hold a " convention or meeting of the three
" orders or eſtates of the iſlands, in imitation
" of thoſe auguſt aſſemblies, known by
" that or ſome other name, in great king-
" doms and monarchies, a ſhadow, and
" reſemblance of an Engliſh parliament."
In which, " the King's governor, or lieute-
" nant, had a negative voice. The great
" buſineſs of which meetings, was the raiſing
" money to ſupply public occaſions. For,
" (Mr. Falle ſays) as in England, money
" cannot be raiſed upon the ſubject, but by
" authority of parliament, ſo here it is a re-
" ceived maxim, that no levies can be made
" upon the inhabitants, but by their own
" conſent, declared by their repreſentatives
" aſſembled in common-council." It was
fortunate, I ſay, for our colonies, that this
was the caſe of Jerſey ; for there can be no
other reaſonable account given, how our colonies preſerved this eſſential right of Engliſhmen, but that it happened to be alſo a conſtitutional right of his Majeſty's foreign
French-Norman ſubjects. This commiſſion
indeed was annulled, and a board of plantations (at the head of which, as a marine
department, the Earl of Warwick was placed,
being admiral) was appointed by an ordinance of parliament ; and after the reſtora-
tion, a council of trade and plantations was
eſtabliſhed,

eſtabliſhed, and upon that being diſſolved
in December, 1674, theſe matters were
conducted by a committee of council, until
after the revolution, when the preſent board of
trade and plantations was appointed. But
although, as political liberty became better
underſtood, and more effectually eſtabliſhed,
in our own conſtitution, the very idea of a
privy council making laws for Engliſh ſubjects, though in America, began to be more
warily touched upon, and was at laſt finally
dropped : Yet the idea of directing, reſtraining, and ſuſpending, in ſome caſes, the exerciſe of their conſtitutional powers of government, by the King's further powers and
inſtructions, and authorities under his ſignet,
or ſign manual, or by his order in privy
council, or even by letters from ſecretaries
of ſtate, doth continue too deeply rooted to this
day ; as alſo this fragment of the Norman
cuſtom of appeal to the King, as Duke in
council, continues to be the corner-ſtone in
the edifice of their judicatories. From the
ſtate of matters as above, it is clear, that ſo
far as refers to the relation between the
King and them, while the King by himſelf,
or by his royal commiſſioners, his council,
or his committee, aſſumed a right to make
and publiſh laws, conſtitutions, and ordinances, as binding upon, and penal againſt,
the people of the colonies, without the intervention

vention of their legiflature. They undoubtedly had a right, and it was their duty to reject them, and to refufe obedience to them ;
as alfo to confider all his royal commands
and inftructions, whether by orders in council, by fign manual, or by letters from fecretaries of ftate, when they affumed the port
of laws or ordinances, to be no otherwife
binding on the colonies and provinces, than
as royal proclamations, which have in many
cafes, a certain authority, *quoad terrorem,*
though not that of law) If the colonifts had
at their migration, as natural liberties as
above defcribed, and were, by the commiffions of government or charters (for I fee
no difference, both equally providing for an
uninterrupted and continual fucceffion of civil government) eftablifhed in the fame ;
no orders or inftructions, which might derive
thus from the King alone, to the fufpending,
reftraining, or obftructing the enjoyment of
thefe rights and liberties, or the exercife of
thefe powers, could take effect, or have the
force of law.

And as thus of the King's power in the
government of the colonies, fo we may with
the ftronger reafon venture to pronounce that
parliament without the King, as by that
committee, or board of plantations, inftituted
by order of parliament in the year 1643,

F   could

could have none of thofe powers which might fupercede the rights and liberties of the colonies.

How far the power of King and parliament, the whole impèrium of Great Britain, may go in conjunction with right, is matter of more difficulty to afcertain ; and of more danger to decide. If the provinces have any rights, however much fubordinate, even this imperium muft be bounded by them. However, I have formed my opinion on this fubject, and I will fpeak it out ;—if I am in an error, even error may give occafion to the rife of truth.---But this is not the place.

Having faid fo much on the liberties of the people in the colonies, it is right, perhaps neceffary, to fay, I am fure it may be faid with the utmoft precifion and conviction, That the King muft retain in himfelf, and in his deputy fet over them in his government of them, all thofe fame preheminences, royal rights, powers and prerogatives, which are vefted in the crown, as part of the government of England. And that whenever the people, or their reprefentatives in the colonies, act towards his royal perfon, or towards his reprefentative, in derogation of thefe rights and powers, they can neither be juftified by right, or the conftitution, or even

good

good policy towards themfelves, whatever fpecious temporary reafons they may affign for it; for this mode of conduct will be permitted to a certain degree only, and for a certain time; but will alway in the end, as it alway hath in fact done, call forth fome remedy, fo far as relates to the colonifts ideas, worfe than the difeafe. I will inftance in one cafe only---The conftant refufal of the Affemblies to fix permanent falaries for the civil eftablifhment of government.

The above is the actual and rightful relation between the King and the American colonies; and by the rule of this relation, we ought to review and decide thofe feveral points wherein the crown, or its Governors acting under its commiffion and inftructions, differ with the people.

Upon fuch review it will appear, under this firft general head, in various inftances, that the two great points which the Colonifts labour to eftablifh, is the exercife of their feveral rights and privileges, as founded in the rights of an Englifhman; and fecondly, as what they fuppofe to be a neceffary meafure in a fubordinate government, the keeping in their own hands the command of the revenue, and the pay of the officers of govern-

F 2

ment,

ment, as a fecurity for the conduct of thofe officers towards them.

Under the firft head come all the difputes about the King's inftructions, and the governor's power, as founded on them.

The King's commiffion to his governor, which grants the power of government, and directs the calling of a legiflature, and the eftablifhing courts, at the fame time that it fixes the governor's power, according to the feveral powers and directions granted and appointed by the commiffion and inftructions, adds " and by fuch *further powers, inftruc-* " *tions,* and authorities, as fhall, at any " time hereafter, be granted or appointed " you, under our fignet or fign manual, or " by our order in our privy council." It fhould here feem, that the fame power which framed the commiffion, with this claufe in it, could alfo iffue its *future orders and in-* *ftructions* in confequence thereof: but the people of the colonies fay, that the inhabitants of the colonies are entitled to all the privileges of Englifhmen; that they have a right to participate in the legiflative power; and that no commands of the crown, by orders in council, inftructions, or letters from Secretaries of State, are binding upon them, further than they pleafe to acquiefce under
fuch,

fuch, and conform *their own actions* thereto;
that they hold this right of legiſlature, not
derived from the grace and will of the crown,
and depending on the commiſſion which
continues at the will of the crown ; that this
right is inherent and eſſential to the community, as a community of Engliſhmen :
and that therefore they muſt have all the
rights, privileges, and full and free exerciſe
of their own will and liberty in making
laws, which are neceſſary to that act of le-
giſlation,—uncontrouled by any power of the
crown, or of the governor, preventing or
fuſpending that act ; and, that the clauſe in
the commiſſion, directing the governor to
call together a legiſlature by his writs, is de-
clarative and not creative ; and therefore he
is directed to act conformably to a right actually already exiſting in the people, &c.
and therefore that ſuch clauſe ought not to
be in the commiſſion, or to be underſtood
as being of no effect, ſo far as concerns the
coloniſts.

When I ſpeak of full uncontrouled independent powers of debate and reſult, ſo far
as relates to the framing bills and paſſing them
into laws, uncontrouled by any power of the
crown or of the governor, as an eſſential
property of a free legiſlature ; I find ſome
perſons in the colonies imagine, that I re-

prefent

prefent the colonies as claiming a power of legiflature independent of the King's or governor's negative.---Thefe gentlemen knowing that it is not my intention to do injuftice to the colonies, wifh me fo to explain this matter, that it may not bear even the interpretation of fuch a charge---I do therefore here defire, that the reader will give his attention to diftinguifh a full, free, uncontrouled, independent power, in the act of legiflation,—from a full, free, uncontrouled, independent power, of carrying the refults of that legiflation into effect, independent either of the Governor's or King's negative. The firft right is that which I reprefent the colonifts claiming, as a right effential to the very exiftence of the legiflature: The fecond is what is alfo effential to the nature of a fubordinate legiflature, and what the colonifts never call in queftion. That therefore the point here meant to be ftated as in debate, is, Whether a fubordinate legiflature can be inftructed, reftricted, and controuled, in the very act of legiflation? whether the King's inftructions or letters from fecretaries of ftate, and fuch like fignifications of his Majefty's will and pleafure, is a due and conftitutional application of the governors, or of the royal negative?---The colonifts conftantly deny it, —and miniftry, otherwife fuch inftructions would not be given, conftantly maintain it.

After

After experience of the confufion and obftruction which this dubitable point hath occafioned to bufinefs, it is time furely that it
were fome way or other determined. Or
whether in fact or deed, the people of the
colonies, having every right to the full powers of government, and *to a whole legiflative
power*, are not under this claim entitled in
the powers of legiflature and the adminiftration of government, to ufe and exercife in
conformity to the laws of Great Britain, the
fame, full, free, independent, unreftrained
power and legiflative will in their feveral corporations, and under the King's commiffion
and their refpective charters, as the government and legiflature of Great Britain holds
by its conftitution, and under the great charter.

Every fubject, born within the realm, under the freedom of the Government of Great
Britain, or by adoption admitted to the fame,
has an effential indefeafible right to be governed, under fuch a mode of government as
has the unreftrained exercife of all thofe
powers which form the freedom and rights
of the conftitution ; and therefore " the
" crown cannot eftablifh any colony upon—
" or contract it within *a narrower fcale* than
" the fubject is entitled to, by the great

" charter

" charter of England*." The government
of each colony muſt have the ſame powers,
and the ſame extent of powers that the government of Great Britain has,---and muſt have,
while it does not act contrary to the laws
of Great Britain, the ſame freedom and in-
dependence of legiſlature, as the parliament
of Great Britain has. This right (ſay they)
is founded, not only in the general principles of the rights of a Britiſh ſubject, but
is actually declared, confirmed, or granted
to them in the commiſſions and charters
which gave the particular frame of their reſpective conſtitutions. If therefore, in the
firſt original eſtabliſhment, like the original contract, they could not be eſtabliſhed,
upon any ſcale ſhort of the full and compleat ſcale of the powers of the Britiſh government,---nor the legiſlature be eſtabliſhed on any thing leſs than the whole legiſlative power ; much leſs can this power of
government and legiſlature, thus eſtabliſhed,
be governed, directed, reſtrained or reſtrict-
ed, by any poſterior inſtructions or commands
by the letters of Secretaries of State. But
upon the ſuppoſition, that a kind of general indetermined power in the crown, to
ſuperadd inſtructions to the commiſſions and
charter be admitted, where the coloniſts do

* Hiſtorical Review of the Conſtitution and Government of Penſylvania, p. 11.

not

not make a queſtion of the caſe wherein it is exerted, yet there are particular caſes wherein both directive and reſtrictive inſtructions are given, and avowedly not admitted by the coloniſts. It is a ſtanding inſtruction, as a ſecurity of the dependence of the government of the colonies, on the mother country, that no acts wherein the King's rights, or the rights of the mother country or of private perſons can be affected, ſhall be enacted into a law without a clauſe ſuſpending the effect thereof, till his Majeſty's pleaſure ſhall be known. This ſuſpending clauſe is univerſally * rejected on the principles above, becauſe ſuch ſuſpenſion disfranchiſes the inherent full power of legiſlature, which they claim by their rights to the Britiſh liberties, and by the ſpecial declarations of ſuch in their charters. It does not remove this difficulty by ſaying, that the crown has already in its hands the power of fixing this point, by the effect of its negative given to its governor. It is ſaid, that if the crown ſhould withdraw that inſtruction, which allows certain bills to be paſſed into laws with a ſuſpending clauſe, which inſtruction is not meant as a reſtriction upon, but an indulgence to the legiſlatures ; that if the crown

---

* In ſome caſes of emergency, and in the caſes of the concerns of individuals, the inſtruction has been ſubmitted to, but the principle never.

ſhould

fhould withdraw this inftruction, and pe-
remptorily reftrain its governor from enacting laws, under fuch circumftances as the
wifdom of government cannot admit of,
that then thefe points are actually fixed by
the true conftitutional power ; but where-
ever it is fo faid, I muft repeat my idea, that
this does not remove the difficulty. For
waving the doubt which the colonifts might
raife, efpecially in the charter colonies, how
far the governor ought, or ought not, to
be reftricted from giving his affent in cafes
contrary only to inftructions, and not to the
laws of Great Britain ; waving this point,
let adminiftration confider the effects of this
meafure. In cafes where the bills, offered
by the two branches, are for providing laws,
abfolutely neceffary to the continuance, fupport, and exercife of government, and where
yet the orders of the crown, and the fenfe
of the people, are fo widely different as to
the mode, that no agreement can ever be
come to in thefe points---Is the government
and adminiftration of the government of the
colonies to be fufpended ? The intereft, perhaps the being of the plantations, to be hazarded by this obftinate variance, and can
the exercife of the crown's negative, in fuch
emergencies, and with fuch effect, ever be
taken up as a meafure of adminiftration ?
And when every thing is thrown into confufion,

9

fufion, and abandoned even to ruin by fuch meafure, will adminiftration juftify itfelf by faying, that it is the fault of the Colonifts? On the contrary, this very ftate of the cafe fhows the neceffity of fome other remedy.

In the courfe of examining thefe matters, will arife to confideration the following very material point. As a principal tie of the fubordination of the legiflatures of the colonies on the government of the mother country, they are bound by their conftitutions and charters, to fend all *their acts* of legiflature to England, to be confirmed or abrogated by the crown; but if any of the legiflatures fhould be found to do almoft every act of legiflature, by votes or orders, even to the repealing the effects of acts, fufpending eftablifhments of pay, paying fervices, doing chancery and other judicatory bufinefs: if matters of this fort, done by thefe votes and orders, never reduced into the form of an act, have their effect without ever being fent home as acts of legiflature, or fubmitted to the allowance or difallowance of the crown: If it fhould be found that many, or any of the legiflatures of the colonies carry the powers of legiflature into execution, independent of the crown by this device,—it will be a point to be determined how far, in fuch cafes, the fubordination of the legiflatures of the colonies to the government of the mother country

country is maintained or fufpended ;—or if,
from emergencies arifing in thefe governments, this device is to be admitted, the
point, how far fuch is to be admitted, ought
to be determined ; and the validity of thefe
votes and orders, thefe Senatus-Confulta fo
far declared. For a point of fuch great
importance in the fubordination of the colony legiflatures, and of fo queftionable a
caft in the valid exercife of this legiflative
power, ought no longer to remain in queftion.

The next general point yet undetermined,
the determination of which very effentially
imports the fubordination and dependance
of the colony governments on the government of the mother country, is, the manner
of providing for the fupport of government, and for all the executive officers of the
crown. The freedom and right efficiency
of the conftitution require, that the executive and judicial officers of government
fhould be independent of the legiflative ;
and more efpecially in popular governments,
where the legiflature itfelf is fo much influenced by the humours and paffions of the
people ; for if they do not, there will be
neither juftice nor equity in any of the courts
of law, nor any efficient execution of the
laws and orders of government in the magiftracy : according, therefore, to the conftitution

tution of Great Britain, the crown has the appointment and payment of the feveral executive and judicial officers, and the legiflature fettles a permanent and fixed appointment for the fupport of government and the civil lift in general: The crown therefore has, *à fortiori*, a right to require of the colonies, to whom, by its commiffion or charter, it gives the power of government, fuch permanent fupport, appropriated to the offices, not the officers of government, that they may not depend upon the temporary and arbitrary will of the legiflature.

The crown does, by its inftructions to its governors, order them to require of the legiflature a permanent fupport. This order of the crown is generally, if not univerfally rejected, by the legiflatures of the colonies. The affemblies quote the precedents of the Britifh conftitution, and found all the rights and privileges which they claim on the principles thereof. They allow the truth and fitnefs of this principle in the Britifh conftitution, where the executive power of the crown is immediately adminiftered by the King's Majefty; yet fay, under the circumftances in which they find themfelves, that there is no other meafure left to them to prevent the mifapplications of public money, than by an annual voting and appropriation of the falaries

ries of the governor and other civil officers,
iffuing from monies lodged in the hands of a
provincial treafurer appointed by the affemblies: For in thefe fubordinate governments,
remote from his Majefty's immediate influence, adminiftered often times by neceffitous
and rapacious governors who have no natural, altho' they have a political connection
with the country, experience has fhewn that
fuch governors have mifapplied the monies
raifed for the fupport of government, fo that
the civil officers have been left unpaid, even
after having been provided for by the affembly. The point then of this very important
queftion comes to this iffue, Whether the
inconveniencies arifing, and experienced by
fome inftances of mifapplications of appropriations (for which however there are in
the King's courts of law, due and fufficient
remedies againft the offender) are a fufficient
reafon and ground for eftablifhing a meafure
fo directly contrary to the Britifh conftitution : and whether the inconveniencies to be
traced in the hiftory of the colonies, through
the votes and journals of their legiflatures,
in which the fupport of governors, judges,
and officers of the crown will be found to
have been withheld or reduced on occafions,
where the affemblies have fuppofed that
they have had reafon to difapprove the nomination,—or the perfon, or his conduct ;---
whether,

whether, I fay, thefe inconveniencies have not been more detrimental, and injurious to government; and whether, inftead of thefe colonies being dependent on, and governed under, the officers of the crown, the fcepter is not reverfed, and the officers of the crown dependant on and governed by the affem- blies, as the Colonifts themfelves allow, that this meafure * " renders the governor, " and all the other fervants of the crown, " dependant on the affembly."---But the operation of this meafure does not end here; it extends to the affuming by the affemblies the actual executive part of the government in the cafe of the revenue, than which no- thing is more clearly and unqueftionably fettled in the crown. In the colonies the treafurer is folely and entirely a fervant of the affembly or general court; and although the monies granted and appropriated be, or ought to be, granted to the crown on fuch appropriations, the treafurer is neither named by the crown, nor its governor, nor gives fecurity to the crown or to the Lord High Treafurer, (which feems the moft proper) nor in many of the colonies, is to obey the governor's warrant in the iffue, nor accounts in the auditor's office, nor in any one colony is it admitted, that he is liable to fuch ac- count. In confequence of this fuppofed ne-

* Smith's Hiftory of New York, p. 118.

ceffity,

ceffity, for the affembly's taking upon them the adminiftration of the treafury and revenue, the governor and fervants of the crown, in the ordinary revenue of government, are not only held dependant on the affembly, but all fervices where fpecial appropriations are made for the extraordinaries which fuch fervices require, are actually executed and done by commiffioners appointed by the affembly, to whofe difpofition fuch appropriations are made liable. It would be perhaps inviduous, and might tend to prejudging on points which ought very ferioufly and difpaffionately to be examined, if I were here to point out in the feveral inftances of the actual execution of this affumed power, how almoft every executive power of the crown lodged in its governor, is, where money is neceffary, thus exercifed by the affembly and its commiffioners. I therefore reft the matter here.

In the firft edition of this book I pointed out the meafure of the government's fettling fixed falaries on the officers of the crown in America, independant of the people. I afterwards withdrew this propofition, from an apprehenfion of the evils which might arife to the fervice by thefe fixed and permanent falaries, having a tendency to render the chief offices finecures, procured by the

the corruptors for the corrupted, in rever-
fions, from generation to generation. This
meafure, hath been fince eftablifhed by parliament. But why, thofe who had the conduct of it would not admit a claufe, providing
that fuch falaries, hereafter to be eftablifh'd, fhould be given to no perfon but to
fuch as actually executed the office; is not
very eafy to conceive, unlefs from fuggeftions
that one would not willingly take up againft
the integrity of their intentions.---If that
act fhould ever be explained, or amended
by any fubfequent law, it is to be hoped,
that this claufe would not again be omitted.

The fame motive, and reafon which
weigh'd with government, to adopt this
meafure of fixing falaries for the civil officers of the crown in America during the
time of their ferving, fhould operate, to induce government to take one ftep further,
in order to render the meafure quite effectual, that is, to fettling fome half-pay or
other penfion, on fuch officers as are from
age or ill health removed; or after long
fervices in that country, are permitted to
return home. The appointments of the
governors &c. are fuch, wherein no fortunes can either be made, or faved with
honor.---If they have no fortunes of their

G   own,

own, they muft, after their fervices, return home to ftarve. " There is no man" (fays an American, the intelligent author of the Hiftorical Review of Penfylvania) " long, or much converfant in this over- " grown city {London] who hath not often " found himfelf in company with the fhades " of departed governors, doomed to wan- " der out the refidue of their lives, full of " the agonizing remembrance of their paft " eminence, and the fevere fenfation of " prefent neglect. *Sir. William Keith,* upon " his return, was added to this unfortunate " lift, concerning whom, the leaft that can " be faid is, that either none but men of " fortune fhould be appointed to ferve in " fuch diftinguifh'd offices; or otherwife " for the honor of government itfelf, fuch " as are recalled without any notorious im- " putation on their conduct fhould be pre- " ferved from that wretchednefs and con- " tempt which they have been but too fre- " quently permitted to fall into, for want " even of a proper fubfiftance."----The means of avoiding this wretched iffue of their fervice, by making up a fortune to live on when they fhall be recalled, is a tempta- tion which ought to be removed from this fituation, by thofe who regard the King's fervice, even if they have no feelings of compaffion for his fervants.---A fmall pit-

tance

tance would pay this, and that very fum might engage the fervices of thefe half pay officers in a way not unufeful to govern-ment.---They might, in confideration of this pay, be directed to attend the Board of trade or whatever board or officer was for the time being, the acting minifter for the bufinefs of America, in order to give expla-nations, or opinions, as they fhould be re-quired; or even to report, if ever they fhould be thought worthy to have any mat-ter, requiring a report, refer'd to them; they might be formed into a kind of fubordinate board for this purpofe.---The benefit of fuch a meafure needs not to be expatiated upon, and to explain the operation of it would be too minute a detail for the curfory mention which I here make of it.

It is a duty of perfect obligation from go-vernment towards the colonies, to preferve the liberty of the fubject, the liberty of the conftitution : It is a duty alfo of prudence in government towards itfelf, as fuch conduct is the only permanent and fure ground, whereon to maintain the dependance of thofe countries, without deftroying their utility as colonies.

The conftitutions of thefe communities, founded in wife policy, and in the laws of

the

the Britifh conftitution, are eftablifhed by
their feveral charters, or by the King's commiffion to his governors, being in the nature of a charter of government. In thefe,
all the juft powers of government are defcribed and defined, the rights of the fubject
and of the conftitution declared, and the modes
of government agreeable thereto eftablifhed.
As thefe pafs under the great feal, no jurifdictions or offices will be inferted in the powers
granted, but what are agreeable and conformable to law, and the conftitution of the
realm. Although the King's commiffion is barely a commiffion during pleafure, to the perfon therein named as governor, yet it pro-
vides for a fucceffion without vacancy, or
interregnum, and is not revoked but by a
like commiffion, with like powers: It becomes the known, eftablifhed conftitution
of that province which hath been eftablifhed
on it, and whofe laws, courts, and whole
frame of legiflature and judicature, are
founded on it: It is the charter of that province: It is the indefeafible and unalterable
right of thofe people: It is the indefeafible
right by which thofe colonies thus eftablifhed, are the colonies of Great Britain, and
therefore not to be altered; but by fuch
means as any reform or new eftablifhment
may take place in Great Britain: It cannot,
in its effential parts, be altered or deftroyed
by

by any royal inftructions or proclamation ; or
by letters from fecretaries of ftate : It cannot be fuperceded, or in part annulled, by
the iffuing out of any other commiffions not
known to this conftitution.

In thefe charters, and in thefe commiffions,
the crown delegates to the governor for the
time being, all its conftitutional power and
authority civil and military—the power of
legiflation fo far as the crown has fuch---its
judicial and executive powers, its powers of
chancery, admiralty jurifdiction, and that
of fupreme ordinary.—All thofe powers, as
they exift and refide in the crown, are known
by the laws and courts of the realm, and as
they are derived to the governors are defined,
declared, and *patent*, by the charters and
commiffions *patent*. It is therefore the duty
and true interefts of the Colonifts to maintain
thefe rights, thefe privileges, this conftitution : It is moreover the duty and true intereft of King, Lords, and Commons, to be
watchful over, to fupport and defend thefe
rights of the colonies : It is the duty of adminiftration to have conftant regard to the
exercife of them, otherwife it will be found
a dangerous thing to have given fo much of
civil power out of the King's hands, and to
have done fo little to maintain thofe into
whofe hands it is entrufted. How far the

efta-

eftablifhment of the office and power of a
military commander in chief, not fubordinate
but fuperior to thefe conftitutional commanders in chief, how far the fuperceding
of the *Confular* power of the Governors, by
eftablifhing, not for the time of war only, but
as a fettled fyftem, this *Dictatorial* power,
with a jurifdiction extending over the whole of
the Britifh empire in America, is conformable
to law, to prudence, or found policy, is matter
of very ferious confideration to thofe who regard the liberties of the conftitution.

All military power whatfoever, as far as
law and the conftitution will juftify the eftablifhment of fuch, is refident in the eftablifhed office of governor, as Captain general and commander in chief. There is no
power here granted, but what is fpecified
and defined by the nature of the conftitution.
The fubject and ftate is duly guarded againft
any extenfions of it, by the feveral laws
which the legiflatures of the feveral colonies
have provided to limit that power; and it
can be exercifed by none but fuch perfons as
are within the jurifdiction of the province,
who deriving their powers from the fupream
powers are amenable to the laws of the province; and to the governor, who is himfelf
fpecially refponfible for the truft. This
power thus limited becomes part of the
conftitution of the province, and unlefs thus
limited,

limited, and thus confidered as part of the conftitution of the government, it may be matter of great doubt, whether the crown would be advifed to erect any military powers whatever. But under fuch limitations, and as a known eftablifhed part of the confti- tution, the crown may fafely grant thefe powers, and the people fafely live under them, becaufe the governor is " required " and commanded to do and execute all " things in due manner, that fhall belong " unto *the truft* repofed in him, according " to the feveral powers and authorities men- " tioned in the charter." That is to fay, according to thofe powers which in charter governments are exprefsly part of the confti- tution; and which from the very nature of the *commiffion patent* in fuch conftitutions as are called King's governments, are like- wife to be confidered in the fame light.—— When this military branch of the governor's office is eftablifhed and received as part of the conftitution, the King may fafely grant, and the people fafely act under " a power " to levy, arm, mufter, command, and " employ all perfons whatfoever refiding " within fuch province; to refift and repell " both at land and fea, all enemies, pirates, " and rebels, and fuch to purfue in or out " of the limits of the province: to erect and " build forts, to fortify and furnifh, and to

" commit

" commit the command of the fame to fuch
" perfon or perfons as to fuch governor fhall
" feem meet—and the fame again to dif-
" mantle or demolifh: and to do and execute
" all and every other thing which to a cap-
" tain general doth or ought of right to be-
" long, as fully and amply as any other the
" King's captains general doth or hath ufual-
" ly done, according to the powers in the
" commiffion and charter granted." It becomes hence a queftion of the higheft import,
and leading to the moft dangerous confequences
—Whether, after the conftitutions and offices
of a colony or province are thus eftablifhed,
the King himfelf can difmember the fame,
fo as to grant to any office or officer not
known to the conftitution, any part whatfoever of thofe powers, as he cannot dif-
franchife a people having fuch powers, under fuch charters, of any the leaft right or
privilege included in, or as derived from,
the eftablifhment of their conftitution of
government ? This is a queftion that it
would behove the crown lawyers well to
confider, whenever it fhall be referred to
their confideration. If every military power
that can legally be included in any commiffion which the crown will be advifed to iffue,
is already included in the office of governor,
as part of the conftitution of thefe provinces
and colonies, what commiffion can fupercede
the

the fame, or give power to any other officer
than the governor to exercife thefe powers
within fuch province? It was fuggefted by
the writer of thefe papers at the beginning
of the late war, that *if the neceffity of the cafe
in time of war* urged to the appointing a military commander in chief of all North America,
who fhould command all military operations,
and prefide in general over all military eftablifhments for the general fervice, independent
of, and fuperior to, the powers and authorities
already granted to the governors and captains
general of the provinces,—it was fuggefted,
that no commiffions under the private feal
and fign manual could fupercede, revoke,
or take precedence of thefe powers granted
by letters patent under the great feal, and it
was determined accordingly, that the military
commander in chief muft have his commiffion patent under the great feal. But when it
came to be confidered what powers fhould be
granted in this commiffion, the wifdom and
prudence of the great ftatefman and lawyer
who was then entrufted with that feal, iffued
the commiffion for the commander in chief,
in general and indefinite terms, " to have,
" hold, exercife, and enjoy the faid office dur-
" ing pleafure, together with all the powers,
" authorities, rights and privileges, thereunto
" belonging, fubject however to fuch reftric-
" tions, limitations, and inftructions, as are
" given, or to be given, from time to time,
" under

" under the royal fign manual, and charging
" and requiring all the governors, lieutenant
" governors, deputy governors, and prefi-
" dents of the council of the refpective co-
" lonies and provinces of North America,
" and all other officers civil or military with-
" in the fame, to be aiding and affifting in
" this command." Thefe general powers
undefined and unknown, and fuch as no
minifter who advifes the iffuing fuch commiffion will venture to defcribe, thefe general words, power and command, either
mean nothing, or fuppofe every thing, when
a juftifiable occafion, or perhaps a coloura-
ble pretext calls for the exercife of them. It
was feen that thefe general defcriptions were
either dangerous or nugatory, and therefore
the commander in chief had at the fame time,
another commiffion under the private feal and
fign manual, in which were inferted all the
powers for governing the forces, &c. which
were not thought proper to be included and
granted by letters patent under the great
feal. I am no lawyer, and do not therefore
prefume to give an opinion of decifion, but
venture to affirm, that it ought well to be
confidered, Whether if this commiffion be
now in time of peace interpreted to extend
to any one purpofe at all, it muft not extend
to much more than can be juftified by either
law or the conftitution? Whether (the conftitutions of the provinces and colonies remaining)

maining) the office of a commander in chief
exercising such powers as are supposed neceffary *to the execution of that command*, can
be eftablifhed over all North America? Thefe
military powers, as they exift in the governor's commiffion, exift and muft be exercifed under the civil limitations and regulations of the conftitution, nor can any law
martial, or any other military ordonnances
be publifhed, without the concurrence of
the other branches of the legiflature. But
the difference of this *dictatorial power* of a
military commander in chief, and the *confular* power of the provincial governor, can
not be better defcribed than in the following
paffage: *Ea poteftas (fcilicet dictatoria) per
fenatum more Romano magiftratui maxima
permittitur, exercitum parare, bellum gerere,
coercere omnibus modis focios atque cives:
domi militiæque imperium atque judicium fum-
mum habere: aliter fine populi juffu nullius
earum rerum confuli jus eft* *.

If it fhould upon confideration and advice,
of which I am no judge, be found that the
dictatorial power and command of a military
commander in chief, fuperior to the provincial governors (however neceffity, in time of
war, might juftify it, *ne quid refpublica ae-
trimenti capiat)* is not agreeable and conformable to law, and to the conftitution ei-

* Salluft, Bellum Catilinarium.

ther

ther of Great Britain or of the colonies in
time of peace; it may be fuppofed that fuch
will not be continued in time of peace, and that
as foon as the * hoftile ftate of Indian affairs
ceafes, this power will be made to ceafe alfo.

In the confiderations above, I have fuggefted the doubt; whether this commiffion
may be right as to law and the conftitution.
But if there be only a doubt of its legality,
and there no longer remains an abfolute
neceffity for the continuance of it; I think
it may be fairly made to appear, that neither
prudence nor found policy can juftify it.

Such powers with fuch a command may
be dangerous to the liberty of the fubject,
to the liberties of the conftitution of the
colonies on one hand: And on the other
hand, there are no people in the whole
world, when their liberties fhall become in-
fected and undermined, fo liable to become
the inftruments of dominion, as a people
who have lived under a free and popular
government. This has been the fate of the
free ftates of Greece and Italy; this the fate
of Rome itfelf:—But may heaven avert,
that this ever becomes the ftate of the Britifh colonies.

* The firft edition of this book was publifhed during the
continuance of the hoftilities of the Indians, after the
General Peace amongft the Europeans. That hath ceafed.

3

There

There is not, there cannot be any danger in this power at prefent in any degree;---but thus planted when it comes to grow, *occulto velut arbor ævo*, when it has taken root, and has fpread its branches through the land, it will foon overtop and overfhadow all the weaker, humbler fhoots of civil liberty. Set once this lord of the foreft on a permanent footing, it will foon have, as Mr. Harrington fays, " Toes that have roots, and arms that " will bring forth what fruit you pleafe."

It is a common obfervation, but it is as trivial as common, which fuppofes the danger of the colonies revolting, and becoming independent of the mother country. No one colony can by itfelf become fo—and no two under the prefent ftate of their conftitutions, have any poffible communion of power or intereft that can unite them in fuch a meafure; they have not the means of forming fuch; they have neither legiflative nor executive powers, that are extended to more than one; the laws of one extend not to the other; they have no common magiftracy, no common command, in fhort, no one principle of affociation amongft them : On the contrary, as I have faid elfewhere, the different manner in which they are fettled, the different modes under which they live, the different forms of charters, grants, and frame of government which they poffefs, the

the various principles of repulsion that these create, the different interests which they actuate, the religious interests by which they are actuated, the rivalship and jealousies which arise from hence, and the impracticability, if not impossibility, of reconciling and accommodating these incompatible ideas and claims, will keep the several provinces and colonies perpetually independent of, and unconnected with each other, and dependent on the mother country. The particular danger here meant to be pointed out, is that of furnishing them with a *principle of union*, disunited from the civil constitution, by establishing a military commander in chief over the whole. If ever the colonies revolt, and set up an empire in America, here begins the history of it; from this period as from the first dynasty, will future historians deduce their narrative. The Romans, as long as they governed their provinces by the vigour of policy, preserved their dependence, and see what that policy was.---I will produce two instances, one in Italy, the other in Greece ; *Cæterùm habitari tantùm, tanquam urbem, Capuam, frequentarique placuit : corpus nullum civitatis nec senatûs, nec plebis concilium, nec magistratus esse, sine consilio publico*, sine imperio, *multitudinem nullius rei inter se sociam ad* consensum inhabilem fore *

* Liv. lib. 26. § 16. lib. 45. § 30.

The

The other is as follows, after the Romans had entirely overcome Perſeus, and reduced all Macedonia, they reſtore it to its liberty; but to diſarm that liberty of all power of revolt, they divide Macedon into four regions or provinces, not barelv by boundary lines, and geographical diſtinctions, but by diſſevering and ſeparating their intereſts; *diviſæ Macedoniæ, partium uſibus ſeparatis, et regionatim commerciis interruptis* ‡.

Under this policy they preſerved their provinces and maintained the empire of Rome; but when they took up the falſe policy of eſtabliſhing and continuing, in time of peace, military commanders in chief in their provinces, the people of the provinces became an army, and that army ſubverted the empire. " By how much the more remote (ſays Machiavell) their wars were, by ſo much they thought thoſe prorogations more convenient, by which it happened that the commander might gain ſuch an intereſt in the army, as might make it diſclaim the

‡ I beg that it may be here underſtood, that while by this example, I mean to point the danger of giving any principle of union amongſt the ſeveral colonies, and the ſure wiſdom of keeping this diſunion of council and imperium amongſt them, I do from principles of policy as well as thoſe of ſtrict juſtice, invariably recommend the preſervation of their reſpective conſtitutions, in the full uſe and exerciſe of all their rights and privileges.

power of the fenate." Publius Philo was the firſt to whom his military commiſſion was prolonged, and this precedent once ſettled, we hear next of the ſoldiers in Spain declaring L. Marcius imperator in the field. *Res mali exempli imperatores legi ab exercitibus et ſolenne auſpicatorum comitiorum in* caſtra et provincias, *procul ab legibus magiſtratibuſque, ad militarem temeritatem tranferri* †. "This " it was that enabled Marius and Sylla to " debauch the army ; this* it was that en- " abled Cæſar to conquer his native country. " It may be objected, that their great affairs " could not have been managed at ſo great " a diſtance, without ſuch commands.—It " is poſſible indeed, that their empire might " have been longer before it came to that " height, but then it would have been " more laſting ; for the adverſary would " never have been able to have *erected a* " *monarchy* and deſtroyed their liberty ſo " ſoon."—This power, monarchical from its very nature, may have been dangerous to a commonwealth, and have ruined the republic by eſtabliſhing a monarchy upon it ; but it will be aſked, How can this ever be the caſe in a regulated monarchy ? Can it be ſuppoſed that any future King can ever wiſh to change that conſtitution in which his power is eſtabliſhed ? Can it be ſuppoſed that

† Lib. 26. § 2.

a free

a free people could ever be fo wild as to put themfelves under an unbounded military power, in order to become independent of a limited and civil power? What may be the turn of future events, Heaven only knows; yet experience has taught us that former Kings have thus miftaken their real intereft, and former people have been driven to this diftraction: And if, on any fuch future occafion, there fhould be found eftablifhed by repeated and continued cuftom, by unrefifted precedents, the office of commander in chief of all North America, not only in the poffeffion, but in the actual exercife of thefe powers:—*Exercitum parare*—*bellum gerere*—*coercere omnibus modis focios atque cives*—He might like another Monck, in fuch critical fituation, give the turn to the balance, and negotiate, either with the prince, or the people, as his inclinations and interefts lead him, for the liberties of Great Britain.— If in any future period of events the fate c war fhould reduce Great Britain to ftruggle for its rights, its power, perhaps, its fafety, on terms hardly equal, with all its force, to its fupport in Europe: And in the courfe of that ftruggle, there be eftablifhed in North America a commander in chief, with an army at his command; with a degree of authority prefiding over the civil power, and civil governors; with an extent of

H   command

command capable of affociating and uniting a number of powers, otherwife, incapable of fuch union; if fuch a man, at
fuch a crifis, fhould have ambition enough
to wifh, and fpirit enough to dare to fet
up an independent empire in America, he
could want, in fuch crifis, no fupport that
a wife and artful enemy to Great Britain
would not give him: *Nunc illud effe tempus
occupandi res dum turbata omnia nová atque
incondítá libertate effent, dum regis ftipendiis
paftus obverfaretur miles, dum ab Annibále
miffi duces affueti militibus juvare poffent in-
cepta*. The enemy could not wifh better
ground, than fuch an eftablifhment fo circumftanced at fuch a crifis, nor could take a
more effectual meafure for the ruin of Great
Britain, than fetting up and fupporting an
American empire; for there could be no
doubt of the fuccefs of the meafure, and no
doubt of its effect.

The prefent government found already
eftablifhed, from the neceffity of things in
the ftate of the laft war, fuch a power—and
as the effects of that war in America can not
be faid wholly to ceafe, † while the Indian
affairs wear fuch an hoftile appearance, this
power is for the prefent continued: But we
may confide in the true genuine principles of

* Liv. lib. 24. § 24.
† This is not the cafe now, 1768.

liberty,

liberty, which animate the royal breaft; we
may truft in the wifdom and prudence of
the King's miniftry;—that no fuch officer as
that of a military commander in chief, prefiding over all North America, and preceeding
in military matters, and in the power *neceffary to the execution of that command*, the
conftitutional power of governor; we may
truft, * I venture to fay, that no fuch office
will ever be made an eftablifhment *in time
of peace*. Regular troops are in the fame
manner and degree neceffary in North America, as in Britain or Ireland ;—but we fhall
fee them eftablifhed there under the fame
relations to the civil power as in Ireland;
we fhall fee again the civil governments, as
eftablifhed under commiffions patent, and
charters, predominate. If I, a private perfon,
and wholly removed from all advice or con-
fultation with miniftry, might be permitted
to indulge a conjecture, I would fuppofe,
from fome leading meafures which are already taken, of dividing the American army
into commanderies, and putting a ftop to
draughts on general contingencies, that the
danger and expence of the office of commander in chief, will foon ceafe: and that
the feveral commandants of the troops appointed, each to their refpective diftricts,
having every power neceffary for the dif-

* I could venture to fay fo much when this was firft
written, and had grounds for what I faid.

cipline

cipline and government of the regular forces
under their command, will be eftablifhed in
the fame relation and fubordination to the
civil power of that government, within which
their command lies, as the commander in
chief in Ireland ftands to the fupream civil
power of Ireland :—and that as a commander
in chief of thofe forces may in cafe of the
commencement of hoftilities, or of actual
open war, be again neceffary ;—if fuch neceffity appears firft here in Europe, his Majefty will immediately appoint fuch, and that
if fuch neceffity fhould appear firft in America, there will be proper provifion and regulations made for the giving effect to fuch
neceffary powers, *without leaving it to the
judgment or will of the army to fay when
that is neceffary, or what powers in fuch
cafe, are neceffary.*—The feveral governors of
the colonies fhould have inftructions, in cafe
of fuch emergency, to meet, and in council
to give effect to this command, with fuch
powers as they fhall judge neceffary and fafe
to a General commanding in chief, until his
Majefty's pleafure can be known ; that is to
fay, power of engaging in general expences,
of ordering embargoes, of demanding veffels
and carriages, of calling upon the feveral governments for their aid in troops, &c. of
preparing an army, of taking poffeffion of
all pofts, forts, and caftles, (which in the
ordinary

ordinary courſe of the King's charters and commiſſions patent to his governors, muſt otherwiſe be under their commands—and cannot be taken from them, unleſs the charters of the government can be ſuperceded) of having the command and diſpoſal of all military ſtores—none of which powers ought to reſide in any one office, whoſe juriſdiction extends over all North America, and preceeds the civil power of governor—unleſs in ſuch caſe of neceſſity—unleſs confirmed (until his Majeſty's pleaſure can be known) by ſuch council, and under ſuch reſtrictions as the prudence of that council would ſee proper. Under ſuch an eſtabliſhment, every caſe of ſervice that could ariſe is provided for, and every caſe of danger that might ariſe from a predominant military power, is guarded againſt,

I muſt the rather ſuppoſe that the military eſtabliſhment will have that mode given to it ; as already the commander in chief, as the commiſſion now ſtands, is inſtructed in " making any ſuch preparations as ſhall be neceſſary, and are not contained in his inſtructions, that he ſhall take the opinion and aſſiſtance of the governors."

A review and ſettlement of doubted points is no where more neceſſary, than in the

maxims

maxims and rules of their law, and the ſtate of their courts. It is a rule univerſally adopted through all the colonies, that they carried with them to America the common law of England, with the power of ſuch part of the ſtatutes (thoſe concerning eccleſiaſtical juriſdiction excepted) as were in force at the time of their eſtabliſhment; but, as there is no fundamental rule whereby to ſay, what ſtatutes are admiſſible, and what not, if they admit all, they admit the full eſtabliſhment of the eccleſiaſtical juriſdiction, from which they fled to this wildern
eſs for refuge ;—if they once make a diſtinction of admitting ſome, and rejecting others, who ſhall draw the line, and where ſhall it paſs ? Beſides, as the common law itſelf is nothing but the practice and determination of courts on points of law, drawn into precedents; where the circumſtances of a country and people, and their relation to the ſtatutes and common law differ ſo greatly, the common law of theſe countries, muſt, in its natural courſe, become different, and ſometimes even contrary, or at leaſt incompatible, with the common law of England, ſo as that, in ſome caſes, the determinations ariſing both from the ſtatute and common law *muſt be rejected.* This renders the judicatories of theſe countries vague and precarious, dangerous, if not arbitrary : This leads neceſſarily (let what care

care will be taken, in forming and enacting
their provincial laws) this leads to the rendering the common law of the country different, incompatible with, if not contrary
to, and independent of, the law of the mother country, than which nothing can be
more difadvantageous to the fubject, and nothing more derogatory from the power of
the government of the mother country, and
from that fundamental maxim, that the colonifts fhall have no laws contrary to thofe
of the mother country.

I cannot avoid quoting here at length, a
very precife and juft obfervation of the author of the hiftory of New York. " The
" ftate of our laws opens a door to much
" controverfy. The uncertainty with re-
" fpect to them, renders property precari-
" ous, and greatly expofes us to the arbi-
" trary decifion of bad judges. The com-
" mon law of England is generally received,
" together with fuch ftatutes as were enact-
" ed before we had a legiflature of our own ;
" but our courts exercife a fovereign autho-
" rity in determining, *what parts of the*
" *common and ftatute law* ought to be ex-
" tended ; for it muft be admitted, that the
" difference of circumftances neceffarily re-
" quires us, in fome cafes, to *reject* the de-
" termination of both. In many inftances,
H 4   " they

" they have alfo extended even acts of par-
" liament, paffed fince we have had a diftinct
" legiflation, which is greatly adding to our
" confufion. The practice of our courts is
" not lefs uncertain than the law. Some of
" the Englifh rules are adopted, others re-
" jected. Two things therefore feem to be
" abfolutely neceffary for the public fecu-
" rity.

" Firft, *The paffing an act for fettling the*
" *extent of the Englifh laws.*

" *Secondly,* That the courts ordain a ge-
" neral fet of rules for the regulation of the
" practice."

From this reprefentation of things, by an
eminent practitioner in thofe courts, it muft
be feen that fomething is wanting, to fix
determinately the judicial powers.———But
from a further review made by government
here, it will be found that much more is
wanting.—Firft, to determine (I do not at
all take into confideration which way it be
determined, only) I fay, to determine fome
points on this head, which are, and will
otherwife remain in difpute ; but which
ought by no means to be fuffered one moment to remain in difpute.

The

The crown directs its governor to erect courts and appoint the judges thereto.--- The actual appointment of the judges is no where *directly* disputed.---But the power of erecting courts, according to this instruction, is, I believe, univerfally disputed; it being a maxim univerfally maintained by the Colonifts, that no court can be erected but by act of legiflature.---Thofe who reafon on the fide of the crown,---fay,---that the crown does not, by erecting courts in the colonies, claim any right of enacting the jurifdiction of thofe courts, or the laws whereby they are to act.——The crown names the judge, eftablifhes the court, but the jurifdiction is fettled by the laws of the realm; ---and " * cuftoms, precedents, and common judicial proceedings of a court are a " law to the court, and the determination " of courts make points to be law."——The reafoning of the Colonifts would certainly hold good againft the erection of any new jurifdiction, eftablifhed on powers not known to the laws of the realm; but how it can be applied to the oppofing the eftablifhment of courts, the laws of whofe practice, jurifdiction and powers are already fettled by the laws of the realm, *is the point in iffue, and to be determined.* It will then be fixed, beyond difpute, whether the crown can, in

* Rep. 16. 4. Rep. 53. fol. 298.

its

its colonies, erect, without the concurrence of the legiflature, courts of Chancery, Exchequer, King's Bench, Common Pleas, Admiralty, and Probate or Ecclefiaftical courts.——If it fhould be determined in favour of the reafoning, and the claims of the Colonifts,—1 fhould apprehend that the confideration of the points under this head, would become an object of government here, even in its legiflative capacity.——In which view it may be of confequence to confider, how far, and on what grounds, the rights of the crown are to be maintained by courts of King's Bench, &c. and how far the revenues by courts of Exchequer, and how far the crown and fubject may have relief by courts of equity.----If in this view we confider the defects which muft be found in Provincial courts, thofe point out the necef-fity of the eftablifhment of a remedial general court of Appeal; but if we view the only mode of appeal, which at prefent exifts, we fhall fee how inapplicable, how inadequate that court is. 1 cannot, in one view, better defcribe the defects of the provincial courts in thefe infant governments, than by that very defcription which my Lord Chief Juftice Hales gives of our county courts, in the infancy of our own government, wherein he mentions,

" *Firft,*

" *First,* The ignorance of the judges, who
" were the freeholders of the county.

" *Secondly,* That these various courts bred
" variety of law, especially in the several
" counties, for the decisions or judgments
" being made by divers courts, and several
" independent judges and judicatories, who
" had no common interest amongst them
" in their several judicatories, thereby in
" process of time, every several county
" would have several laws, customs, rules,
" and forms of proceedings.———

" *Thirdly,* That all the business of any
" moment was carried by parties and fac-
" tions, and that those of great power and
" interest in the county did easily overbear
" others in their own causes, or in such
" wherein they were interested, either by
" relation of kindred, tenure, service, de-
" pendence, or application."

Upon the first article of this parallel, it
will be no dishonour to many gentlemen sit-
ting on the benches of the courts of law in
the colonies, to say, that they are not, and
cannot be expected to be lawyers, or learned
in the law. And on the second article it is
certain, that although it be a fundamental
maxim of colony administration, that the

colonies

colonies fhall have no laws contrary to the
laws of Great Britain, yet, from the fluctuation of refolutions, and confufion in the
conftruction and practice of the law in the
divers and feveral colonies, it is certain, that
the practice of their courts, and their common law, muft be not only different from
each other, but in the confequence different
alfo from that of Great Britain. In all the
colonies the common law is received as the
foundation and main body of their law; but
each colony being vefted with a legiflative
power, the common law is thereby continually altered; fo that (as a great lawyer of
the colonies has faid) " by reafon of the di-
" verfity of the refolutions, in their refpec-
" tive fuperior courts, and of the feveral
" new acts or laws made in them feverally;
" the feveral fyftems of the laws of thofe
" colonies grow more and more variant,
" not only from one another, but alfo from
" the laws of England."

Under the third article, I fear experience
can well fay, how powerfully, even in
courts, the influence of the leaders of party
have been felt in matters between individuals.
But in thefe popular governments, and where
every executive officer is under a dependence
for a temporary, wretched, and I had almoft
faid, arbitrary fupport to the deputies of the
people,

people,---it will be no injuſtice to thé frame of human nature, either in the perſon of the judges, of the juries, or even the popular lawyer to ſuggeſt, how little the crown, or the rights of government, when oppoſed to the ſpirit of democracy, or even to the paſſions of the populace, has to expect of that ſupport, maintainance, and guardianſhip, which the courts are even by the conſtitution ſuppoſed to hold for the crown---Nor would it be any injuſtice to any of the colonies, juſt to remark in this place, how difficult, if ever practicable it is in any of their courts of common law to convict any perſon of a violation of the laws of trade, or in any matter of crown revenue. Some of our acts of parliament direct the proſecution and puniſhment of the breach of the laws of trade, to take its courſe in the courts of Vice-admiralty: And it has been thought by a very great practitioner, that if the laws of trade were regulated on a practicable application of them to the ſtate of the colony trade, that every breach of them ſhould be proſecuted in the ſame way. That there ſhould be an advocate appointed to each court from Great Britain, who, having a proper ſalary independent of the people, ſhould be directed and empowered to proſecute in that court, not only every one who was an offender, but alſo every officer of the cuſtoms, who

through

through neglect, collusion, oppression, or any other breach of his truft became fuch. --- Here I own, was it not for the precedent already eftablished by fome of the laws of trade, I fhould doubt the confiftency of this meafure with the general principle of liberty, as eftablished in the trials by a jury in the common law courts. If thefe precedents can reconcile thefe proceedings to the general principles of liberty, there can be no more effectual meafure taken; yet fuch precedents fhould be extended with caution. The defect in moft, and actual deficiency in many of the colonies, of a court of equity, does ftill more forcibly lead to the neceffity of the meafure of fome remedial court of appeal and equity.———In all the King's governments fo called,—the governor, or governor and council are the chancellor, or judges of the court of chancery.———But fo long as I underftand that the governor is, by his general inftruction, upon found principles of policy and juftice, reftrained from exercifing the office of judge or juftice in his own perfon, I own I always confidered the governor, taking up the office of chancellor, as a cafe labouring with inexplicable difficulties. How unfit are governors in general for this high office of law; and how improper is it that governors fhould be judges, where perhaps the confequence of the judg-

ment

ment may involve government, and the administration thereof, in the contentions of parties. Indeed the fact is, that the general diffidence of the wifdom of this court thus conftituted, the apprehenfion that reafons of government may mix in with the grounds of the judgment, has had an effect that the coming to this court is avoided as much as poffible, fo that it is almoft in difufe, even where the eftablifhment of it is allowed. But in the charter governments they have no chancery at all. I muft again quote the opinion of a great lawyer in the colonies,—— " there is no court of chancery in the char- " ter governments of New England," [and I believe I may add alfo in Penfylvania] " nor " any court vefted with power to determine " caufes in equity, fave only that the juf- " tices of the inferior court, and the juftices " of the fuperior court refpectively, have " power to give relief on mortgages, bonds, " and other penalties contained in deeds ; in " all other chancery and equitable matters, " both the crown and the fubject are with- " out redrefs. This introduced a practice " of petitioning the legiflative courts for re- " lief, and prompted thofe courts to inter- " pofe their authority. Thefe petitions be- " coming numerous, in order to give the " greater difpatch to fuch bufinefs, the le- " giflative courts tranfacted fuch bufinefs by
" orders

" orders or resolves, without the solemnity
" of passing acts for such purposes; and
" have further extended this power by re-
" solves and orders, beyond what a court of
" chancery ever attempted to decree, even
" to the suspending of public laws, which
" orders or resolves are not sent home for
" the royal assent. The tendency of these
" measures is too obvious to need any ob-
" servations thereon." Nor do I see how
this measure of proceeding can be ventured
upon in the colonies, or suffered to continue
by the government here, if it be supposed
that by 1 Hen. 4. 14. " it is accorded, and
" assented, that no appeal be from hence-
" forth made, or in any wise pursued in
" parliament in time to come." The general apprehension of these defects occasioned,
that at the first planting of the colonies, the
King in council here in England was established as a court of appeals from the provincial judicatories.——At the time of set-
tling these colonies, there was no precedent
of a judicatory besides those within the realm,
except in the cases of Guernsey and Jersey,
the remnants of the dutchy of Normandy,
and not united within the realm: according
to the custom of Normandy, appeals lay to
the Duke in council; and upon this ground,
appeals lay from the judicatories of these islands
to the King here, as Duke in council; and
upon

upon this general precedent (without perhaps attending to the peculiar cafe of the appeal, lying to the Duke of Normandy, and not to the King) was an appeal from the judicatories of the colonies to the King in council fettled.———But, befides the inapplicablenefs of fuch appeal to the modes of the Englifh law; befides, that this appeal does not actually take place in general, and is in fome of the charter colonies actually excluded, except in perfonal actions, wherein the matter in difference exceeds 300 *l.* fterling;———befides the difficulty of this appeal, and inefficiency of this redrefs,—the King in council never being, by the conftitution, in any other cafe, between fubject and fubject, formed as fuch a court of appeal. This body fcarce ever, in the temporary and occafional fittings, looks like a court; but is rather accidentally or particularly, than officially attended.

. Thefe general apprehenfions and reafonings, upon experience, have led many very knowing and difpaffionate men in the colonies, into a conviction of *the neceffity of fome eftablifhed and conftitutional court of appeal* and redrefs: and the following meafure has not only been fuggefted, but even taken up as matter of confideration by fome of the ableft lawyers in that country;---namely, the

I   efta-

establishment of a supreme court of appeal
and equity, not confined to any one government, but circuiting through a certain diftrict of governments; perhaps as follows;
one to Nova Scotia and New England; one
to New York, New Jerseys, Penfylvania, and
Maryland---one to Virginia, the Carolinas,
and Georgia. It has been imagined, that this
court should be established by a commission
issued to two or more persons for each district,
learned in the law, not only of the mother
country, but of the several governments in its
said district: that this commission should give
full powers of a court of chancery, with
power also of judging on matters of law, to
be brought before this court, by writ of error, from the several superior courts of the
district, which this extended to. Such court
would become an established court of appeals and redress, would regulate all the
courts of law, so that they could not exceed their jurisdiction; would have a general
superintendency over all inferior courts;
would tend to establish some regularity, and
introduce a conformity, not only amongst
the courts themselves, of the different colonies, but a conformity also to the courts of
the mother country, in the construction and
dispensation of law: such court would, more
than any other measure, not only tend to
preserve the laws, and practice of law in the
colonies,

colonies, under a conftitutional conformity to the laws of the mother country; but would alfo maintain that dependency therein, which is of the effence of colony adminiftration.

There are gentlemen on this fide the water, who feeing that this meafure is not without defect, and not feeing the neceffity of a court of chancery at all, as there is nothing contrary to the fundamentals of law, that thefe law-courts already eftablifhed fhould equatize; (if I may fo exprefs myfelf)---think, that inftead of eftablifhing any new courts of chancery,---it would be very proper to abolifh even thofe already eftablifhed, extending the power which the law-courts already take in chancering bonds, &c.———by impowering them to equatize : and after that to take fuch meafures as may beft eftablifh a fixt and conftitutional court of appeals here in England.

Senfible of the danger of innovations, and abhorrent from tampering in experiments of politics, I mention the following rather as a matter of fpeculation, than to recommend the trial : yet I cannot but obferve, that while the conftitutions of the governments of the colonies take fo exactly the model of the Britifh conftitution, it always ftruck me as a ftrange deviation in this one particular, that the governor's council of ftate, although

a difa diftinct, and I had almoft faid, an incompatible board,—with the council, one branch of the legiflature, is yet always conftituted of the fame perfons, in general nominated and liable to be fufpended by the governor.——— One may fee many advantages, befides the general conformity to the government of the mother country, in having thefe boards diftinct in their perfons, as well as their office. If the council of ftate remaining under the fame conftitution as at prefent, was compofed of men of the beft experience, fortune, and intereft in the colony, taken in common from the legiflative council, the houfe of reprefentatives, or the courts, while the members of the legiflative council, independent of the governor for their exiftence, had all and only thofe powers which are neceffary to a branch of the legiflature, much weight would be added to adminiftration in the confidence and extent of intereft that it would thereby obtain ; and to the legiflature a more true and political diftribution of power, which, inftead of the falfe and artificial lead, now held up by expedients, would throw the real and conftitutional balance of power into the hands of government.

There is a matter which at firft or laft will be found abfolutely neceffary to be done, and I would wifh to recommend it at this time ;

5   that

that when the Lords of council fhall take under confideration the general ftate of the adminiftration of the King's delegated powers
in America, they would order a general revifion of the feveral powers granted by the
feveral boards here in England, to the officers
of different kinds, under their refpective departments: If upon fuch revifion they fhall
find that thefe powers are given and granted
without any general concert, or any reference
to that union which they ought to have, as
parts of the one power centering in, and derived from the crown ; if they fhall find that
the feveral officers and offices in America,
though all branches of the one united power
of the crown, are by mifchievous rivalfhip
of departments, perpetually croffing and obftructing each other ; if they fhall find them
alternately labouring to deprefs and to depreciate that part of the crown's power,
which does not fall within their own delegation; if they fhall find that while the feveral
powers of the crown are thus by parts im-
peached, and rendered contemptible in the
eyes of the people, the whole cannot long
remain with that authority which fhould be
able to exert an equal and univerfal adminiftration throughout the colonies : if this
difconcerted delegation of powers, accompa-
nied with this diftraction in the exercife of
them, fhould be found to lead to fuch con-

I 3   fequence,

fequence, it will be found, as I have repeatedly faid elfewhere, " That it is a dan-
" gerous thing to have trufted fo much of
" civil power out of the hands of the crown;
" and to have done fo little to maintain thofe
" to whom it is intrufted." If this fhould
be found to be the ftate of things, and there
fhould arife a ferious intention of putting the
adminiftration of the colonies on a practicable footing, their Lordfhips will advife,
that thefe powers of the crown, delegated
through the powers of the feveral boards and
offices in England, fhall be fo granted as not
to interfere with each other; fo granted as
not to ferve the power or purpofes of individuals, either board offices, or officers; but
in fuch manner as fhall unite, ftrengthen,
and maintain the powers of the crown, in
the true and conftitutional eftablifhment of
them; and in fuch manner as fhall render
the adminiftration of them in the colonies,
uniform, equable, and univerfal, the common bleffing and protection of the whole.

Having thus far examined into the principles of the conftitutions of the colonies in
that relation, by which they ftood connected with the King, as Sovereign: and having reviewed thofe points of colony adminiftration which derive from thence, marking, in the courfe of that review, fuch
matters

matters as feem to require the more immediate attention of government: I will proceed to examine thofe conftitutions, in that
relation, by which the colonies have become connected to the parliament, to the
Empire, not only of the King, as Sovereign,
but to the Empire of King, Lords, and
Commons, *collectively taken*, as having the
whole fupream power in them, have become
connected to the Realm. In whatever predicament the colonies may ftand, as to their
allegiance to the King, which muft mark out
the mode of adminiftration, by which they
fhould be governed; yet the precife fettlement of this relation and connection, is
what muft decide and determine thofe
points, which have come into difpute between the government of Great Britain,
and the people of the colonies.

And firft, how much foever the colonies,
at their firft migration, may be fuppofed
to have been, or were in fact, without the
Realm, and feparated from it: Yet, from
the very nature of that union of the community, by which all civil fociety muft
fubfift, they could not have migrated, and
been abfolved of their communion and
connection to the Realm, without leave or
licence; they had fuch leave, according to
the then forms of the conftitution, and the

I 4 terms

terms were, that the fociety, community, or government which they fhould form, fhould neither act nor become any thing repugnant or contrary to the laws of the Mother Country. Here therefore is an exprefs fubordination to a certain degree—— The Colonifts allowed the fubordination, but held their allegiance, as due only to their fovereign Lord the King.---The direct and neceffary confequence of this fubordination muft be, that the legiflature of England (afterward Great Britain) muft have power to make laws which fhould be binding upon the Colonies; contrary or repugnant to which the Colonies could not act, either in their legiflative, or executive capacity--- contrary to which they could neither fettle nor trade.

In the firft attempts, indeed, which parliament made to exercife this power, in af- ferting the right which the people of the realm had, to the ufe of certain poffeffions in America, againft the exclufive claim, which the King affumed in the property of it---They were told, that it was not proper for them to make laws about America, which was not yet annexed to the realm, but was of the King's foreign dominions, in the fame manner, as Gafcoigne or Nor- mandy were, that they had no jurifdiction over

over thofe dominions; and the attempt was dropt. In a fecond attempt, wherein they took up the petition of fome fettlers of Virginia, upon the Speaker's reading a letter from the King, the petition was withdrawn,---and we find no more of the parliament, as the conftitutional legiflature of the kingdom, interpofing in thefe affairs until after the reftoration.

In the year 1643, when the two Houfes of Lords and Commons, had affumed the fovereign executive power of government, and were, in fact, the acting fovereign, they made an ordinance Nov. 2. * " Where- " by Robert Earl of Warwick is made " Governor in Chief, and Lord High- " Admiral of thofe Iflands and other plan- " tations, inhabited, planted or belonging " to any, his Majefty's the King of Eng- " land's fubjects, within the bounds, and " upon the coafts of America." At which time, a † committee was appointed, for *regulating the Plantations.* The colonies indeed, by this ordinance, changed their Sovereign. But the fovereignty was exercifed over them in the fame manner, and

---

* Scobel's Acts, and Journals of the Houfe of Commons, Nov. 2.

† Journals of the Houfe of Commons, Nov. 2.

in

in the fame fpirit as the King had attempted to exercife it, by his commiffion
of 1636, for regulating the Plantations.---
That is the parliament, not as legiflature,
but as fovereign, affumed the fame power
of making laws, ordinances, &c. for the
Plantations: nay, went one ftep further, in
1646, and charged them with a tax by excife. In 1650 this patent, or commiffion,
was revoked, and the fame power was
lodged in the council of ftate, who had
power ‡ " to grant commiffion or com-
" miffions to fuch perfon or perfons as they
" fhall think fit, with power to enforce all
" fuch to obedience, as do or fhall ftand in
" oppofition to the parliament, or their
" authority; and to grant pardons, and to
" fettle governors in all, or any of the faid
" iflands, plantations and places, and to do
" all juft things, and to ufe all lawful
" means to fettle and preferve them in
" peace and fafety, until the parliament
" fhall take further, or other order therein,
" any letters patent, or other authority,
" formerly granted or given, to the con-
" trary notwithftanding."

During the adminiftration of this fo-

‡ Scobell's Acts.

vereignty,

vereignty, an * act paffed in 1646, exempt-
ing the plantations from all cuftoms, fubfidies, taxation, impofition, or other duty,
except the excife: provided, their trade was
carried on in Englifh bottoms, *otherwife,*
they were made liable to all thefe duties.
Alfo, in * 1650, when the Iflands of Bar-
badoes, Bermudas, and Antego, and the
country of Virginia, continuing to hold for
the King, were confidered as in rebellion;
all commerce with them was prohibited.
At which time alfo, in the fame act, " all
" fhips of foreign nations, were forbid and
" prohibited to come to, or trade in, or
" traffic with any of the Englifh plantations
" in America, or any iflands, ports, or
" places thereof, which are planted by, or
" in the poffeffion of the people of this
" commonwealth, without licenfe firft
" had or obtained from the parliament,
" or council of ftate."

If we confider the parliament acting here,
as the fovereign, not the legiflature, if we
could look upon it as lawful, or de facto
fovereign for the time being, yet we fhould

---

* Note, Thefe acts or ordinances became the
ground-work of that act of parliament, after the reftoration, which was called the navigation act, of
which we fhall take notice, in its proper place.

certainly

certainly view every exertion of its power,
in the fame light, and fhould examine it by
the fame principles, as we did thofe of the
King, as fovereign, exercifed in the iffuing
his grants, charters, or commiffions. And
if we doubt whether the King, as lawful
fovereign, could legally himfelf, exercife or
commiffion other perfons to exercife thofe
powers, affumed in his commiffion of 1636,
of making laws, ordinances and conftitutions for the plantations; confidering the inherent, natural and eftablifhed rights of the
colonifts—we may *à fortiori* by much more
powerful objections, doubt the right of
thefe powers in the two houfes called then
the parliament acting as fovereign.—No
precedent therefore can be drawn from this
period. —

We have feen above how at one time
the King as fovereign, without the intervention of the parliament, affumed a right,
both adminiftrative and legiflative, to govern
the colonies.—We have feen how the parliament, without the intervention of the
King's commiffion, affumed as fovereign
the fame powers. But whatever the natural or eftablifhed rights and liberties of
the colonies were, at their firft migration,
they could not be faid, to be legally fufpended,

ed, abridged or altered by thefe affumptions of power.

Upon the reftoration of the monarchy, when many of the rights of the fubject, and of the conftitution were fettled, the conftitution of the colonies, received their great alteration : the King participated the fovereignty of the colonies with the parliament, the parliament in its proper capacity, was admitted to a fhare in the government of them : The parliament then firft, taking up the idea, indeed very naturally, from the power they had exercifed during the commonwealth, that all thefe, his Majefty's foreign dominions, and " all thefe, " his Majefty's fubjects," were of or belonging to the realm, then firft, in the proper capacity of legiflature, fupreme legiflature of the realm, interpofed in the regulation and governing of the colonies.---And hence forward, from time to time, fundry acts of parliament were made, not only 1ft, for regulating the trade of the colonies, but alfo 2dly, for ordering and limiting their internal rights, privileges and property, and even 3dly, for taxing them.—In the courfe of which events, while the Colonifts confidered this principle, that they were to be ruled and governed only by acts of parliament, together with their own laws, not

contrary

contrary to the laws of England, as the palladium of their liberties, the King from time to time, by his minifters, called in the aid of parliament to enable him to regulate and govern the colonies.—The Britifh merchants at times applied to parliament, on the affairs of the colonies, and even the Weft India Planters applied to the fame power, to carry a meafure againft the continent of North America. Hence we find enacted,

I. The navigation act, the fugar and other acts for regulating and reftraining the trade of the colonies.

II. Alfo Acts, 1. altering the nature of their eftates, by treating real eftates as chattels. 2. Reftraining them from manufactures. 3. Regulating their money. 4. Altering the nature of evidence in the courts of common law, by making an affidavit of a debt before the Lord mayor in London, &c. certifyed in writing, an evidence in their courts in America. 5. Diffolving indentures, by difcharging fuch of their fervants as fhould enlift in the King's fervice.

III. Alfo Acts, fixing a tax upon American failors, payable to the Greenwich Hofpital.

pital. 2. Likewise impoſing taxes, by the
ſeveral duties payable on ſundry goods,
if intended as materials of trade, to be
paid *within the province*, or colony, *before*
they can be put on board, for exportation.
3. Alſo, the revenue ariſing from the *duties*
payable on the poſtage of letters. 4. Alſo,
the tax of quartering ſoldiers, and ſupplying
them in their quarters. Laſtly, eſtabliſhing the claim which Great Britain makes,
of taxing the colonies in all caſes whatſoever,
by enacting the claim into a declared right,
by act of parliament.

From the uncontroverted, and univerſal
idea of the ſubordination of the colonies to
the government of the mother country,
this power, by which the parliament mak-
eth laws that ſhall be binding on the colonies, hath been conſtantly exerted by the
government of England, (afterwards Great-
Britain) and ſubmitted to by the colonies.
The fundamental maxim of the laws of
thoſe countries, is, that 1ſt, the common
law of England, together with ſuch ſtatutes
(the eccleſiaſtical laws and canons excepted)
as were enacted before the colonies had a
legiſlature of their own. 2dly, The laws
made by their own legiſlature; together
with 3dly, ſuch acts of parliament, as by a
ſpecial clauſe are extended to America, ſince

that

that time, are the laws of each province or Colony. The jurifdiction and power of every court eftablifhed in that country; the duty of every civil officer; the procefs of every tranfaction in law and bufinefs there, is regulated on this principle. Nay further, every * act of parliament paffed fince the eftablifhment of the colonies, *which refpects the general police of the realm, or the rights and liberties of the fubjects of the realm,* although not extended by any fpecial claufe to America by parliament, although without the intervention, or exprefs confent of their own refpective legiflatures or reprefentatives, hath been confidered, and I may venture to fay, adopted as part of the law and conftitution of thofe countries; but by what principle of our conftitution, by what maxim of law, this laft practice hath been eftablifhed, is not fo eafy to afcertain, any more than it will be eafy to fix any rule, when the colonies fhall adopt, or when they may refufe thofe kind of laws of the mother country. This arifes, as I have faid, from fome vague indecifive idea---That the colonies are of, or fome parts of, the realm; but how or what parts, or whether any parts at all, has never yet been thoroughly examined.——

* As the bill of rights, the 7th Wil. 3. &c.

We

We have feen what was, in reality, the dependance and fubordination of the colonifts to the King, while they were fuppofed to be fubject to him in a feignoral capacity. ——We have feen what muft have been the fame fubordination, while they were fuppofed to be fubject to the two houfes of Lords and Commons, as fovereign in the fame capacity.

Let us take up the next idea, that while they are not of the body of the realm, are no parts or parcel of the fame, but bodies corporate and politick, diftinct from and without the realm : * " They are neverthelefs, and " of right ought to be fubordinate unto, and " dependant upon the imperial crown of " Great Britain ; [i. e. the realm,] and that " the King's Majefty, by and with the ad- " vice and confent of the Lords fpiritual " and temporal, and Commons of Great " Britain affembled in parliament, had, hath, " and of right ought to have full power " and authority to make laws and ftatutes " of fufficient force and validity, to bind " the colonies and people of America, fub- " jects of the crown of Great Britain, in all " cafes whatfoever."——In this idea we have a very different ftate of the relation, namely, the imperial crown of Great Britain, the

* 6 Geo. III. c. 12.

K   King,

King, Lords and *Commons, collectively taken,* is stated *as sovereign,* on the one hand, and *the Colonists as subjects* on the other.——

There is no doubt, but that in the nature, reason, justice and necessity of the thing, there must be somewhere, *within* the body politic of every government, an absolute power. The political freedom of Great Britain, consists in this power's being lodged no where but in King, Lords and Commons in parliament assembled. This power is absolute throughout the realm,—and yet the rights and liberties of the subject are preserved, as the *Communitas Populi* is the *body,* of which this *Imperium* is the soul, reasoning, willing, and acting, in absolute and intire union with it, so as to form one political person.

There can be no doubt but that this power is absolute throughout the dominions of the realm; yet in the exercise of this power, by the imperial crown of Great Britain, that is, by the King's Majesty, with the Lords and Commons in parliament assembled---towards the colonies, if they are not of this body of the realm, but are still to be considered as distinct bodies, foreign, or extraneous parts without the realm, and the jurisdiction of this kingdom *.——There

* Blackstone, B. i. c. 5.

4
i9

is furely fome attention due to the nature of this abfolutenefs in this cafe.

If the people of the colonies are no part of the people, or of the body, of the realm of Great Britain,---and if they are to be ftated in the argument, as fubject to the King, not as the head of that compound political perfon, of which they are in part the body, *fed ut caput alterius populi*, as wearing the imperial crown of Great Britain, as the head to which the realm of Great Britain is the body, and of which body the parliament is the foul, but of which the colonies are no part; then this imperial fupreme magiftrate, the collective power of King, Lords and Commons, may be ftated as fovereign on the one hand, while the people of the colonies ftand as fubjects on the other.---

Taking the relation of the colonies to the mother country in this view, when the argument is ftated in this manner, we furely may fay with exactnefs and truth, that if the colonifts, by birthright, by nature or by eftablifhment, ever were entitled to all the rights, privileges, liberties and franchifes of an Englifhman, the abfolute power of this fovereign muft have fome bounds: muft from its own nature, from the very nature of thefe rights of its fubjects, be limited in its extenfion and exercife.

Upon

Upon this ſtate of the caſe, queſtions will neceſſarily ariſe, which I will not take upon me to decide, whether this ſovereign can diſfranchiſe ſubjects, ſo circumſtanced, of their rights becauſe they are ſettled beyond the territorial limits of the realm; whether theſe ſubjects, thus circumſtanced can, becauſe they are ſuppoſed not to be of the realm, loſe that intereſt in the legiſlative power, which they would have had if they were of, or within the realm.——Whether this natural right which they have to perſonal liberty, and to political freedom is inherent in them " to all intents and pur-" poſes, as tho' they had been born within " the realm:" Or whether " * it is to be " underſtood, with very many *and very* " *great reſtrictions.*" Whether theſe people, from the nature of theſe inherent rights and liberties, are intitled to have, and have a right to require a conſtitution of the ſame political liberty as that which they left; or whether ‡ " the whole of their conſtitutions " are liable to be new modelled and re-" formed,"---at the will of this ſovereign. Whether the legiſlative part of their conſtitution is, they being diſtinct, altho' ſubordinate, dominions, and no part of the mother country, an inherent right of a body of Engliſhmen, ſo

* Blackſtone, Introduction § 34.
‡ Ibid.

cir-

circumftanced, or whether it can be fufpended, or taken away at the will of this
fovereign. In ftating thefe doubts I do not
here add the queftion, which in time paft
hath been raifed, on the right which this
fovereign hath, or hath not, to impofe
taxes on thefe fubjects, circumftanced as
above ftated, without the intervention of
their own free will and grant.—Becaufe,
let thefe other queftions be decided how
foever they may, this ftands upon quite
other ground, and depends upon quite
other principles.

So long as the government of the mother
country claims a right to act under this
idea, of the relation between the mother
country and the colonies; fo long as the
colonies fhall be efteemed in this relation, as
" *no part of the mother country*;" fo long
will the colonifts think they have a right
to raife thefe queftions; and that it is their
duty to ftruggle in the caufe, which is to
decide them; and fo long will there be faction and oppofition inftead of government
and obedience.

But the matter of perplexity is much
ftronger, in the queftions which have been
raifed, as to the right of impofing taxes
on the fubject, fo ftated.

In

In the fame manner as in the act of granting a general pardon, the King alone is the
originating and framing agent; while the
other two branches of the legiflature, are
only confenting thereto, that it may be an
act of parliament: fo in the fame manner in
the act of granting fupplies, by impofing taxes
on the people, the houfe of commons is the
fole originating and framing agent, " as to
" the matter, meafure and time;" while the
King and lords act only as confentients, when
it becomes an act of parliament. In one cafe
the King acts as chief magiftrate, reprefenting
and exercifing the collective executive power
of the whole realm: in the other, the commons
act, as " granting for the counties, cities and
" boroughs whom they reprefent *."

If in the act of taxing, the parliament
acted fimply in its capacity of fupream legiflature, *without any confideration had to the
matter of reprefentation* vefting in the commons, I know of no reafon that can be
affigned, why the refolve to give and grant
fhould not originate from, and be framed
or amended by another branch of the legiflature as well as by the commons. The
only reafon that I find affigned, and the
only one I venture to rely upon, for explain-
ing that right of the commons to originate,

* Comm. Journ. 1672.

and

and form the refolve of giving and granting; and to fettle the mode of charging, and im-pofing taxes on the people, to make good thofe grants; and to name commiffioners, who fhall actually levy and collect fuch taxes; " as a fundamental conftitution," is that which the commons themfelves have given, that " the commons grant for the " counties, cities and boroughs *whom they* " *reprefent*,"—and that the word " grant," when fpoken of the lords, " muft be un-" derftood only of the lords affent, to what " the commons grant; becaufe the form of " law requires, that both join in one bill, to " give it the force of law."——Therefore, previoufly inferting this caution, that I do not prefume to form an opinion, *how* they reprefent the property of, or grant for the lords; and without reafoning on *this mode* of the right: " for it is a very unfafe thing " in fettled governments, to argue the rea-" fon of the fundamental conftitutions!" The fact is, that this right is ab initio, a funda-mental conftitution, in that the commons grant for the counties, cities and boroughs whom they reprefent; and that they do, in fact, reprefent the property of the realm; although copyholders, and even freeholders within the precincts of boroughs, or within the counties of cities, not being freemen or burgeffes in fuch boroughs, have no vote in

the

the election of them:——For the property
of the copyholder is reprefented by it's lord;
and the property within the borough or city,
is actually reprefented by the corporation or
body of freemen in fuch borough or city,
who chufe the member of parliament.

Although it fhould be willingly acknowledged without difpute, by the Americans,
even upon this ftating of the cafe, that the
legiflative power of parliament extends
throughout America in all cafes whatfoever; yet, as to the matter, meafure and
time, in the article of taxes, originating
with, and framed by the commons; " grant-
" ing for the counties, cities and boroughs
" whom they reprefent;" it would greatly,
relieve the perplexity and doubts, which
have raifed queftions, much agitated, if any
one could, according to this ftate of the cafe,
and according to this reafoning, fhow how
the commons do reprefent the property in
America, when ftated as being without the
realm; and no part of any county, city or
borough of the fame: and how the freeholders of that property are reprefented,
even as the copyholder and landholder within a borough or city is reprefented. For,
fo long as the cafe fhall be fo ftated, that
the Colonies are neither within the realm,
nor any part of it; or of any county, city
or

or borough within the fame; until it can be
pofitively demonftrated, either that in granting fupplies, by impofing taxes, the commons
do not act in virtue of their reprefenting the
counties, cities and boroughs for whom they
grant; or that in granting for the counties,
cities and boroughs whom they reprefent,
they do alfo reprefent the property of America; the people of America will diftinguifh
their not acknowledging the power of the
commons of Great Britain in the cafe of
granting for them, as a very different cafe,
from that under which they acknowledge
their fubordination to the legiflative power of
parliament.—Nay, further, every reafon
which the commons give for that fundamental right of granting fupplies, and impofing
taxes on the counties, cities and boroughs
whom they reprefent; and every precedent
which the commons alledge for the exercife
of this right; the people of America will
ufe, and alledge for and apply to their own
fpecial cafe, in a way that may be very per-
plexing, unfafe and dangerous to fundamental conftitutions. But all this perplexity
and danger arife from ftating the Colonifts
as fubjects of the realm, at the fame time
that the Colonies are ftated as being no part
of the realm, as no otherwife connected to
it than by their fubjection.

On

On the other hand, let us review the ſtate of this matter as it ſeems actually to have ſtood. If the ſtate of it which we ſhall repreſent, cannot and muſt not be ſuppoſed right in law ; may we be permitted to ſtate it, at leaſt, as an hypotheſis.

The Colonies, from their remote diſtance, and local circumſtances, could not have been incorporated into any county, city or borough ; at leaſt ſo it is ſaid : and yet, at the ſame time, they are ſuppoſed to be, and conſidered as, within the dioceſs of London. The Coloniſts were conſidered as having gone forth from, and having *quitted the realm*; as having ſettled on lands *without the realm*.

The Colonies thus remote and ſeparate from the realm, were formed, and incorporated into diſtinct communities ; were erected into provinces ; had the jura regalia granted to them ; were, in conſequence thereof, to all intents and purpoſes, *counties palatine*, in like and as ample manner as the county palatine of Durham was, ſome matters of form excepted. They were dominions of the King of England ; although, according to the language of thoſe times, " not yet annexed to the crown." They were under the juriſdiction of the King,
upon

upon the principles of fœdal sovereignty: although considered " * *as out of the jurif-* " *diction of the kingdom.*" The parliament itself doubting, at that time, whether it had jurisdiction to meddle with those matters, did not think proper to pass bills concerning America.——The Colonies had therefore legislatures peculiar to their own separate communities ; subordinate to England, in that they could make no laws contrary to the laws of the mother country ; but in all other matters and things, free uncontrouled and compleat legislatures, in conjunction with the King or his deputy as part thereof.

When the King, at the restoration, participated this sovereignty over *these his foreign dominions*, with the lords and commons, the Colonies became *in fact*, the dominions of the realm——became subjects of the kingdom.——They came, in fact, and by an actual constitutional exercise of power, under the authority and jurisdiction of parliament. They became connected and annexed to the state: By coming as parts of the British realm, not as a separate kingdom, (which is the case of Ireland) under subjection to the parliament, they became par-

* Blackstone, B. 1. c. 5.

ticipants

ticipants of the rights and liberties on which
the power of parliament is founded. By
the very act of extending the power of parliament over the Colonies, the rights and
liberties of the realm muft be alfo extended
to them, for, from the nature of the Britifh
conftitution, from the conftitution of parliament itfelf, they, as parts, can be fubject
by no other mode, than by that in which
parliament can exercife its fovereignty; for,
the nature of the power, and the nature of
the fubjection muft be reciprocal.) They
became therefore *annexed*, although perhaps
not yet united parts of the realm. But to
exprefs all that I mean, in a propofition that
can neither be mifunderftood nor mifinter-
preted; they from that moment (whatever
was their prior fituation) ftood related to the
crown and to the realm literally and precifely in the fame predicament, in which
the county Palatine of Durham ftood; that
is, fubject to be bound by acts of parliament
in all cafes whatfoever; and even " liable
" to all rates, payments and fubfidies granted
" by parliament;" although the inhabitants
of thefe countries, " have not hitherto had
" the liberty and privilege of fending
" knights and burgeffes to parliament of
" their own election." And, in the fame
manner alfo, becaufe in that, the inhabitants
of the county Palatine of Durham were
liable

liable to all rates, payments and fubfidies
granted by parliament; and were therefore
concerned, with others the inhabitants of
this kingdom, to have knights and burgeffes
in parliament, *of their own election*; to reprefent the condition of their country, as the
inhabitants of other countries had,——it
was by act of parliament enacted, that they
fhould have fuch : in the fame manner, I fay,
whenever thefe colonies fhall be confidered
in parliament, as objects of taxation, and be
rendered liable to rates, payments and fubfidies granted by parliament out of their
property——they will become concerned
equally with others the inhabitants of this
kingdom, to have knights and burgeffes in
parliament, *of their own election,* to reprefent the condition of their country, as the
inhabitants of other countries have,——and
of right ought to have; although a right in
parliament, to make laws for governing,
and taxing the Colonies, may and muft, *in
the order of time*, precede any right in the
Colonies, to a fhare in the legiflature: yet
there muft arife and proceed pari paffu, a
right in the Colonies to claim, by petition,
a fhare in the reprefentation, by having
knights and burgeffes in parliament, of their
own election; to reprefent the condition of
their country. And as in fuch circumftances, this right fhall arife on one hand,

fo on the other, it may become a duty in
government, to give them power to fend
fuch reprefentatives to parliament; nay,
could one even fuppofe the Colonies to be
negligent in fending, or averfe to fend fuch
reprefentatives, it would, in fuch cafe, as
above fettled, become the duty of government to require it of them.

Although from the fpirit and effence of
our conftitution, as well as the actual laws
of it, " the whole body of the realm, and
" every particular member thereof, either
" in perfon, or by reprefentation, (upon
" their own free election) are, by the laws
" of the realm, deemed to be prefent in the
" high court of parliament †." Yet as the
circumftances of the feveral members of this
body politic muft be often changing; as
many acquifitions and improvements, by
trade, manufactures and Colonies, muft
make great changes in the natural form of
this body; and as it is impoffible, both
from the gradual nature of thefe changes,
and from the mode of the reprefentative
body, that this reprefentative body can, in
every inftance and moment, follow the
changes of the natural paffibus æquis; it
muft neceffarily at times, from the nature

† 1 Jacobi I.

of

of things, *not be an actual reprefentative.*——
Although, from the nature of the conftitution of government, it muft, in the interim,
continue to be a juft and *conftitutional reprefentative.* And hence, from the laws of
nature, as well as from the nature of our
own laws and conftitution, arifes the juftice
and right, which parliament always hath
had to render feveral members of the realm
liable to rates, payments and fubfidies,
granted by parliament; although fuch
members have not, as yet, had the liberty
and privilege to fend knights and burgeffes
to parliament, of their own election. Yet
on the other hand, as the principle, that no
free people ought to be taxed, but by their
own confent, freely originating from, and
given by themfelves or their reprefentatives,
is invariable, abfolute and fixed in truth and
right, fo the mode of the reprefentation in
parliament, hath from time to time, altered,
fo as to extend to, and to fuit the mode,
under which the reprefented were, from
time to time, found to exift. Hence it was,
that many towns, boroughs, counties, and
even dominions, which from any thing
that did exift, or was to be found in their
antiquas libertates, and liberas confuetudines,
were not previoufly reprefented by members
of parliament of their own election; have,
as they acceded to the realm, or encreafed
within

within the realm, ſo as to be equally concerned, to have knights, and burgeſſes in parliament of their own election, to repreſent
them equally as other inhabitants of the
realm have, according to ſuch modes as
were at the time admitted to be legal and
conſtitutional, been called to a ſhare in the
common-council of the realm. Hence it
was that the county Palatine of Durham, after many tryals, and a long ſtruggle, was
admitted to the privilege of ſending knights
and burgeſſes to parliament;—but of this
caſe enough has already been ſaid.

In the time of King Henry VIII, we find
parliament *reaſoning and acting* upon this very
principle in the caſe of the county of Cheſter.
—The *reaſoning of parliament* ſets forth †,
" that the King's county Palatine of Cheſ-
" ter, had hitherto been excluded out of
" his high court of parliament, to have any
" knights within the ſaid court.—By rea-
" ſon whereof, the inhabitants had ſuſ-
" tained manifold diſheriſons, loſſes and da-
" mages, as well in their lands, goods and
" bodies, as in the good, civil and politic
" government of their ſaid county.———
" That foraſmuch as they have alway hi-
" therto *been bound by the acts and ſtatutes,*

† 34 and 35 of Henry 8.

" made

" made and ordained by the King, by au-
" thority of the faid court, as far forth as
" other counties who had knights and bur-
" geffes in parliament;——and yet had nei-
" ther knights nor burgeffes :—The inhabi-
" tants for lack thereof have been often times
" grieved with acts and ftatutes, made within
" the faid court derogatory to their ancient
" privileges and liberties, and prejudicial to
" the common-wealth, quietnefs, reft and
" peace of the King's bounden fubjects in-
" habiting within the fame. For remedy
" whereof, the parliament *acts*—and it is
" enacted, that the county of Chefter
" fhould have two knights, and the city
" two burgeffes, which knights and bur-
" geffes are to have the *like voice and autho-*
" *rity*, to all intents and purpofes,——the
" like liberties, advantages, dignities, pri-
" vileges, &c. with other knights and bur-
" geffes."

Hear alfo, *the reafoning*, and view the *acts*
of parliament, in the cafe of the acquifition
of the dominions of Wales *, fubject to the
imperial crown of, although not yet incorporated or annexed to, the realm.——The
reafoning fets forth, that Wales ever had
been united and fubject to the imperial

* 27th of Hen. 8. cap. 6.

crown

crown of the realm, and to the King, *its
very Head, Lord and Ruler*.———That the
principality and *dominions* had rights, laws
and cuftoms, different from the laws, &c.
of *this realm.*

That the people of *that dominion* had a
fpeech different from the tongue ufed in
this realm.

———Thence fome *ignorant people made a
diftinction* between the King's *fubjects of the
realm,* and *his fubjects of the principality.*———
His Highnefs, therefore, out of love to his
fubjects of the principality, and to bring *his
fubjects of the realm* and *his fubjects of the
principality* to *concord and unity*, by advice
of Lords and Commons, and by authority
of the fame hath enacted, that henceforth
and for ever, his faid *country and dominion
of Wales*, fhall be incorporated, united and
annexed to *this realm of England*; and that
all, fingular perfon and perfons, born, and
to be born in the faid principality of Wales,
fhall have, and enjoy all the fame freedoms,
liberties, rights, privileges and laws within
this his realm, and *other* the King's dominions, as other the King's fubjects, naturally
born within the fame, have, enjoy and in-
herit; and that knights and burgeffes fhall
be elected, and fent to reprefent them in
par-

parliament, with all the like dignity, pre-
eminence and privilege as other knights and
burgeſſes of the parliament have and be
allowed.

We alſo find, upon the acquiſition of
Calais to the King's dominions, that King
Edward turned all the French inhabitants
out of it; planted *an Engliſh Colony
there*, with all the rights, freedom, privileges, &c. of natural born ſubjects within
the realm, and that *this Colony ſent burgeſſes*
to parliament.

Seeing then how exactly, and to the mi-
nuteſt circumſtance, ſimilar the caſe of the
Colonies erected into provinces, is to theſe
counties Palatine, to thoſe acquired and annexed dominions; can the ſtateſman, whether in adminiſtration or in parliament, reaſon or act towards the Colonies in any other
mode, or by any other acts, than what the
foregoing give the wiſeſt and happieſt examples of?

It is a firſt and ſelf-evident truth, without
which all reaſoning on political liberty is
certâ ratione inſanire. That a free people
cannot have their property, or any part of it,
given and granted away in aids and ſubſidies,
but by their own conſent; ſignified by them-

ſelves

felves or their legal representatives. It is also (as hath been marked before) an undoubted principle and law of our constitution, that the whole body of the realm, and every particular member thereof, either in perfon, or by reprefentation, (upon their own free elections) are deemed to be perfonally prefent in the high court of parliament: And, that the King, Lords and Commons affembled in parliament, are the commune concilium, the common-council of the realm;——the legal and conftitutional reprefentative of the whole body of the realm, and of every particular member thereof: having perfect right, and full power and authority to make laws and ftatutes of fufficient force and validity to bind the Colonies and people of America, fubjects of the crown, in all cafes whatfoever.——But as various external acquifitions and dominions, may accede to this body, ftill remaining without the realm, out of its jurifdiction; not yet annexed, united and incorporated with the realm:—As various and divers new interefted individuals, may arife and increafe within the realm; which, although *conftitutionally reprefented* in parliament, cannot be faid to have there *actually* reprefentatives of their own free election.——
Let us look and fee how government, to be

con-

confiftent with itfelf and its own principles, hath acted in fuch cafes.

Parliament hath never ceafed to be deemed the conftitutional reprefentative of the whole dominions of the realm : Hath never ceafed to act as the commune concilium, both in the cafe of making laws, which did bind thefe fubjects under this predicament; as alfo, in the cafe de auxilio affidendo; and render'd them liable to all rates, payments and fubfidies granted by parliament : Yet on the other hand, parliament (thefe fubjects being equally concerned to have reprefentatives in parliament, of their own election, equally as other inhabitants of the realm) hath always given them power to fend fuch; as they have arifen to an importance and a fhare of intereft in the ftate, which could juftify the meafure. On this principle, and by this proceeding, has the number of reprefentatives in parliament, increafed from between two and three hundred, to above five hundred.

In other cafes, as in the cafe of the American Colonies, where thefe acquifitions in partibus exteris, have been deemed fo far feparate from the kingdom; fo remote from the realm, and the jurifdiction thereof; that they could not have been incorporated

L 3   into

into any county, city or borough within the realm; that the ftate and condition of their country could fcarcely be faid to be within the actual cognizance of parliament: Where the local internal circumftances of their property could fcarce fall within the ways and means adopted by parliament for taxes;—where the peculiar nature of their eftablifh-ment required the conftant and immediate prefence of fome power to make orders, or-dinances and laws for the prefervation and well government of thofe countries: There government hath conftantly and uniformly eftablifhed and admitted the governor, council and reprefentatives of the freeholders of the country affembled, to be a full and perfect legiflature, for the making laws and impofing taxes in all cafes whatioever, ari-fing within, and refpecting the body of that community;—full and perfect within itfelf, to all the purpofes of free debate, free will, and freedom of enacting;——although fub-ordinate to the government of the mother, as being bound by its laws, and not capable to act, or to become any thing contrary or repugnant to it. Although parliament hath, in fome cafes, as before recited, impofed taxes, arifing from cuftoms and duties, paid by the trade and intercourfe of the inhabi-tants of the Colonies: Yet, from the firft moment that they have been confidered as

capable

capable of paying a certain quota to the extraordinary fervices of government, and as being in circumftances proper to be required fo to do;——government fixed the mode, and hath hitherto invariably continued in the fame, of doing this by requifition from the crown, to be laid before the affembly by his Majefty's commiffioner the governor.——

If it be the fpirit and fenfe of government, to confider thefe Colonies ftill as thus feparate unannexed parts ; as incapable, from their local circumftances, of having reprefentatives of their own election, in the. Britifh parliament;—the fame fenfe and fpirit will, I fuppofe, continue to the Colonies this liberty *; " which, through a tender- " nefs in the legiflature of Great Britain, to " the rights and privileges of the fubjects " in the Colonies, they have hitherto al- " way enjoyed; the liberty of judging, by " their reprefentatives, both of the way and " manner in which internal taxes fhould be " raifed within the refpective governments, " and of the ability of the inhabitants to pay " them :" will think it wife, if not juft alfo, from its having become, I had almoft faid, a conftitutional mode of adminiftration,

* Petition of the general affembly of the Maffachufett's-bay.

L 4   through

through the eftablifhment and invaried continuance of the precedent, to raife the Provincial quota of taxes, by making, in each
cafe, a requifition to the affemblies, to grant
fubfidies, adequate to the fervice of government, and in proportion to the circumftances
of the Colony or province which they reprefent.

This is the alternative, either to follow
the fober temper and prudence of this eftablifhed mode, or to adopt the wifdom, juftice and policy of the reafoning and acts of
parliament, in the cafes of Chefter, Wales
and Durham. There is no other practicable or rational meafure.

If thefe external circumftances of our
American dominions, and the internal circumftances of our police and parties, lead
adminiftration to this meafure, of continuing to derive aids and fubfidies from the Colonies by the eftablifhment of general affemblies of the ftates in each Colony, upon the
precife model of the parliament in the mother
country: It may be very well juftified by
example, and from precedent, in the government of the Roman Colonies.

Although the Romans governed their
provinces by an abfolute imperium, which
fuperceded all civil government, properly fo
called;

4

called; yet the inhabitants of their *Colonies* were, in their civil conftitution *, divided into Senate and People, exactly according to the conftitution of the city itfelf: And conform exactly to the model of the fovereign fenate. As the order of the patres confcripti were the conftituents of that body,—fo the order of the decuriones, the tenth part from amongft the people were, for the purpofe of forming a like council, enrolled by the triumvirs whom the Roman ftate had created, to lead out Colonies either of Citizens or Latins.—By this eftablifhment, a fenate, for this council is literally fo called in the Pompeian law de Bithynis, was formed in every Colony—and latterly, in every municipal corporation alfo.—

As the ordinary fupply of the fenate in the city, was from the annual election of magi-

---

* Conftituendum eft ad urbis inftar, in Coloniis Plebem a Patribus difcriminatum ; & ad exemplum Senatus ampliffimi ordinis, decurionum ordinem (quem et Senatum dictum in Pompeia lege de Bithyniis Plinius fcribit) in civitatibus orbis Romani ex decimâ parte Colonorum, concilii publici gratiâ, confcribi folitum fuiffe a triumviris quos S P Q R creabat ad Colonias aut latinorum aut civium ducendas; cumque in Coloniis veluti in fpeculo effigies Repub. Rom. cerneretur fimulachrum quoddam Senatûs in illis, & demum in municipiis ex decurionum ordine fuit.

Marcus Vetranius Maurus de jure liberorum. Cap. 8.

ftrates,

ſtrates, who, in conſequence of their having
been inveſted with ſuch magiſtracy, acquired
a ſeat there; as the extraordinary ſupply
of ſenators, was by Kings, Conſuls, Cen-
ſors, or Dictators (according to the different times and periods of the Roman government) propoſing good and true citizens
to the people,—of whom thoſe, who were
approved, were enrolled Conſcripti, Sena-
tores, juſſu populi: So the ordinary ſupply of
the members of this Colony ſenate or curia
was from the decuriones, the magiſtracy of
that community,—while the extraordinary
ſupply was by the triumvirs enrolling, in
like manner, the ſenator at the firſt eſtabliſhment, or the ‡ governors, upon extraordinary caſes, which might afterwards
ariſe,——propoſing honeſt and honourable
men, from whom the people choſe thoſe
who were enrolled.—Both council and reſult were left to the community.——The
council in the ſenate, the reſult in the
people;—who made, and were governed
by their own laws, ſubordinate to the laws
of the empire; who created, and were governed by their own magiſtrates.—

When this iſland was itſelf, in a provincial ſtate, under the empire of Rome, ſeve-

‡ Vide Plinii Epiſt. et Trajani Reſp. lib. x.
Epis. 80 and 81.

ral

ral Colonies and municipal diftricts within the fame, were happy under this very conftitution of being governed by a reprefentative, magiftracy, and legiflature,—which the Britifh Colonies now contend for. The manufcript of Richard of Cirencefter, lately difcovered, tells us which they were.——— The Colonies were, London, Colchefter, Sandwich with Richborough, Bath, Caërleon in Wales, Weft Chefter, Gloucefter, Lincoln and Chefterford. The municipal diftricts, York and St. Albans. To which perhaps we may add, from the fame lift, as Civitates, Latio jure donatæ, Old Sarum, Cirencefter, Carlifle, Burton north of Lancafter, Cafter by Peterborough, Alkmanbury and Catteric in Yorkfhire, Perth, Dunbritton and Invernefs.

If this mode of adminiftration for the Colonies be adopted by government, efpecially in the article of taxation—It will behove adminiftration, to be thoroughly informed of, and acquainted with the circumftances of the Colonies, as to the quota or fhare of the taxes which they are capable to bear, and ought to raife, not only in proportion to thofe raifed by the mother country, but amongft themfelves: It will become the duty of miniftry, to endeavour to perfuade the Colonies to eftablifh, *as far as their circumftances will*

will admit of it, the fame mode of taxation, by ftamp duties, excifes and land tax, as is ufed in this country:—That the property and manufactures of the Colonies may not, by an exemption from thefe, have a preference and advantage over the property and manufactures of the mother country. It will require all the wifdom and intereft, all the firmnefs and addrefs, of a thoroughly eftablifhed miniftry, to carry thefe points:—As the Colonies, no doubt, will keep off fuch incumbrances as long as they can; and as the affemblies of the Colonies, will, under this conftitution, reafonably argue, that as to the matter, extent, mode and time of taxes, they, the reprefentative of the people for whom they grant, are the only proper and conftitutional judges.

Government ought at all times to know the numbers of the inhabitants, diftinguifhing the number of the rateable polls.

2. The number of acres in each province or Colony, both cultivated and lyeing in wafte.——The number of houfes—and farms, &c.

3. The numbers and quantity of every other article of rateable property, according to the method ufed by the provinces themfelves, in rateing eftates, real and perfonal.

4. Go-

4. Government ought alway to know what the annual amount of the several province taxes are, and by what rates they are raised, and by what estimate these rates are laid.

From whence, by comparing the estimation with the real value, for the time being, of each article, they may alway collect nearly the real value of the property of such province or Colony. All which, compared with the prices of labour, provisions and European goods imported, with the value of their manufactures, the interest of money, and their exports, will fully and precisely mark their abilities to bear, and the proportion which they should bear, of taxes, amongst one another, and with the mother country.

The following estimates of the provinces, Massachusett's-Bay to the northward, of South-Carolina to the southward, and of New Jersey in the center, are founded in the tax-lists of each province; which tax-lists, being of * ten years standing, must, in encreasing countries as the Colonies are, fall short of the numbers and quantity which

* That is ten years back from the time of the publication of the first edition of this book.

would

would be found on any tax-lift faithfully made out at this time. The eftimates which I have made thereon are in general at fuch an under-valuation, that I fhould think no man of candour in the provinces will object to them; although they be, in fome articles, higher than the valuation which the legiflatures directed fo long ago to be made, as the fund of the taxes that they order to be levied on them. This valuation of the eftates, real and perfonal, gives the grofs amount of the principal of the rateable property in the province. I think I may venture to affirm, that no man, who would be thought to underftand the eftimation of things, will object that I over-rate the produce of this property, when I rate it at fix *per cent.* only of this moderate valuation; when he confiders that money, in none of thofe provinces, bears lefs than fix *per cent.* intereft; and that under loans of money, at five *per cent.* moft of the beft improvements of the country have been made.

The valuation of the provinces, New-York and Penfylvania, lying on each fide of New-Jerfey, are calculated in a different manner, by taking a medium between the fuppofed real value and the very loweft rate of valuation. Without troubling the reader, or encumbering the printer with the detail

of

of thefe tax-lifts, and the calculations made thereon, I will infert only the refult of them, as follows.

The provinces under-mentioned could annually raife, by one fhilling in the pound on the produce of the rateable property, eftates real and perfonal in each province:

	£.	s.	d.
Province Maffachufett's-Bay,	13172	7	11
New-York, - -	8000	0	0
New-Jerfey, - -	5289	17	0
Penfylvania, - -	15761	10	0
South-Carolina, -	6971	1	11
Sterling, £.	49395	16	10

Suppofe now the reft of the colonies to be no more than able to double this fum:

The fum-total that the colonies will be able to raife, according to their old tax-lifts, and their own mode of valuation and of rating the produce of eftates, real and perfonal, will be, at one fhilling in the pound on the produce, *per annum.* - - £. *s.* *d.* 98791 13 8

In

In juftice to the reft of the provinces, par-
ticularized above, I ought to obferve that,
by the equalleft judgment which I can form,
I think that the province of South-Carolina
is the moft under-rated.

I fhould alfo point out to the American
reader, that, as the calculations and lifts
above referred to, are taken from the private
collections of the writer of thefe papers,
without any official communication of fuch
papers as miniftry may be poffeffed of, I
defire him to give no other credit to them,
than fuch as, by referring to his own knowledge of the ftate of things in the Colonies,
he finds to be juft and near the truth. I
fhould, on the other hand, inform the Englifh reader, that thefe were collected on the
fpot, and communicated by perfons leading,
and thoroughly converfant in the bufinefs of
their refpective provinces.

Another remark is neceffary, That, except what relates to Penfylvania, thefe collections were made nine years ago; fo that,
wherever any difference may arife, from the
different proportion in which thefe provinces
have encreafed, that ought to be carried to
account; at the fame time, that a certain addition may be made to the whole from the
certain encreafe of all of them.

If

If this moderate tax, raifed by the above moderate valuation, be compared with the internal annual charge of government in the refpective provinces, that charge will be found much below the fupplies of this fund. The whole charge of the ordinary expence of government in the province of Maffachufett's-Bay, which does, by much, more to the fupport of government, and other public fervices than any other province, is, in time of peace, fterling 12937 *l*. 10 *s*. whereas that of New-York is not more than about, fterling, 4000 *l*. annually.

When thefe points fhall be fettled, there cannot be a doubt but that the fame zealous attention, which all parties fee and confefs to be applied in the adminiftration of the Brit fh department to the public revenue, will be applied to the eftablifhing and reforming that of America.

A proper knowledge of, and real attention to, the Crown's quit-rents in America, by revifing the *original defects*, by remedying the almoft infurmountable difficulties that the due collection of them is attended with, may render that branch a real and effective revenue, which at the fame time will be found to be no inconfiderable one.

M   By

By proper regulations for fecuring the Crown's rights in waifs and wrecks, in fines and forfeitures, and by proper appropriations of the fame, that branch of revenue may be made effective: But, whenever it is taken up in earneft, whenever it fhall be refolved upon to give a real official regard to the revenue in America, the office of *Auditor General of the Plantations* muft ceafe to be a mere finecure benefice, and be really and effectively eftablifhed with fuch powers as will carry the duty of it into execution, yet under fuch cautions and reftrictions as fhall fecure the benefit of its fervice to the ufe of the crown.

If it fhould be thought difficult and hazardous, to extend the legiflative rights, privileges and preeminences, the true Imperium of government, to wherefoever the dominions of the ftate extend,—the adminiftration muft be content to go on in this ptolomaïc fyftem of policy,—as long as the various centers and fyftems fhall preferve their due order and fubordination: Or to fpeak in a more appofite idea;—if we would keep the bafis of this realm confined to this ifland, while we extend the fuperftructure, by extending our dominions: We fhall invert the pyramid (as Sir William Temple expreffes it) and muft in time fubvert

the

the government itſelf. If we chuſe to follow the example of the Romans, we muſt expect to follow their fate.

Would ſtateſmen, on the other hand, doubt for a while, the predetermined modes which artificial ſyſtems preſcribe; would they dare to look for truth in the nature of things; they would ſoon adopt what is right, as founded upon fact.———They would be naturally led into the true ſyſtem of government, by following *with the powers of the ſtate*, where the actual and *real powers of the ſyſtem of things* lead to. They would ſee, that by the various and mutual interconnections of the different parts of the Britiſh dominions, throughout the Atlantic, and in America; by the intercommunion and reciprocation of their alternate wants and ſupplies; by the combination and ſubordination of their ſeveral intereſts and powers; by the circulation of their commerce, revolving in an orbit which hath Great Britain for its center: That there does exiſt, in fact, in nature, a real union and incorporation of all theſe parts of the Britiſh dominions, *an actual ſyſtem of dominion*; which wants only to be avowed and actuated by the real ſpirit in which it moves and has its being: By that ſpirit, which is the genuine ſpirit of the Britiſh conſtitution: By that ſpirit from

which

which the Britifh government hath arifen
to what it is: By the fpirit of extending the
bafis of its reprefentative legiflature, through
all the parts to wherefoever the rights, intereft or power of its dominions extend; fo
as to form (I cannot too often inculcate the
idea) A GRAND MARINE DOMINION, CON-
SISTING OF OUR POSSESSIONS IN THE
ATLANTIC, AND IN AMERICA, UNITED
INTO A ONE EMPIRE, IN A ONE CENTER,
WHERE THE SEAT OF GOVERNMENT IS.

This meafure has been, and I dare fay
will be generally treated as impracticable and
vifionary *. I wifh thofe declarations of
power, with which we mock ourfelves,
may not be found the more dangerous delufion. Such is the actual ftate of the really
exifting fyftem of our dominions; that
neither the power of government, over thefe
various parts, can long continue under the
prefent mode of adminiftration; nor the
great intereft of commerce extended thro'-
out the whole, long fubfift under the prefent fyftem of the laws of trade: Power,

---

* On repealing the ftamp-act, an act pafs'd, declaring the power of parliament to bind thefe Colonies
in all cafes whatfoever: This, however, was only
planting a barren tree, that caft a *fhade* indeed over the
Colonies, but yielded *no fruit*. Penfylvania Farmer's
Letters, Letter 10th.

3   when

when ufed towards them, becoming felf-de-
ftructive, will only haften the general ruin.

To this meafure, not only the Briton but
the American alfo *now* objects, that it is
unneceffary, inexpedient and dangerous:
But let us confider their feveral objections.

The Briton fays that fuch meafure is unneceffary, becaufe the power of parliament
extends to all cafes and purpofes required.—
Be it allowed, that this power does, in
right and theory, thus extend: Yet furely
the reafoning, the precedents, the Examples,
and the practice of adminiftrations do fhow,
that fomething more is neceffary in this cafe.

The American fays it is unneceffary, becaufe they have legiflatures of their own,
which anfwer all their purpofes.——But
each Colony having rights, duties, actions,
relations, which extend beyond the bounds
and jurifdiction of their refpective communities; beyond the power of their refpective
governments: The colonial legiflature does
certainly not anfwer all purpofes; is incom-
petent and inadequate to many purpofes:
Something therefore more is neceffary, *ei-*
ther a common union amongst themfelves; or
a one common union of fubordination, under
the one general legiflature of the ftate.

M 3 The

The Briton fays that it would be inexpedient to participate with, and communicate
to the Colonifts, the rights and privileges of
a fubject living and holding his property
within the realm; to give thefe rights to
people living out of the realm, and remote
from it, whofe interefts are rival and contrary, both in trade and dominion, to thofe
of this realm. But the fcheme of giving
reprefentatives to the Colonies, annexes them
to, and incorporates them with the realm.
Their intereft is contrary to that of Great
Britain, only fo long as they are continued
in the *unnatural artificial* ftate of being confidered *as external provinces*; and they can
become rivals only by continuing to increafe
in this feparate ftate: But their being united
to the realm, is the very remedy propofed.

The American fays, that this meafure is
inexpedient; becaufe, if the Colonies be
united to the realm; and have participation
in the legiflature, and communication of the
rights and privileges of a fubject within the
realm: They muft be affociated in the burden of the taxes, and fo pay a fhare of the
intereft and principal of the national debts,
which they have no concern in.———This is
literally the objection which was made by
the Scots, at the propofal of the union of
the two kingdoms; and came indeed with
reafon

reaſon and propriety, from an independent
ſovereign kingdom, which had no concern
in the debts of England. But the like objection can never be made with propriety,
reaſon or juſtice, by Colonies and provinces
which are conſtituent parts of a trading nation, protected by the Britiſh marine. Much
leſs can it be ſaid, that they have no concern
in theſe debts, when they are debts contracted, by wars entered into, the firſt for
the preſervation of the proteſtant intereſt
and independency of the ſovereignty of the
mother country; the two latter, ſolely in
defence, and for the protection of the trade
and actual exiſtence of the Colonies. However, if the Colonies could, on any reaſonable grounds of equity or policy, ſhow any
inequality, or even inexpediency in their
paying any part of the taxes, which have a
retroſpect to times, before they were admitted to a ſhare in the legiſlature.—There
is no doubt but that the ſame moderation
and juſtice which the kingdom of England
ſhowed towards Scotland, in giving that *an
equivalent*, would be extended to the Colonies, by the kingdom of Great Britain.
And I cannot but think, that it would not
be more than ſuch equivalent, that the
government ſhould grant them a ſum of
money ſufficient to pay off all their debts,
which were contracted, in conſequence of

M 4   the

the laſt war, and were ſtill out-ſtanding;
unleſs Great Britain engaged from henceforth to conſider theſe as the debts of the
ſtate in general. I cannot but think that it
would not be more than ſuch equivalent,
that the crown ſhould give up all its right to
quit rents; and that every act, whereby any
ſpecial revenue was raiſed upon the Colonies,
ſhould be repealed.

The Briton ſays, that this meaſure would
be *dangerous*; as it might prove a leading
ſtep, to the finally removing of the ſeat of
Empire to America.———To which the true
anſwer is, that the removing of the Seat of
the Empire to America or not, depends on
the progreſſive encreaſe of the territories,
trade and power of the American Colonies;
if continued in the ſame unnatural ſeparate
rival and dangerous ſtate, in which they
are at preſent.——That this is an event not to
be avoided.——But this meaſure of uniting
the Colonies to the realm, and of fixing the
legiſlature here in Britain, is the only policy
that can obviate and prevent this removal.
For, by concentring the intereſt and power
of the ſeveral parts in this iſland, the Empire muſt be fixed here alſo.——But if this
removal cannot finally be prevented,——is it
better that a new Empire ſhould ariſe in
America, on the ruins of Great Britain; or
that

that the regalia of the Britifh Empire ex.
tending to America, fhould be removed
only to fome other part of the dominions,
continuing however in the fame realm?

The American fays, that this meafure
might be dangerous to their liberties; as this
calling the American reprefentatives to a
parliament, fitting in Great Britain, would
remove their reprefentatives at too great a
diftance from their conftituents, for too long
a time; and confequently from that communication and influence, which their conftituents fhould have with them; and therefore transfer the will of the Colonies out of
their own power, involving it, at the fame
time, in a majority, againft which their
proportion of reprefentatives would hold no
ballance. This objection, if it hath any
ground for its fears, is a direct anfwer to
the Britifh objection laft mentioned:—But it
proves too much; as, according to this argument, no remote parts of a ftate ought to fend
reprefentatives, as the feat of Empire is alfo
remote; the truth and fact is, that the mutual fituation of Great Britain and America,
very well allows every communication,
which a member of parliament ought to
have with his conftituents; and any influence beyond that, is unparliamentary and
unconftitutional.

As

As to all objections which arise from apprehenfions of what effect fuch an additional number of members, acceding all at once to the Houfe of Commons, might have on the politics, conduct and internal management of that body.—They arife from an unwarranted and (one fhould hope) groundlefs fufpicion of fome undue influence operating there —But fhould this be a fuppofition, that could ever be admitted to be true, even amongft the fœces Romuli; the contrary apprehenfions, from the different quarters, are fuch as mutually deftroy each other.—The Americans fear, that the number of reprefentatives which will be allowed to them, will have no power proportionable to their fhare of intereft in the community. That this union to the Britifh legiflature, will only involve them in the conclufions of a majority, which will thence claim a right to tax them, and to reftrain their trade, manufactures and fettlements as they pleafe. The Briton fears, that thefe reprefentatives may be an united phalanx, firmly oppofing every tax propofed to be laid upon the Colonies; and every regulation meant to keep their actions and intereft in due fubordination to the whole.——That they will be a party, a faction, a flying fquadron, alway ready, and in moft cafes capable, by uniting with oppofition to adminiftration, or with

com-

commercical factions, to diftrefs government and the landed intereft of the kingdom.
The Americans again on the other hand,
fear that fome future Britifh miniftry, in
fome future days of corruption, will fucceed
in bribing their reprefentatives, againft which
the Colonies will have no remedy, but muft
fubmit to the betraying confequences.———
Thefe are objections which, on the very
fuppofition, mutually counteract and deftioy
one another.——They are objections which
have had fair trial upon experience, in the
cafe of the Scots members,——and are directly
contradicted by truth and fact.

As to all objections raifed on the fuppofed
impracticability of the meafure; they are too
contemptible to deferve an anfwer.——There
is but one which hath any fenfe in it,——it is
faid, that the Colonies are too remote, upon
a diffolution, to receive the writs and return
their reprefentatives within the time limited
by law; and that, if the parliament fhould
be affembled immediately on its election,
the Colonies could not have their reprefentatives in the houfe for fome time. The
portion of time limited by law, is fixed in
proportion to the diftance of the remoteft
parts concerned at prefent, to fend members to parliament. A fpecial time might
be

be fixed by law, in proportion to the fpecial cafe of the diftance of the Colonies. And as to their having their reprefentatives in a new parliament, upon its being affembled immediately ; in the fame manner, as upon the demife of the King, the parliament, then fitting, is by law, to continue fix months, unlefs diffolved by the fucceffor : fo the old reprefentatives of the Colonies, might by law, be permitted to fit in the new parliament, if affembled within fix months ; until they were reelected or others fent in their room ; the doing of which, might be limited to fix months.

Notwithftanding, I know that this propofal will be confidered as utopian, vifionary, idle, impertinent and what not :—I will proceed to confider the juftice and policy of this meafure, of this invariable truth, this unavoidable confequence ; that in the courfe and procedure of our government, there muft arife a duty in government to give, a right in the Colonies to claim, a fhare in the legiflature of Great Britain.

While we confider the realm, the government of Great Britain, as the *Sovereign*, and the Colonies as the fubject, without full participation in the conftitution ; without participation in the legiflature ; bound implicitly

citly to obey the orders of government; and
implicitly to *enact or register* as an act of
their own, those grants which we have by
our acts required them to make, as a tax
imposed on them: They say that their obedience in this case, without the interposition
of their own free will, is reduced to the
lowest predicament of subjection, wherein
they are not only required to *act*, but to
will, as they are ordered. Yet, however
too strongly they may be supposed to state
their case, surely there is a species of injus-
tice in it.

Supplies granted in parliament, are of
good will, not of duty, the free and voluntary act of the giver, not obligations and
services which the giver cannot, by right,
refuse. Whatever therefore is given out of
the lands and property of the Colonies,
should some way or other, be made their
own act.

The true grounds of justice whereby the
parliament grants supplies, and raises them
by taxes on the lands and property of themselves and their constituents, is, that they
give what is their own ; that they lay no tax,
which does not affect themselves and their
constituents; and are therefore not only the
proper givers, but also, the best and safest
judges,

judges, what burdens they are beſt able to bear: They do not give and grant from the property of others, to eaſe themſelves. Let the ſtateſman apply this reaſoning to the caſe of the Colonies, and he may be lead up to the true ſources of the diſcontents, murmurings, proteſts and counteractings againſt government, which divert its effect, which undermine its eſtabliſhment, and tend to its utter diſſolution.

Whereas on the other hand, we ſhall find, as hath ever been found, that univerſal participation of council, creates reciprocation of univerſal obedience. The ſeat of government will be well informed of the ſtate and condition of the remote and extreme parts: And the extreme and remote parts, by participation in the legiſlature, will, from ſelfconſciouſneſs, be informed of, and ſatisfied in, the reaſons and neceſſity of the meaſures of government: Theſe parts will conſider themſelves as acting, in every grant which is made, and in every tax which is impoſed: This conſideration alone, will give efficiency to government; and will create that *conſenſus obedientium*, on which only, the power and ſyſtem of the Imperium of a ſtate can be founded: This will give extention and ſtability of Empire, as far as we can extend our dominions.

I could

I could here proceed to juftify this propofition, as founded in fact, by fhowing,
that *this principle of eftablifhing the Imperium
of government, on the bafis of a reprefentative
legiflature*, hath been, from the earlieft and
* firft inftance of the eftablifhment of a
BRITISH SENATE, under the government
of Caraufius, founded on its native and natural bafis, a marine dominion, invariably
through all times, *the fpirit of this country* :
The fpirit of that conftitution, by which
government hath been alway the moft furely
and happily eftablifhed in the Britifh dominions. It is a native plant of this foil,
which, although at various times, it hath
been trodden and cut down, almoft to the
very roots, hath alway again broken forth
with a vigour fuperior to all falfe culture and
all force. Although it was fuppreffed for a
while, under the laft defpairing efforts of
the Roman corrupted ftate; yet having taken
root, it revived : Although it was, in part,
oppreffed by the feudal fyftem, in the latter
times of the Saxons, as well as under the
Normans ; yet I could here fhow, not only
how, by its native vigour, it rofe again
from ruin, but alfo mark the progrefs of
its reftoration, to the time of Henry the
third.

* Anno Dom. 291.

But

But thefe are arguments only to thofe who feel their hearts united to this fpirit, who revere the inftitutions of their anceftors, as the true fources of the original liberty, and political happinefs of this country. In thefe days, when it is the wifdom of ftatef-men to raife objections to this fpirit of po-licy; when the learned fortify their under-ftanding againft conviction of the right of it; when the love of liberty, nay, the very mention of fuch a feeling is become ridicu-lous, fuch arguments muft of courfe become ridiculous alfo.

It would be a melancholy, and but an ufelefs confideration, to look back to that ftate of political liberty, on which the Bri-tifh Empire hath extended itfelf; or to look forward to that ftate of political glory, li-berty and happinefs on which it might be extended and eftablifhed. When we find bounds fet to the principle of this fpirit; thus far fhalt thou extend and no further: When we fee a fyftem of policy adopted, under which this country muft continue for a while, entangled in a feries of hoftile dif-putes with its Colonies, but muft at length lofe them; muft be finally broken in its commercical intereft and power, and fink by the fame pride, and fame errors, into the fame infignificance and dependence, as all

other

other commercial ftates have done, one
after another; one has only left to hope,
that the ruin is not inevitable, and that
heaven may avert it.

I decus: I noftrum: melioribus utere
    fatis.

Let us here clofe this view, and let us
return to the examination of matters, which
form the internal adminiftration of the Colonies. And firft their money.

The Britifh American Colonies have not,
within themfelves, the means of making
money or coin. They cannot acquire it from
Great Britain, the balance of trade being
againft them. The returns of thofe branches
of commerce, in which they are permitted
to trade to any other part of Europe, are
but barely fufficient to pay this balance.—
By the prefent act of navigation, they are
prohibited from trading with the Colonies of
any other nations, fo that there remains nothing but a fmall branch of African trade,
and the fcrambling profits of an undefcribed
traffic, to fupply them with filver. However, the fact is, and matters have been fo
managed, that the general currency of the
Colonies ufed to be in Spanifh and Portu-
guefe coin. This fupplied the internal cir-
       N   culation

culation of their home bufinefs, and always
finally came to England in payments for
what the Colonifts exported from thence. If
the act of navigation fhould be carried into
fuch rigorous execution as to cut off this fupply of a filver currency to the Colonies, the
thoughts of adminiftration fhould be turned
to the devifing fome means of fupplying the
Colonies with money of fome fort or other :
and in this view, it may not be improper to
take up here the confideration of fome general principles, on which the bufinefs of money and a currency depends.

SILVER, *by the general confent of mankind,*
has become a DEPOSITE, *which is,* THE COM-
MON MEASURE *of commerce.* This is a general effect of fome general caufe. The experience of its degree of fcarcenefs compared
with its common introduction amidft men,
together with the facility of its being known
by its vifible and palpable properties, hath
given this effect: Its degree of fcarcenefs
hath given it a value proportioned to the
making it a DEPOSITE, and the certain quantity in which this is mixed with the poffeffions and tranfactions of man, together with
the facility of its being known, makes it a
COMMON MEASURE amongft thofe things.
There are perhaps other things which might
be better applied to commerce as a common

mea-

meafure, and there are perhaps other things which might better anfwer as a depofite; but there is nothing except filver known and acknowledged by the general experience of mankind, which is a depofite and common meafure of commerce. Paper, leather, or parchment, may, by the fanction of government, become a common meafure to an extent beyond what filver could reach; yet all the fanction and power of government never will make it an adequate depofite. Diamonds, pearls, or other jewels, may in many cafes be confidered as a more apt and fuitable depofite, and may be applied as fuch, to an extent to which filver will not reach; yet their fcarcity tends to throw them into a monopoly; they cannot be fubdivided, nor amaffed into one concrete, and the knowledge of them is more calculated for a myftery or trade, than for the forenfic ufes of man in common, and they will never therefore become a common meafure.

This truth eftablifhed and rightly underftood, it will be feen that that ftate of trade in the Colonies is the beft, and that adminiftration of the Colonies the wifeft, which tends to introduce this only true and real currency amongft them. And in this view I muft wifh to fee the Spanifh filver flowing into our Colonies, with an ample and unin-

ter-

terrupted ftream, as I know that that ftream, after it hath watered and fupplyed the regions which it paffeth through, muft, like every other ftream, pay its tribute to its mother ocean: As this filver, to fpeak without a metaphor, after it hath paffed through the various ufes of it in the Colonies, doth always come to, and center finally in Great Britain.

The proportion of this meafure, by the general application of it to feveral different commodities, in different places and circumftances, forms *its own fcale*. This fcale arifes from the effect of natural operations, and not from *artificial impofition*: If therefore filver was never ufed but by the merchant, as the general meafure of his commerce and exchange, coin would be (as it is in fuch cafe) of no ufe; it would be confidered as bullion only. Although bullion is thus fufficient for the meafure of general commerce, yet for the daily ufes of the market fomething more is wanted in the detail; fomething is wanted to mark to common judgment its proportion, and to give the fcale: Government therefore, here interpofes, and by forming it into COIN *gives the fcale*, and makes it become to forenfic ufe AN INSTRUMENT in detail, as well as it is in bullion a MEASURE in general.

This

This *artificial marking* of this fcale on a *natural meafure,* is neither more nor lefs than marking on any other rule or meafure, the graduate proportions of it : And this artificial marking of the fcale, or graduating the meafure is of no ufe but in detail, and extends not beyond the market;——for exchange reftores it again in commerce. No artificial ftandard therefore can be impofed.

Having this idea of money and coin, I could never comprehend to what general ufes, or to what purpofes of government, the proclamation which Queen Ann iffued, and which was confirmed by ftatute in the fixth year of her reign, could be fuppofed to extend, while it endeavoured to rate the foreign coins current in the Colonies by an artificial ftandard. It would feem to me juft as wife, and anfwering to juft as good purpofe, if government fhould now iffue a proclamation, directing, that for the future, all black horfes in the Colonies fhould be called white, and all brindled cows called red. The making even a law to alter the names of things, will never alter the nature of thofe things; and will never have any other effect, than that of introducing confufion, and of giving an opportunity to bad men of profiting by that confufion.

N 3   The

The fafeft and wifeft meafure which government can take, is not to difcourage or
obftruct that channel through which filver
flows into the Colonies,—nor to interfere
with that value which it acquires there ;—
but only fo to regulate the Colony trade, that
that filver fhall finally come to, and center
in Great Britain, whither it will moft certainly come in its true value ;——but if
through any fatality in things or meafures,
a medium of trade, a currency of money,
fhould grow defective in the Colonies, the
wifdom of government will then interpofe,
either to remedy the caufe which occafions
fuch defect, or to contrive the means of fupplying the deficiency. The remedy lies in a
certain addrefs in carrying into execution the
act of navigation ;——but if that remedy is
neglected, the next recourfe muft lie in
fome means of maintaining a currency
fpecially appropriated to the Colonies, and
muft be partly fuch as will keep a certain
quantity of filver coin in circulation there,—
and partly fuch as fhall eftablifh *a paper
currency*, holding a value nearly equal to
filver.

On the firft view of thefe refources, it
will be matter of ferious confideration, whether government fhould eftablifh a mint and
coinage fpecially appropriated for the ufe of
the

the Colonies; and on what bafis this fhould be eftablifhed. If it be neceffary that filver, which in bullion is a common meafure of general commerce, fhould, that it may be inftrumental alfo to the common ufes of the market, be formed into coin, it fhould be fo formed, that while it was the duty of the public to form this coin, it may not be the intereft of the individual to melt it down again into bullion.

If a certain quantity of coin is neceffary for the forenfic ufes of the Colonies, it fhould be fo formed as *in no ordinary courfe* of bufinefs to become the intereft of the merchant to export it from thence.

This coin fhould be graduated by alloy, fomewhat below the real fcale, fo as to bear a value in tale, fomewhat better than the filver it contains would fetch after the expence of melting down the coin into bullion,— fomewhat better *as an inftrument*, in common forenfic ufe, than the merchant *in ordinary cafes* could make of it, in applying it *as a meafure* by exporting it.

I have here inferted the caution againft ordinary cafes only, as I am not unaware that the lowering the intrinfic worth of the coin for America, will have in the end no other

N 4   effect,

'effect, than to raise the price of the European goods carried thither, while the coin will be exported to Great Britain the same as if it were pure silver.

If such a necessity of an artificial currency should ever exist in the Colonies, and if such a coinage was established, the Colonists would, for the purposes of their forensic business, purchase *this instrument* either in gold or silver, in the same manner as they do now purchase copper coin for the same purposes.

There are two ideas of *a paper currency*. The one adopts a measure for establishing a bank in the Colonies, which is quite a new and untried measure; the other turns the view to the regulating the present paper money currency, which the Colonies have had experience of in all its deviations, and to the establishing the same on a sure and sufficient basis.

I have seen this plan for *a provincial bank*, and think it justice to the very knowing person who formed it, to say, that it must be because I do not understand it, that many objections arise in my mind to it. Whenever he shall think fit to produce it, it will come forth clear of all objections, with that force

force of conviction with which truth always
flows from a mind in full and perfect poffeffion of it.

In the mean while, I will recommend to
the confideration of thofe who take a lead in
bufinefs, a meafure devifed and adminiftered
by an American affembly.—And I will venture to fay, that there never was a wifer or
a better meafure, never one better calculated
to ferve the ufes of an encreafing country,
that there never was a meafure more fteadily
purfued, or more faithfully executed, for
forty years together, than the loan-office in
Penfylvania, formed and adminiftered by the
affembly of that province.

An encreafing country of fettlers and
traders muft alway have the balance of trade
againft them, for this very reafon, becaufe
they are encreafing and improving, becaufe
they muft be continually wanting further
fupplies which their prefent circumftances
will neither furnifh nor pay for :—And for
this very reafon alfo, they muft alway labour
under a decreafing filver currency, though
their circumftances require an encreafing one.
In the common curfory view of things, our
politicians, both theorifts and practitioners,
are apt to think, that a country which has
the balance of trade againft it, and is continually

nually drained of its filver currency, muft be in a declining ftate; but here we may fee that the progreffive improvements of a commercial country of fettlers, muft neceffarily have the balance of trade againft them, and a decreafing filver currency; that their continual want of money and other materials to carry on their trade and bufinefs muft engage them in debt——But that thofe very things applied to their improvements, will in return not only pay thofe debts, but create alfo a furplus to be ftill carried forward to further and further improvements. In a country under fuch circumftances, money lent upon intereft to fettlers, creates money. Paper money thus lent upon intereft will create gold and filver in principal, *while the intereft becomes a revenue that pays the charges of government.* This currency is the true Pactolian ftream which converts all into gold that is wafhed by it. It is on this principle that the wifdom and virtue of the affembly of Penfylvania eftablifhed, under the fanction of government, an office for the emiffion of paper money by loan.

A plan of a general paper currency for America, which was intended to have been inferted in the firft edition of this work, hath been witheld from publication now four years, for reafons, which, I was in hopes, might

might have led to more publick benefit, than the making it public in this work could do. I have inferted it in this edition, but firft—I proceed to the confideration of the ordinary mode of making paper-money, by the legiflatures of the Colonies iffuing government-notes, payable at a certain period by a tax. It may be ufeful to give fome defcription of this, and to point out fuch regulations as will become neceffary in this cafe, fhould the other not be adopted.

This paper-money confifts of promiffory notes, iffued by the authority of the legiflature of each province, deriving its value from being payable at a certain period, by monies arifing from a tax proportioned to that payment at the time fixed. Thefe notes pafs as lawful money, and have been hitherto a legal tender in each refpective province where they are iffued.

As any limitation of the USES of thefe notes as a currency, muft proportionably decreafe its value; as any infecurity, infufficiency, or uncertainty in the FUND, which is to pay off thefe notes, muft decreafe their value; as any QUANTITY emitted more than the neceffities of fuch province calls for as a medium, muft alfo decreafe its value; it is a direct and palpable injuftice,

that

that that medium or currency which has depreciated by any of thefe means from its *real value*, fhould continue *a legal tender at its nominal value.*

The outrageous abufes practifed by fome of thofe legiflatures who have dealt in the manufacture of this depreciating currency, and the great injury which the merchant and fair dealer have fuffered by this fraudulent medium, occafioned the interpofition of parliament to become neceffary :— Parliament very properly interpofed, by applying the only adequate and efficient remedy, namely, by prohibiting thefe Colony legiflatures from being able to make the paper currency *a legal tender.* And government has lately for the fame prudent reafons made this prohibition general to the whole of the Colonies. For, *when this paper-money cannot be forced in payment as a legal tender,* this very circumftance will oblige that legiflature which creates it, to form it of fuch internal right conftitution, as fhall force its own way by its own intrinfic worth on a level nearly equal to filver. The legiflature muft fo frame and regulate it as to give it *a real value.*

Thefe regulations all turn upon *the fufficiency and certainty of the* FUND, *the extent*
of

of the USES, and the proportioning the
QUANTITY to the actual and real necessities
which require such a medium.

The FUND should at least be equal to the
payment of the principal *in a limited time*;
and that time should be certainly so fixed, as
that the legislature itself could not alter it.
Where the paper currency is treasurer's notes
given for specie actually lent to government,
the fund whereon it is borrowed should be
also capable of paying, *ad interim*, a certain
interest, as is the case of treasurer's notes in
the province Massachusetts-Bay.

This medium ought to be applicable to
all the equitable as well as legal USES of silver
money within the Colony or province, except that of being a legal tender.

The QUANTITY ought always to be proportioned to the necessity of the medium
wanted; which (the *fund and uses* being
fairly and absolutely fixed) may always be
judged of by the rise or fall of the *value* in
its general currency or exchange : for where
the quantity issued is more than necessity requires, the value will depreciate : and where
the fund is good, and all proper uses of the
medium secured, so long as no more paper
is issued than necessity does require, it will
always

always hold a value near to, though some-what lefs than filver. On this fubject I here refer the reader to the following very judi-cious tract, written and given to me, feve-ral years ago, by *Tench Francis*, Efq; late attorney-general of the province of Penfyl-vania, converfant in thefe matters, both as a lawyer and a merchant. I print and pub-lifh it by leave of a near relation, and fubjoin it as containing the moft exact and decifive fentiments on this fubject that I have any where met with. I entitle it, CONSIDERA-TIONS ON A PAPER-CURRENCY.

ALL value is given to things for their fitnefs or power to anfwer or procure the neceffary conveniences or pleafures of hu-man life.

This value may be confidered as abfolute or relative. Abfolute value terminates in our efteem of any thing, without referring to any other; relative is that which it has compared with another. The latter only I fhall have occafion to treat of.

Men have power to difcover qualities in a thing, which fhall give it value. They can by laws, cuftoms, or fafhions, greatly in-

creafe

creafe that value; yet, to know or fix its
worth or price, compared with other things
à priori, has always been found beyond
their reach and capacity.

This is owing to an inability to forefee,
eftimate, and govern exactly all the points
and circumftances, on which the value of
things turns, which are fuch as are in, or
follow the nature and order of things in general, and then may be forefeen and judged
of with fome certainty; or which confift of
the paffions, prejudices, and mifapprehen-
fions of mankind, whofe number and influences we cannot rate or calculate.

From the *natural* ftate and order of things,
I think it may be affirmed, that the worth
or price of any thing will always be, as the
quantity and ufes amongft mankind; as the
ufes directly, and as the quantity reciprocally
or inverfely. Ufe is the fole caufe of value,
and value the neceffary effect of ufe. Abat-
ing thefe diftinctions of caufe and effect,
ufelefs and worthlefs, are fynonymous terms.
Every man muft agree, that if you add to a
caufe, you muft increafe the effect; fubftract
from it, and the contrary effect muft follow. Let the quantity of any thing be as
20, and the ufes as 20, and let it have a value; let the ufes be increafed to 30, without
in-

inlarging the quantity; it is plain, the equal
proportion that every man can enjoy will be
as 20 divided by 30, $\frac{2}{3}$ds only. But this
being lefs by $\frac{1}{3}$ than each man requires, the
demand for it, and confequently the value
muft rife. Subftract 10 from the ufes when
20, and then under an equal diftribution,
each fhall have double the value he wants,
which muft leffen the demand, and the value
dependent upon it.

Governing the ufes is one of the rational
powers, that men have over the value of
things.

Experience teaches the meaneft underftanding, that price depends on quantity, and
that they are to each other inverfely, or the
more of one the lefs the other. Water is
as neceffary as any thing, and a diamond
perhaps as little; yet the fuperfluous plenty
of one has rendered it of no worth in moft
places, and the fcarcity of the other has carried it to an extravagant price.

Limiting the quantity is another rational
power men have over the value of things;
and I do not know a third.

From hence it appears, that increafing
the ufes, and leffening the quantity, and leffening

fening the ufes, and increafing the quantity, muft always have the fame influence upon the rates and prices of things. Therefore, whenever I fhew the effect of one, for brevity's fake, let it be underftood, that I fuppofe the fame confequence will attend the other refpectively.

Although I affirm, that variation in quantity or ufe fhall caufe a change in the price of a thing, yet I do not fay, that this change fhall be in proportion equal to the variation in the quantity or ufe; for I think the contrary. To inftance in quantity, let it be in any thing as 30, and let the ufe be as 30, and it fhall then have a mean value. The ufe unchanged, let the quantity be at one time as 20, at another 40. Whoever confiders the prevalence of men's appetites for a fcarce commodity, under the dreads and apprehenfions of wanting it, with their different abilities to procure it, on one hand, and their great contempt of ufelefs excefs on the other, muft agree it is more than probable, that the difference between the means and the extremes fhall not be the fame in the prices, as in the quantities. Merchants, by experience, have found the truth of what I advance. I think they have obferved, that leffening a commodity one third from the mean quantity, *cæteris paribus*, nearly

O   doubles

doubles the value; adding a third, fubftracts
one half from it; and that by further increafing or diminifhing the quantity, thefe
difproportions between the quantity and
prices vaftly increafe.

It is extremely difficult, if not impoffible,
to inveftigate thefe proportions mathema-
tically; but events fpringing from ufe and
experience have equal certainty in them, and
to all practical purpofes are as much to be
relied and depended upon.

It is further worth obfervation, that whatever fluctuates much in quantity, and confequently in worth, will fink beneath its mean
value.

Suppofe the quantity of any thing produced in every 50 years be exactly the fame:
let the annual product be as *one* anfwerable
to the neceffities of mankind, then the value
in each year fhall be as one, and the whole
equal to 50. But if the quantity of the annual product fluctuates, there will be annual fluctuations in the value; but as the
proportions of the decreafe of value, from
experience above ftated, will be greater than
the proportions of the increafe of value, this
fluctuation will caufe a deficiency in the
mean value, which deficiency will always be
in proportion to the greatnefs and quicknefs
of

of the changes. This, I prefume, is occafioned by the defire of mankind in general to
reft on certainty, rather than rely on what
is fluctuating and inconftant, though they
fhould expect gain equal to the rifque, and
by the low circumftances of the majority of
men, whofe fortunes, in all prudence, direct
to the firft, rather than the latter. The cafe
of infurances is an evident proof of this remark. If the infurers gain, which I think
muft be admitted, then they receive a premium beyond the value of the rifque, and
this again the infured pay for *certainty* againft
contingent loffes.

Thefe few rules of eftimating the value
of things, well applied, will, I prefume,
fhew when it is convenient to introduce paper-money into a country, and when it will
prove hurtful; what are its advantages and
inconveniencies, general and particular, when
introduced; of what great importance it is
to prevent an excefs in quantity, and to extend the ufes; and nearly what its value
will be in any given ftate.

If a nation has a quantity of money equal
to its commerce, the lands, commodities,
and labour of the people fhall bear a middle
price. This ftate is the beft, and tends
moft to enrich the people, and make their

hap-

happinefs lafting. If they fhould mint paper to pafs for money, the increafe of quantity in the former will leffen the value of the
latter, will raife the price of lands and rents,
and make the labour of fuch a people, and
the commodities, be *rated* higher than in
other places. Men's fortunes will rife in
nominal, not real value; from whence idle-
nefs, expence and poverty fhall follow. Under thefe circumftances, their *real money*, inftead of their commodities, fhall be exported
from them. Here the paper will be their
bane and deftruction. But if their commerce, or ufes of money, exceed the quantity of it, their lands, labour, and commodities fhall fink beneath their worth in other
countries. Few purchafers of lands will be
found in regard to the fuperior profit that
muft attend the ufe of money in trade: the
wealthy merchant fhall be at the head of affairs:
with few competitions; he fhall be able to
grind down the farmer in the fale of his commodities, and, when thofe fail to fupport
him, in the purchafe of his lands. The
artifan's labour fhall be depreciated by the
merchant who exports it, or the needy farmer that ufes it. The wealthy only fhall
accumulate riches, the commonwealth fhall
decline, and in time farmers and artifans
muft defert the place for another, where
their labour fhall be better rewarded. Here
the

the ufe of paper-money will fhake off the
fetters and clogs of the poor. Merchants
will multiply; they will raife the price of
labour, and of the fruits of the earth, and
thereby the value of lands. An equal diftribution of gain and profit fhall fucceed,
and deftroy the partial accumulations of
wealth.

I think thefe marks, taken from the
value of lands, labour, and commodities,
compared with their worth in other countries, will be found the only infallible rules
to judge of an equality, excefs, or defect of
money in any place wherefoever; and confequently will, at all times, unerringly fhew
the neceffity of increafing coins, or the contrary. Had a neighbouring province well
underftood and weighed thefe points, they
had not created a paper credit far exceeding
all their ufes for money, when they were
able to fupply themfelves with gold equal to
their trade, nor at the fame time have
dammed up fo many ufes for it, which now
cover them with clouds and confufion, that
no man can fee his way through. The beft
method they can ufe is to fink it as faft as
poffible, and not let their fund lie in Britain
at an intereft lefs than 4 *per cent.* when it is
worth 6 in their own country, and their
paper paffes 50 *per cent.* lefs than the nomi-

nal

nal value. But to return: when it is found neceſſary to add *paper-money* to the coin of any country, to ſupport its value ought to be the main and principal view. This will turn upon the FUND, the USES, and the QUANTITY.

All value ariſing from the uſe, I beg leave to call *extrinſick*.

Having ſhewn that paper-money acquires its extrinſic value from the uſes, which uſes apparently may be encreaſed or diminiſhed; I think it would be needleſs and miſpending the reader's time, to demonſtrate, that this value muſt be in direct proportion to the uſes ; for it would really amount to no more than the proof of an axiom univerſally acknowledged, that the effect ſhall always be adequate to the cauſe. Therefore, in all future arguments, I ſhall take it for granted.

The fund ought to be as ſatisfactory to mankind as human wiſdom can deviſe and furniſh.

The community ſhould become ſecurity to anſwer all deficiencies in the FUND; this is not only the higheſt juſtice, but the beſt policy. It is juſt, becauſe it is a creature of their

their own, calculated for their private utility
and advantage, and is in the management
of the country by their reprefentatives and
officers. But when they receive an intereft
from the money, the equity of it is unan-
fwerable: for it feems wholly inconfiftent
with juftice, that one fhould receive the intereft, and another run the rifque of the
principal. Policy requires it, becaufe the
community will certainly receive more profit from its credit under their fupport, than,
with due caution, they can probably lofe by
accidents in the fund.

Our next confideration, with refpect to
the value, turns on *what* the fund is to pay,
and *when*. Thefe are arbitrary, being within the power of thofe by whofe authority the
money is emitted. But for the prefent purpofe: Let us fuppofe it is to pay filver money,
according to the late Queen's proclamation,
to the value of 1000 *l*. for fo much of the
paper, as, according to the *nominal value*,
amounts to that fum at the end of 15 years.
In this ftate the 1000 *l*. paper, *with regard
to the fund alone*, at the time of its emiffion,
is worth no more proclamation money than
what will produce 1000 *l*. of that money at
the end of the term, at compound intereft,
under as good fecurity.

For

For example, take a 1000 *l.* paper, and let it reprefent that the poffeffor fhall receive 1000 *l.* proclamation money for it at the end of 15 years, and let the ufe of money be worth 6 *per cent. per annum*; rebate 6 *per cent. per annum* with compound intereft for 15 years, and you have the value of the 1000 *l.* proclamation money in hand, which appears to be but 417 *l.* 5 *s.* $3\frac{1}{2}$; more it cannot be worth, becaufe 417 *l.* 5 *s.* $3\frac{1}{2}$, with 6 *per cent. per annum* compound intereft for 15 years added, will amount to 1000 *l.*

On this ftate it appears, that the longer the term, the lefs the value, with regard to the fund alone. From whence it follows, that by increafing the term, this value may be reduced to a degree beneath eftimation. But whatever the value thus proved be, I call it *intrinfick.*

The FUND eftablifhed, I proceed to the USES as they next require our attention in regard to the value of the paper-money.

If value, in refpect to the ufes of things, fhall always be in direct proportion to thofe ufes, (which I prefume I have heretofore proved in general, and fhall hereafter fhew is true in relation to paper-money) and we defign to raife the power, it follows clearly, that

that to bring this to pafs, we ought to give it all the ufes of money, or coined gold and filver in other countries. From thefe ufes alone it muft derive all the worth it fhall bear beyond what I called the *intrinfick* value. For the purpofe *take the cafe ftated* on the Fund only, that the poffeffor of 1000 *l*. paper fhall receive 1000 *l*. proclamation money in exchange for it, at the end of 15 years. On this account the paper appeared to be worth but 417 *l*. 15 *s*. 3 $\frac{1}{2}$. But fuppofe this 1000 *l*. paper may be immediately exchanged for 800 *l*. proclamation money, which is 382 *l*. 14 *s*. 8 $\frac{1}{2}$ more than the intrinfick worth, how has it acquired this exceeding price or value? I think plainly from the ufes. To prove the truth of this, fuppofe all the ufes as money taken away; unqueftionably then the worth of 1000 *l*. paper in proclamation money will be reduced to what I call the intrinfick value; becaufe, depending upon the fund alone, it will be exactly in the ftate of a fund to be paid at a future day; for in neither cafe can the creditor ufe it in the mean time. But if the creditor can by any contrivance ufe the fum in that time, as he may the paper when it paffes for money, that ufe muft be fomething worth. And when experience fhews, that under this ufe the value advances from 417 *l*. 15 *s*. 3 $\frac{1}{2}$ to 800 *l*. I apprehend it is evident to a demonftration,

that

that the difference is derived from the ufe. To deny it muſt be as irrational and abſurd, as if, upon adding and extracting an ingredient to and from a compoſition, we perceived properties in the compoſition appear and diſappear, and yet were to deny that ſuch ingredient was the cauſe of thoſe properties. This leads me to attempt the ſolution of a queſtion I have known frequently made. If we in Penſylvania, upon a ſufficient fund anſwerable in ſilver, at a future day, mint a quantity of paper equal to the uſes of the people for money, and they willingly and univerſally accept of the paper in all payments, why ſhould it not, at all times, have *value* equal *to the nominal value*, or to the ſum chargeable on the fund at the day to come. This reaſon, urged by many, to ſupport the paper to this degree, is drawn from the nature of money in general. Money, ſay they, is but a ticket or counter, which repreſents to the mind of the poſſeſſor a quantity or degree of power. No man, on the receipt of it, ever examines how, or from whence it acquired that power, but in order to diſcover its reality and duration. For inſtance, when an Engliſh crown is received, does the acceptor regard any properties in the metal, or the figures of it, but thoſe which are to convince him that it is what it appears to be? a crown. It muſt

be

3

be confeffed, he does not. If fo, then why may not a piece of paper, under diftinguifh-ing characters and impreffions, affixed by law and common confent, have the power of an Englifh crown annexed to it? It is to pafs in the fame manner as a crown does, and in the end will as certainly be a crown as the real one.

Therefore they conclude, that the paper may, and ought at all times, to be efteemed equal to the quantity of filver the fund is to yield for it at the end of the term.

I confefs I think this reafoning fair, and the conclufion juft and fatisfactory, if we do not ufe filver in our *commerce, foreign or do-meftick:* otherwife not. The fact is, we do ufe filver *in our foreign commerce.* I pre-fume it will be eafily admitted, as the paper reprefents the filver in the fund, and from thence obtains its credit, that it fhall always be at leaft of equal ufe with, or be as readily received as paper. Then if filver in hand has one power, *one ufe more* than the paper, to wit, that of procuring foreign commodi-ties, it is impoffible we can efteem them equally. For that would be to controul the different virtues and influences of things over the mind of man, which neceffarily depend-ing upon the things themfelves, no laws or
con-

confent can, by any means, vary or direct. Wherefore, in the cafe ftated, it feems to me certain and undeniable, that the paper muft have lefs worth than the filver.

Having faid, that the ufes of the paper fhould be as many as poffible, it may be proper for me to fpeak of fome of thofe ufes, the equity and advantage of which have been very much controverted. But here let it be underftood, that I proceed upon the cafe laft ftated, that the quantity of paper is to be equal to all the ufes of money *within* the country. For that ftate, and a partial fupply of paper credit, differing in principles, require different reafoning, and infer quite oppofite confequences.

Firft, then, it feems juft and reafonable to compel all perfons contracting for filver money, after the law, that raifes the paper money to be paid in the country is enacted, to receive the paper in lieu of it, and at the value ftruck from the fund, although that be inferior to the real value. This perhaps may not be ftrict equity *between the contracting parties*, but it is juft *from the community*, who have power from the confent of every member, by laws, to prohibit the exercife of a particular natural right inconfiftent with the welfare of the whole, and to inflict a penalty

nalty upon difobedience to the law. To ufe
filver or gold with the paper, muft depreciate the latter. Therefore the law forbids
it. This can't be unfair, becaufe every man
has notice of what coin he is to be paid in,
and *is not obliged to exchange more* for the
paper, than he thinks agreeable to the *real
worth.* And if any fhould endeavour fuch
ufe, the lofs of the difference between gold
or filver and paper, is a kind of penalty for
violating the law, which muft be as juft as
any other penalty impofed on an act, *not
evil in itJelf, but prohibited* only.

Again, upon breach of contracts for payment of money in foreign countries, I think
it both convenient and right, that fatisfaction
fhould be made in the paper. The convenience of it will appear, if we fuppofe the
debtor a member of the fociety amongft
whom the paper paffes ; for as fuch, being
reftrained by law from trafficking for gold
or filver, and thereby difabled from procuring them, he muft either pay paper in
compenfation, or lie in a goal, if the feverity of his creditors requires it. In thefe circumftances, no man in his fenfes would
dare to contract a foreign debt, or transfer
foreign money in the ufual manner, by exchange ; the bad confequences of which are
too numerous and obvious to admit of, or
need

need particular mention, and evidently prove the convenience of allowing fatisfaction to be made in paper.

The equity of this fatisfaction will be indifputable, if the debtor pays a fum of paper really of equal value with the foreign money. It is the common cafe on breach of fpecifick contract. If it cannot be performed, the moft exact juftice requires no more than *an equivalent compenfation*.

Some perfons imagining the real worth of the paper equal to the nominal, have affirmed, that it ought to difcharge thefe debts *at the nominal value*; others confeffing a difference between thefe values, under fome political views, have afferted the fame. As I fhall have occafion to fpeak on thefe opinions hereafter, upon a point fimilar to this I fhall only add here, that if this mode of payment fhould take place, it would as effectually deftroy foreign credit and negociations by exchange, as if gold or filver were to be infifted on here, to difcharge a foreign debt. In one cafe, it would be the higheft imprudence to be the debtor, in the other, it muft be equally indifcreet to become a creditor.

Pur-

Purfuing the ufes, I come to that of difcharging by paper, the filver debts contracted antecedent to the law that raifes the
paper.

To fhew the neceffity of admitting this,
I fuppofe it will be granted me, that there
muft at all times be a very great number
of debtors who depend on their future labour and induftry to pay their debts. This
dependence is reafonable and juft, founded
on the natural right of all fairly to purchafe
filver, the then current money of the country. The debtor has the continuation of
this right in view and expectation at the time
of his contract; without it he cannot be fuppofed either prudent or honeft to borrow.
If then, for the convenience and advantage
of the whole fociety, this right muft be
taken away by a fubfequent law which he
could not forefee, it cannot be agreeable either to reafon or good confcience, to exact
a payment in fpecie; for that would be requiring a performance when we had exprefsly taken away the means. Therefore I
think it clear in refpect to the debtor, that
the paper fhould have this ufe. But how
will this ftand with the right of the creditor,
who upon the contract as certainly expected
to be paid filver, as the debtor did the opportunity of acquiring it to pay.

I pre-

I prefume, if he receives as much paper as fhall be equal in power or value to the filver, it will be juft in itfelf, and perfectly fatisfactory to him. But can any man offer fo high a degree of violence to his own reafon, and the underftanding of others, as to affirm, if he is forced to accept lefs, that ftill he has juftice difpenfed him. If I borrow 100 *l.* in filver before the law, under agreement to repay it at the end of the enfuing year, and before the day of payment comes, the law takes place, commanding the lender to receive 100 *l.* paper for it, which fhall be worth, or have power to procure 82 *l.* filver money only ; with truth can this be called a rational or upright law? Certainly no. Nor fhall it be any juftification to me in confcience to detain 18 *l.* of my creditor's money.

The rules of natural juftice flowing from our fixed and unchangeable relations to each other, and the invariable nature and order of things, inforced by the exprefs commands of God, are of eternal and indifpenfible obligation. No laws, no combinations of human power, cuftoms, ufages, or practice, can controul or change them. We may, by the confent of a majority, tie up the compulfory hand on the civil magiftrate, and thereby diffolve the power of coercive laws,

laws, but can no more abfolve from the moral duty, than we can reverfe decrees inrolled in heaven. If my debtor fhould be fo extremely weak, as to fuppofe this not criminal becaufe it is legal, (which I think next to impoffible to imagine of a rational creature, and I make bold to affirm, never was the cafe of a creditor of underftanding, fufficient to know the meafure of his demand) his opinion perhaps may ferve for an excufe, or extenuation of his crime, but never can prove the rectitude of the act, and ftill the guilt muft reft fomewhere. The law-makers, the authors of this miftake, are culpable, unlefs they are under the fame delufion, which is yet more difficult to apprehend. Some, who gave up the juftice of the law, defend their practice under it, by faying, they are creditors as well as debtors: and as they are obliged to receive, fo they fhould have liberty to pay. Alas! what feeble arguments fatisfy, when they are caft into the fcale of intereft, and gain is the confequence of conviction. If the actions of men towards us are to be the meafures of our dealing with others, then he that is cheated by any perfon, may juftly plunder the next he meets. And truly I can't fee why it fhould ftop here; for as we may be many times defrauded, and not know it, to be fecure, and keep the ballance on the right

P fide,

fide, we fhould pillage our neighbours as often as an opportunity offers. This may feem fevere reafoning, but really I think it fair from the firft pofition; that becaufe one keeps back part of another's due, therefore he may honeftly detain the right of a third innocent perfon.

Again, paying an equivalent cannot be injurious to the debtor. For fuppofe he pays 120 *l.* paper. If 100 pounds worth of coin'd filver, reduced to bullion, will then yield him fo much, what does he more than perform his contract to pay 100 *l.* of coin'd filver? feeing a compleat recompence is perfectly confiftent with the right of each contracting party. Any remaining objections muft arife from its being hurtful or injurious to the fociety in general. This has been afferted, and endeavours have been ufed to fupport the truth of it, by this kind of reafoning.

Firft, if the law fhould oblige the debtor (for the purpofe) to pay 120 *l.* paper in lieu of 100 *l.* filver, the legiflature would thereby confefs the inferior worth of the paper, which will be attended with this ill confequence, that the general current value of the paper fhall be lefs than if the law had declared it equal to filver.

Secondly,

Secondly, That leſſening the current value will be a loſs to the ſociety in general. To the firſt, That obliging to pay a larger ſum of paper for a leſs of ſilver, acknowledges an inequality of value under the like denominations, is ſelf-evident. But from thence to infer, that the paper ſhall paſs in general, at leſs value than if they had been declared equal, with ſubmiſſion, I think miſtaken, and inconcluſive reaſoning.

To be clearly underſtood, permit me to examine this upon the fact. Suppoſe the law, in the ſtrongeſt terms, enacts that the paper ſhall be in value equal to ſilver money, according to their ſeveral denominations. Carry the paper from thence to uſe, by offering it in exchange or payment for ſome commodity, and then I aſk a ſhort queſtion, Who it is that really ſets a value on the paper, the legiſlature, or the perſon that has the commodity to ſell? If it be anſwered, the firſt, then I ſay, this cannot be, unleſs they alſo limit the price of the commodity. For if the ſeller can raiſe and porportion the price of it to what he thinks the real worth of the paper, the law-maker's declaration notwithſtanding, it is he that ſtrikes the value, and not they. For inſtance, put the caſe; a farmer, juſt upon emitting the paper, has a buſhel of wheat to ſell, which he rates at,

and

and will not part with under, three silver
shillings. The future current worth of the
paper being unknown to him, let him by
guess imagine these three shillings equal to
four shillings paper. A purchaser then
presses him, under the influence of the law,
to accept of three paper shillings for this
wheat; but he, without regard to the law,
according to his own opinion, demands and
receives four shillings for it. Will any man
say, the legislature determined the value of
the paper here? Apparently the seller did.
For the legislature commanded, that the three
paper shillings should be valued at three of
silver, but the farmer has made his estimate
at three fourths of that value only. Un-
questionably the vender must always have
this power, unless, as I said before, the
law-makers can limit the price of all commodities, which is not practicable, consistent with the order of things, or the pre-
servation of men's properties. But it may be
alledged, although the receiver of the money is not bound to observe the legislative
command, yet still it may have some weight.
He may consider it to be the impartial opinion of the wisest part of the society, what
the future current value of the paper shall
be, and thereby add, in some degree, to its
worth.

In

In anſwer I muſt obſerve, firſt, this gives up the point of power, and changes it to a matter of meer advice. Then, ſuppoſing that of any import, ſurely delivering it in a man-datory way, will be very little able to pro-duce the deſired effeđt. Imperative advice (pardon the expreſſion) favours too much of ſelling the rabbit, to prevail or perſuade. In ſhort, the words command and adviſe, convey two ideas ſo widely different, and ſo oppoſite and repugnant to each other, that it is abſolutely impoſſible we ſhould take the firſt for the laſt. But granting it to be in-terpreted as a piece of cordial advice. Shall it be received implicitly, and paſs without any examination ? I preſume not. When it comes to be examined, if the people ſhould be informed, that, upon a nice examination, the legiſlature had found a fourth, fifth, or ſixth difference between ſilver and paper, as ſuch calculations are generally out of the reach and comprehenſion of moſt people, it ſeems not improbable that the paper might paſs at firſt, agreeable to the given difference. *I ſay at firſt*; for I contend, if the calcula-tion ſhould be erroneous, (which the uſe of the money in time will diſcover) this effeđt ſhall not be laſting. But if, on the contrary, they learn that the paper, without any cal-culation, by gueſs, was pronounced equal to ſilver, which every man's judgment, who

P 3　　　　　knows

knows the superior power of the last, must disapprove of, what influence can the legislative advice then have? Undoubtedly it will be universally rejected, and each person turned at large to make his estimate as well as he can, without the least regard to the legislative opinion.

Once more, take it, that the quantity of silver in 100 shillings proclamation money is now worth 120 paper shillings in Pensylvania, and suppose this requisite had hitherto been omitted in all laws relating to the paper: let the supreme authority to-day enact, that from henceforth all persons shall give as much for 100 shillings paper as they do now for that quantity of silver, would this make the least alteration in the current value of the paper? Might a man, with reason, expect to buy more bread or wine to-morrow with 100 paper shillings, than he can to-day? if the legislative power can bring this to pass, perhaps it may prove more than some people desire; for I conjecture it will shew, that we never had any occasion for paper. Whatever quantity of silver we had amongst us, when the paper was struck, might have been extended in value proportionable to our wants, and all the business of paper-money done at once. The absurdity of this lies open to the meanest capacity;

yet

yet I aver, that to raife the value of paper by authoritative words or commands, is equally irrational and unfeafible.

I know no juft means whereby mankind can give value to things, but increafing or leffening the *ufes* or *quantity*. The paper derives its *intrinfick worth from* THE FUND which is ftable and fixed. The *ufes* give it further value, but that fhall always be in inverfe proportion to the quantity. The quantity is abfolutely under the direction of the legiflature, but the ufes not. As they are raifed, fo they muft be limited, by our neceffities, and the difpofition and order of things. The utmoft the legiflature can do, or is needful to be done, is to make the paper anfwer *all thofe ufes*. When they have afcertained the FUND, the *ufes* and *quantity*, their power expires. And the current value, if the people receive it, flows from them by fo unavoidable and a neceffary confequence, that whatever the legiflature or others will or do, (if it alters not the fund, ufes, or quantity) can work no change in it in general. For a time, as long as people are ignorant, I confefs it may; but when experience, that excellent miftrefs, has difclofed what worth they give, all imaginary value fhall ceafe and vanifh, and on the three re-

qui-

quifites, as on a folid and firm foundation, it fhall ultimately reft and fettle.

I conclude what I have to fay on this point with a fhort obfervation. That all the attempts of affemblies in America in this way even by penalties on difobedience, have proved fruitlefs and abortive. And it has been extremely remarkable, that although tranfgreffing the law, by making a difference between filver and paper, has been every day's practice, not in fecret, but openly, I have never heard, that any perfon has been fo much as queftioned publickly, or has loft any degree of reputation privately for doing it. So far do the dictates of juft and right reafon furpafs and tranfcend the force and power of any human device or inftitution, that oppofes or contradicts them.

I come now to confider the fecond pofition ; that leffening the current value will be difadvantageous to the fociety in general.

This cannot be maintained without proving, that it will occafion a lofs, or obftruct fome gain.

A fociety can gain but two ways, from the earth, and from their neighbours. When I
fay

fay from the earth, I do not mean from her
fimple productions only; for I include
therein men's labour and manufactures upon
them afterwards: and they can lofe only by
the contrary, neglecting the fruit and product of the earth, and fuffering their neighbours to carry away their wealth.

I prefume it will be very hard to fhew,
how a different valuation of the money can
influence the induftry of the land-holder or
the artifan.

Upon the quantities of the fruits of the
earth, and manufactures produced, entirely
depend the wealth of the country. A farmer and tradefman, for a certain portion of
their commodities one year, receive 8 fhillings, and with them can purchafe an ounce
of filver. The money being raifed in value
next year, they can get but 7 fhillings
for the fame quantities; but ftill that fum
will buy an ounce of filver. Can this difference, in the value of the paper, caufe
the one to till the more or lefs ground, or the
other to make a greater or lefs quantity of
his manufacture? What is it to them how
the money is rated, if they receive and part
with it at the fame value? Gold, comparing
quantity to quantity, is more valuable than
filver. If filver was to vanifh out of the
world,

world, and gold fhould be made the only
medium of commerce, can any one imagine
that mankind would grow more induftrious
to procure it, becaufe more valuable than
filver, when the quantity they fhall get muft
be proportionably lefs ? Do we in fact find
thefe different effects from gold or filver at
prefent ? I think we may as reafonably expect, that varying the meafure of the bufhel
or yard, will induce people to make more
or lefs corn or cloth, as that changing the
value of the money, which is another kind
of meafure for commodities, fhould excite
or abate men's diligence to raife and make
them.

All gain from our neighbours muft be by
getting their money or their goods. Thefe
are to be acquired only by conqueft or commerce. The firft I pafs over as impertinent
to this purpofe. Then let us fee whether
advancing the value of the money can reflect
any gain to us from them in the latter. Gain
in trade may be confidered as derived from
the manner or the meafure of it. The manner of trade in general is of fhort circuit,
and confifts of importing foreign money or
commodities, and the exportation of our own.
In thefe negociations we fhall find the worth
of the paper affords us no advantage over, or
an opportunity to get from our neighbours.

Sup-

Suppofe a foreigner imports 8oo *l*. proclamation money, and finding That not the
medium of our commerce, propofes to exchange it for paper. Let the value of the
paper be fuch, that he can get but 800 *l.* of
it for his filver. With the paper he pur-
chafes corn, which he tranfports. What
have we got from this foreigner? 8oo *l.* in
filver. Should we have got lefs had he received 1000 *l.* for his filver, and with it
bought the fame quantity of wheat? Certainly no. Neither cafe makes us richer or
poorer than the other; and the fame confequence will be found to attend all foreign
imports whatever.

When we export our commodities, the
value of the paper is quite out of the queftion; for in their fales, or the returns, it is
in no fort concerned. If we fend the paper abroad, and fell it, unlefs it be kept in
expectation of what the fund will yield for
it at the end of the term (which I intend to
fpeak to hereafter) we fhall find it but an
exchange of merchandizes between us and
them. For the feller brings the goods he
receives here, and the buyer, by means of
the money, carries back our goods; the
paper is but a meafure, as it was in the
cafe of imports and exports in return; and
if it be rated alike abroad and at home, no

lofs

lofs or gain can enfue to either country, or to the traders, from a high or low valuation of it.

He that is not fatisfied by thefe reafons, may perhaps be convinced by the experience of others. The coins of England being finer than thofe of Holland, quantity to quantity, are of more value; but was it ever thought the Englifh had therefore more power or traffick, to obtain the money and merchandize of other nations, than the Dutch?

Were it poffible that the profit of trade could be affected by lowering the coin, that cunning and fkilful generation would hardly have debafed theirs by defign, much lefs have continued for fo long a time as they have done. * The paper-currency of New England, by a great excefs in the quantity, is funk to a fhameful degree. From hence we hear of much fraud and difhonefty amongft them; but it was never yet objected that it injured them in trade. In truth, if it had, as they principally fubfift by com-

* * Thefe facts muft be referred to the time in which this treatife was written, twenty years ago.——Thefe evils have been remedied by the acts of parliament reftraining the affemblics from making their money a legal tender.

merce,

merce, they muſt have been ruined and un-
done long ago.

* The currencies of North and South
Carolina are in the ſame condition; but ſtill
their trades go on as uſual, without the leaſt
alteration. In reſpect to the meaſure of our
commerce, it is evident that cannot be impaired by reducing the value of our money,
unleſs we are thereby deprived of a ſufficient quantity to carry it on: for inſtance, if
60,000 *l.* proclamation money be neceſſary to
carry on all our trade, and we ſtrike 60,000 *l.*
paper, in hopes it ſhall have the value, upon
experience it proves worth but 50,000 *l.* proclamation. Then, for want of the remaining 10,000 *l.* ſome of the wheels of trade
muſt ſtand ſtill or move ſlower, which apparently will obſtruct a part of our gain.
But the impediment vaniſhes, by raiſing an
additional ſum of paper equal to the 10,000 *l.*
deficiency. The power of doing this we
have hitherto enjoyed and exerciſed without any reſtraint; and probably ſhall retain
as long as we uſe it with diſcretion and prudence.

Seeing then, that by raiſing the value of
our money, we are not likely to get any thing
from our neighbours, let us now try whether
by lowering it they can get any thing from
us.

us. I prefume I have proved, that in common commerce, receiving and returning the money for merchandizes, they cannot; confequently no method remains, but keeping the money to receive filver from the fund at the end of the term. By thefe practices they can gain from us only upon one fuppofition; that they purchafe the money at lefs than what I call the intrinfick worth: for if at more they lofe by it, and we gain from them. I have fhewn, rating intereft at 6 *per cent. per annum*, that 1000 *l.* payable at the end of 15 years, is worth 500 *l.* to take a round fum, in hand. If our neighbour can buy it for 400 *l.* he gets 100 *l.* from us. But on the contrary, if he gives 800 *l.* for it, he lofes 300 *l.* For he lends us 800 for 15 years, at 2 *l.* 8 *s. per cent. per annum*, when it is really worth 6 *l.* and the difference, which on computation will be found in the whole to amount to 300 *l.* or nearly, we gain from him. But neither of thefe cafes can poffibly happen while men have the leaft capacity to difcern and preferve their own intereft. Indeed I have never heard one found reafon, either moral or political, for this manifeft deviation from juftice and equity. So far is it from good policy, that if I am not miftaken, it muft work an effect contrary to the defign; and
inftead

3

inſtead of ſupporting the credit of the paper,
undermine and diminiſh it.

The public authority is guarantee for the
payment of all juſt debts. Every body muſt
agree, that the value of paper money is
nothing but ſo much public credit. Now, is
it poſſible for the public authority to break
its own engagements, in reſpect of the payment of the debts, without in ſome degree
blaſting that credit which is to be the ſupport
of the money? Public and private faith are,
in this reſpect, exactly alike; and it is as
eaſy to ſee how violating one public obligation ſhall impair the value of the paper-money, as how a known breach of private contract in a goldſmith ſhould leſſen the worth
of his bills or notes.

A ſecond inconvenience attending it, is
loſs of foreign credit, which muſt be a great
misfortune to a trading country. This is
occaſioned in the ſame manner, by which I
juſt now ſhewed the value of the money
might be affected; and let it not be thought
amiſs that I mention a third inconvenience,
namely, proſtituting and debaſing the dignity and excellence of the divine and moral
laws in the eyes of the people, and encouraging them, by ill practices and examples, to
depart from true honeſty and virtue. For
if

if a man can once believe, he may juftly, by human authority, tranfgrefs thofe laws, he lofes much of the due and neceffary refpect that ought to be paid them, and fhall afterwards be able to refift their checks and admonitions with greater eafe and facility : and he that owes to 20 people, and pays them with five fixths of their due, and fees his neighbour do the like, under colour of law to-day, will, I am afraid, with lefs regret and compunction, defraud his creditors without a law to-morrow.

But now, granting entire recompence ought to be made, it may be afked how the quantum of paper to be paid for antecedent filver debts fhall be afcertained.

The legiflature cannot fettle it with exact juftice, becaufe no fkill can difcover what the future current value fhall be; and if the people are left to do it themfelves, it will introduce many law-fuits and oppreffions, and ftill they may be as far from right as if the legiflature had done it. The greater inconveniences in the latter, rationally determine the power to the former. When they come to exercife it, if it is the firft experiment of the kind, I imagine they can do little more than guefs at the value. But as it is within demonftration, that the paper cannot be
equal

equal to silver, surely it ought not to be rated so. Impartiality requires the guess to be as near as may be, and then, although it may be mistaken upon the laws of change, it may be perfectly equal, because either party may lose or gain. It is a common case in life, and must be always so in untried things, and no man can justly complain of the event, because all errors are owing to our weakness, not our faults.

If any of our neighbours have issued paper-money, the value of theirs will afford us strong lights to discover the worth of our own, and allowing for different circumstances, we ought to rate ours as they have found theirs upon trial. But when experience has taught us the true worth of the money, all difficulty ends, and whatever debts or pre-contracts remain (as many from their growing nature must) should be satisfied according to that value.

I have now run through all the uses that occur to me worthy of observation; and therefore shall proceed to the quantity.

When it is designed, that paper shall be the only money of a country, the quantity, according to the nominal value, ought to be, as near as possible, adequate to the uses,

Q

or

or in other words, to all commerce, foreign
and domeſtick. It is eaſier to ſee the truth
of this rule in ſpeculation, than to reduce
it to practice; becauſe the number and extent of the uſes of money, in a populous
and induſtrious country, are far beyond our
knowledge and comprehenſion. From the
circumſtances of other places, the quantity
of money current before iſſuing the paper,
and the value of their exports, rational con-
jectures may be formed, but experience alone
can teach us what ſum will ſuffice. To
ſtrike the neceſſary quantity at once, would
be moſt advantageous to the ſociety, and
equal with reſpect to individuals; but as that
cannot be known, let it be approached as
near as may be. And ſince we may expect
to err, I preſume it will be better to err on
the ſide of deficiency than exceſs, ſeeing ad-
ditions are eaſy, but ſubſtractions oftentimes
very difficult after the emiſſion.

FROM what I have ſaid above, which
the foregoing treatiſe doth fully confirm
and eludicate, the following propoſitions,
which I apprehended to be truths, do ariſe.
That in Colonies, the eſſence of whoſe nature requires a progreſſive increaſe of ſettle-
ments and trade, and yet who, from the balance

lance of trade with the mother country being again them, mu suffer a confantly
decreasing quantity of filver money, *a certain quantity of paper-money is necefary.* It
is necefary to keep up the increasing operations of this trade, and thefe fettlements ;
it is alfo necefary, in fuch circumftances,
to the equal diftribution and general application of thefe benefits to the whole Colony,
which benefits would otherwife become a
monopoly to the *monied merchant only* : it is
prudent, and of good policy in the mother
country to permit it, as it is the fureft means
of drawing the balance of the Colony trade
and culture to its own profit.

Thefe reafonings further fhew, how, by
fecuring the *fund*, extending the *ufes*, and
regulating the *quantity*, this meafure of a paper-currency may be carried to the utmoft
extent of which it is capable. Nor do they
ftop here ; for as they give the rule whereby
to judge of the excefs or defe&ct of money
in any place whatfoever, fo do they, at all
times, fhew the necefity of encreafing it, or
the contrary.

Although the reafonings, which from my
own fentiments of the matter, I have applied
to this fubje&ct, and thofe, with which I am
able to oblige the world, by publifhing the

Q 2   above

above very judicious and able tract, do perfectly coincide in thefe points: yet upon the
point of the USES, in confidering the remedies to be provided againft the quantity of any
fallacious depreciation of this paper-money,
our reafonings feem to divide on quite different fides of the queftion. The author of
the above tract afferts, that in Colonies, where
paper-money is. created, the people of that
Colony *fhould be compelled by law to receive*
it in payments: and he ftates two or three
different cafes in proof of his affertion: My
opinion fuggefts, that this paper-money
ought *by no means to be a legal tender:* and
yet, different as thefe propofitions may appear, they will be found to coincide in the
application of the remedy; in the only proper and radical remedy, *the not permitting
the paper-money to be a legal tender*. This
gentleman experienced in the politicks of the
Colonies, and knowing the danger, if not
the impracticability, of any legiflature in
thefe Colonies adopting this maxim, takes up
the reafonablenefs and neceffity of this paper-
money being forced into payments by law;—
but then, in all the cafes wherein he ftates
the remedy in equity, againft the injuftice,
which may arife from the artificial value of
this paper-money thus declared, he firmly
and juftly declares, that the payment thus
by law forced upon the creditor *in paper,*
ought

*ought not to be according to the nominal legal
value* of that paper, but according to the
real value, an equivalent to the debt.———
This judgment totally deſtroys the maxim
of its being a legal tender. In the application therefore of the remedy, our opinions
do not differ, but the truth of them becomes
the more elucidated by this coincidence of
two thus ſeemingly different propoſitions.——
I will therefore proceed in ſaying, that by
the reaſonings above it appears, that the only
and proper remedy, againſt the iniquities
of a fallacious, depreciating paper-currency,
is *that radical one, of not permitting this paper-money to be a legal tender.*—On the other
hand, ſo confirmed am I in my opinion of
the neceſſity and propriety *of a certain quantity* of paper-money in the Colonies, that
were I not convinced, that the reſtraining of
it from being a legal tender, will not deſtroy
the exiſtence of it, but, on the contrary,
amend its currency ; I would even ſacrifice
my conviction to this point of utility : but
whatever apparent value this paper-money
may ſeem at firſt view to loſe by reſtraint of
this one uſe, this very reſtraint, (if the Colonies will have paper-money) muſt become
an occaſion of ſo meliorating and ſecuring
the *fund,* of ſo exactly regulating *the quantity,* and of adding ſome *other valuable uſe,*
namely an intereſt, or ſome premium equiva-

lent

lent to it; that the paper-money shall become
thus intrinsically, and of its own nature, a
better and furer currency than all the power
and authority of Colony-government could
make it. For not being forced into currency, by any external value derived from
authority, it must, like bullion in coin, derive its currency from its intrinsick value and
applicableness to the purpofes of money;—
fo that thus becoming, from neceflity, a
more determinate meafure, a more practical inftrument of trade, and a more beneficial depofit, as bearing an intereft even
while in currency, it becomes to have *all
the ufes* of bullion in coin, and one more,—
fo as even to bear a premium,—which in
fact is the cafe of the treafurer's notes in the
province of the Maffachufetts-Bay in New
England, though they are not a legal tender.

As the inconvenience of permitting the
affemblies of the Colonies to iffue paper-
money, under the fanction of its being a
legal tender, had been complained of and
confeffed; an act of parliament was made,
to reftrain that part of the Colonies, againft
which the complaint chiefly lay. Since that
time, a general reftraint hath been lain upon
all the Colonies, by a like act of parliament,
extending to the whole. The majority of
the

the men of bufinefs and property in the
Colonies, have ever heretofore wifhed to
have the affemblies reftrained by act of parliament, from the power of giving the fanction of a legal tender to their paper-money:
They efteemed that reftraint to be the only
effectual means of preventing the many bad
practices, which have arifen fiom this illu-
fory falfe coin; to the detriment of real
bufinefs and real property. On the other
hand, feeing the abfolute neceffity of fome
paper currency, fchemes of the like nature,
as that of the following propofal, have been
thought of. I have had opportunities, not
with governors and crown-officers, but with
the leading men of bufinefs in the Colonies,
of examining and confidering feveral of thefe
fchemes. The following propofal may be
confidered as the refult of thefe difcuffions,
containing and comprehending, according
to my beft judgment, all which was thought
confiftent with the liberties of the people,
fafe in refpect of their intereft, and effectual to the point required. So far am I from
affuming any merit in the invention or framing of it, that I defire it may be confidered,
as founded on what hath been actually practifed in Penfylvania, by the good fenfe and
good policy of the affembly of that province,
with fuccefs and with benefit to the public.
That the particular propofal, as it is now

formed,

formed, and applied to the prefent exigences of America and Great Britain, was drawn up fome years ago, in conjunction with a friend of mine, and of the Colonies. It was, by us, jointly propofed to government, under fucceffive adminiftrations, in the years 1764, 1765, 1766, during which time, the publication was fufpended. It is now given to the publick, not by way of appeal againft adminiftrations, but as a fcheme which, although not attended to by a Britifh miniftry at prefent, may yet fuggeft fomething that may be of ufe to better politicians than we pretend to be.

We are fully apprifed how much we have rifqued, both in the propofing, and in the now publifhing this fcheme.—If the Britifh ftatefmen fhould ftill think that they can turn it to no good ; and if the American patriots fhould think that a dangerous ufe might have been made of it by government: We fhall be thought by the one to have been impertinent, and by the others to be mifchievous meddlers. If our ftatefmen fhould have the happinefs to find out the right ufe of it, and, like the humbler, but not lefs wife politicians in the Colonies, to apply it to the mutual benefit of government, and of the people ; then we fhall not be allowed to have the leaft fhare, much lefs

any

any merit in the forming of it, or in the application of it: twenty different people will prove, that it has been their fcheme. About this we are not anxious, any more than difappointed that our Britifh ftatefmen could not find their way to the ufe of it. We now propofe it to the fober fenfe and experience of the Colonies. Who will know how to profit by it, how to convert this fpecies of credit, into a real efficient currency; how to benefit *and to take the lead of that power and political intereft,* which their taking the management of this will neceffarily throw into their hands. *We need not point out to them* how that will arife.——They have the means, whenever our bad policy, or their own prudence fhall lead them to make ufe of fuch, of giving this currency a general value throughout America, by eftablifhing an intercommunion and reciprocation of credit, under acts paffed by each particular affembly, all having reference to this one point;—regulating the quantity which each province or Colony fhall iffue—by the ftate of its depreciation; and regulating the proceedings in their feveral courts of law, as to the fpecialty of all bargains and contracts made in this fpecial note-money. They alfo will know, which hath hitherto puzzled our ftatefmen, how to give it a *real intrinfick value*, without

calling

calling in the aid of the government of Great Britain, to give it *an artificial one*, by making it a legal tender ; and without paying to that government *forty thousand pounds per annum*, which sum, at least, the interest of this money would have produced as a revenue.

As the paper-money act made and passed in Pensylvania, in 1739, was the compleatest of the kind, containing all the improvements which experience had from time to time suggested, in the execution of preceding acts: An account of that act will best explain and recommend the measure contained in the following proposal.

The sum of the notes, by that act directed to be printed was 80,000 *l.* proclamation money : This money was to be emitted to the several borrowers, from a loan-office established for that purpose.

Five persons were nominated Trustees of the *loan-office*, under whose care and direction, the bills or notes were to be printed and emitted.

To suit the bills for a common currency, they were of small and various denominations, from 20 shillings downwards to one shilling.

Va-

Various precautions were taken, to prevent counterfeits, by peculiarities in the paper, character, manner of printing, signing, numbering, &c.

The truftees took an oath, and gave fecurity for the due and faithful execution of their office.

They were to lend out the bills on real fecurity of at leaft double the value, for a term of fixteen years, to be repaid in yearly quotas or inftallments, with intereft: Thus one 16th part of the principal was yearly paid back into the office, which made the payment eafy to the borrower: *The intereft was applied to public fervices,* the principal, during the firft ten years, let out again to frefh borrowers.

The new borrowers, from year to year, were to to have the money only for the remaining part of the term of 16 years, repaying, by fewer, and of courfe, proportionably larger inftallments, and during the laft fix years of the 16, the fums paid in, were not to be remitted, but the notes burnt and deftroyed; fo that at the end of the 16 years, the whole might be called in and burnt, and the accounts completely fettled.

The

The truftees were taken from all the
different counties of the province, their
refidence in different parts, giving them
better opportunities of being acquainted with
the value and circumftances of eftates offered
in mortgage.

They were to continue but four years in
office ; were to account annually to com-
mittees of affembly ; and, at the expiration
of that term, they were to deliver up all
monies and fecurities in their hands, to their
fucceffors, before their bonds and fecurities
could he difcharged.

Left a few wealthy perfons fhould engrofs
the money, which was intended for more
general benefit, no one perfon, whatever
fecurity he might offer, could borrow more
than 100 *l.*

Thus, numbers of poor new fettlers were
accommodated and affifted with money to
carry on their fettlements, to be repaid in
eafy portions yearly, as the yearly produce
of their lands fhould enable them.

Great inconveniencies had arifen in other
Colonies, from a depreciation of their paper
money, occafioned by emitting it in too
great quantities.

It

It was difficult to know beforehand, what quantity would be fufficient for a medium of exchange, proportioned to the trade of the country, and not to exceed the occafions.

To prevent the mifchiefs attending an over quantity; the government of Penfylvania began with a fmall fum of 15,000 *l.* in 1723, proceeded to increafe it gradually, in following years, and thus prudently *felt* for a proportion they could not previoufly *calculate*; and, as they never exceeded a moderate fum, the depreciation was never fo great as to be attended with much inconvenience.

The advantages that arife from this act, were from a view thereof, in 1752, thus expreffed, by a committee of affembly, in their report of Auguft, 19th.

" Furnifhing the country with a medium
" of trade, and of a kind that could not, to
" any purpofe, be exported; as it facilitated
" mutual commerce, *leffened cur taxes by*
" *the intereft it produced*; and made it more
" eafy for every one to obtain ready pay for
" his labour, produce or goods, (a medium
" fo evidently wanted at the time paper-
" money was firft iffued) has doubtlefs,
" been

" been one great means of the fubfequent
" increafe of our trade and people, by in-
" ducing ftrangers to come and fettle among
" us. But your committee conceive that
" the manner of iffuing this medium, con-
" tributed no lefs to thofe happy effects,
" than the medium itfelf. It was by the
" law directed to be emitted on loans, in
" fums of 12 *l.* 10 *s.* and upwards, not ex-
" ceeding 100 *l.* to one perfon for a long
" term, on eafy intereft, and payable in
" yearly quotas, which put it in the power of
" many, to purchafe lands and make planta-
" tions; (the loan-office enabling them to
" pay the purchafe fo eafily) and thereby to
" acquire eftates to themfelves, and to fup-
" port, and bring up families, but who
" without that affiftance, would probably
" have continued longer in a fingle ftate,
" and as labourers for others, or have quit-
" ted the Colony in fearch of better fortune.
" This eafy means of acquiring landed
" eftates to themfelves, has, we fuppofe,
" been one principal encouragement to the
" great removal hither of people from *Ger-*
" *many,* where they were only (and could
" fcarce ever expect to be other than) ten-
" ants. That it fhould be eafy for the in-
" duftrious poor to obtain lands, and acquire
" property in a country, may, indeed, be
" charge-

4

" chargeable with one inconvenience, to
" wit, that it keeps up the price of labour,
" and it makes it more difficult for the *old*
" *fettler* to procure working hands; the
" labourers very foon fetting up for them-
" felves, (and accordingly we find, that
" though perhaps not lefs than 30,000 la-
" bourers have been imported into this pro-
" vince, within thefe twenty years, labour
" continues as dear as ever) yet this inconve-
" nience is perhaps more than ballanced by
" the rife and value of his lands, occafioned
" by increafe of people : and to the public in
" general numbers of fubftantial inhabi-
" tants, have been always reckoned an ad-
" vantage. In fine, by rendering the means
" of purchafing land eafy to the poor, the
" dominions of the crown are ftrengthened,
" and extended ; the propietaries difpofe of
" their wildernefs territory, the Britifh na-
" tion fecures the benefit of its manufac-
" tures, and increafes the demand for them ;
" for fo long as land can be eafily procured
" for fettlements, between the *Atlantic* and
" *Pacific* Oceans, *fo long will labour continue*
" *to be dear in America* ; and while labour
" continues dear, we can never rival the
" artificers, or interfere with the trade of
" our mother country."

But

But the act being expired, and the pro‑
prietors and the people differing about the
terms of renewing it, the former, though
they and their deputies had received annual
presents out of the interest, amounting to
near 40,000 *l.* yet, infisting on greater fu‑
ture advantages, which the assembly did not
chuse to allow, *this excellent machine for set‑
tling a new country, now no longer subsists.*
And as by the late act of parliament, no
more paper-money can be issued in the Co‑
lonies, that shall be a *legal tender*, it may
perhaps be necessary for government here to
make some provision of a currency for the
Colonies. If this should be necessary, the
Pensylvania scheme, which has by long ex‑
perience, been found so practicable, and so
useful, may, with a few changes, to accom‑
modate it more to general purposes, be
safely and advantageously extended to all
the Colonies, by an act of parliament as
follows.

Let   millions, in bills of credit (or
paper-money) be printed here, for the use
of the Colonies.

Let a loan office be erected in each Co‑
lony, to issue the bills, take the securities,
and to receive the quota's yearly paid in.

Let

Let the bills be iffued for ten years, payable a tenth part of the fum yearly with intereft, at 5 *per cent.*

Let the Bills be made by the act, a *legal tender* in all the Colonies, and the counterfeiting made death. I defire to mark the very material difference of a paper currency created by act of parliament, and one iffued to the Colonies, as the neceffities only of the Colonifts have occafion for it, from a paper currency poured like a deluge over a country, by act of affembly only: In the one cafe, the mifchief of its being a legal tender, has been feverely felt, and therefore forbidden: In the other cafe, the making it a legal tender, is not only beneficial but neceffary.

Let there be no limitation of the fums to be borrowed by one perfon, but that every one may borrow as much as he can give double fecurity for, by a mortgage of real clear eftate.

And to prevent an over quantity being extant at one time, let an intereft of 4 *per cent.* be allowed, for all fums lodged in the office, during the time the owner fuffers it to remain there. *By this means, it is fuppofed, the due proportion of money that fhall*

R

be

be current, will find itself; and adapt itself from time to time, to the occasions of commerce.

The effects of this scheme would be, that although the silver and gold acquired by the Colonies, would be all sent to England: Yet they would have among them, in consequence of this measure, a legal tender.

They would also have a sufficiency of cash current for all purposes.

They would not have too much current at one time, as the allowance for interest for sums lodged in the office, would always bring in the surplus.

The settlement and improvement of new tracts of land would be greatly encouraged and promoted, population encreased, trade extended, &c.

The means of remittance to England would be always at hand, and the commerce thereby facilitated.

A great annual sum, continually increasing, will arise to the crown for interest,
which,

which, after deducting charges, may be
applied to American purpofes, in eafe of this
kingdom; and become *a permanent and effective revenue.* A confiderable profit will
alfo arife to government, from the wearing
out, and total lofs of a great deal of fmall
money.

It will operate as a general tax on the
Colonies, *and yet not actually be one*; as
he who *actually* pays the intereft, *has an
equivalent,* or more, in the ufe of the principal. But the tax, if it can be fo called,
will, in effect, fpread itfelf more equally on
all property, perhaps more fo than any other
tax that can be invented; fince every one
who has the money in his hands, does from
the time he receives it, to the time he pays
it away, *virtually* pay the intereft of it, the
firft borrower having received the value of
it (to ufe for his own profit) when he parted
firft with the original fum. Thus the rich
who handle moft money, would in reality
pay moft of the tax.

Thefe bills having thus *full* credit, the
government can iffue, on occafion, any
quantity for fervice, in cafe of an American
war, without needing to fend *real, cafh thither, by hurtful contracts.*

Plenty

Plenty of money thus continued in the Colonies, will keep labour high, and thereby prevent the apprehended danger of interfering manufactures.

For the more eafy afcertaining of titles, there fhould be a claufe in the act, requiring that all transfers, conveyances and incumbrances whatfoever fhould be recorded,—this of itfelf would be a great advantage to the Colonies.

The manner of carrying this propofal into execution may be as follows.

An office to be eftablifhed in London, to be managed by two Commiffioners, appointed by the treafury; their falaries   per annum, with   per annum, for clerks and incidents of office, to be paid out of the revenue only, arifing from the intereft.

The bufinefs of this office to be

1. The printing of the paper-money.

2. The figning of it by the Commiffioners.

3. The diftribution of it to the offices in America.

4. The

4. The entering of what is sent, according to its number and denomination.

5. The communication and correspondence with the several loan-offices in the Colonies.

6. The drawing up the instructions for the same.

7. The receiving from these offices, accounts of the issuing the paper bills, these accounts to contain, 1. Account of the numbers and dates of bills issued. 2. State of the mortgages and securities. 3. Account of interest received. 4. Account of interest paid for deposited money. 5. Account of government drafts paid by the loan-office, and salaries paid to its several officers. 6. Account of bills exchanged, for those that are over-worn. 7. Account of receipts of principal money by instalments, &c.

And in general, the Commissioners from the monthly reports of the several offices in America, of every branch of their duty, are to form monthly abstracts and reports for the treasury, of the state of the money current, of the amount of the interest money in the loan-offices, at the government's disposal, of the state of each office, and the

R 3   far-

farther regulations from time to time neceſſary to be made, either by orders from the
treaſury, inſtructions from the Commiſſioners, or further legal powers, or. directions
by act of parliament, or by inſtructions neceſſary to be ſent to the governors in America, recommending acts of aſſembly proper
to be made in that country.

The Commiſſioners are alſo to draw up
directions and inſtructions to the *Inſpectors,*
whoſe office will be hereafter deſcribed.

And they are to ſuperintend all the other
parts of the adminiſtration and execution of
this ſcheme, as will be more particularly
pointed out hereafter, in the deſcriptions of
the ſeveral offices and officers in America,
with their reſpective duties.

Loan-Office in each province.

To conſiſt of *Truſtees, Solicitor,* and
Clerk. The province to be divided into
diſtricts. A large province into eight diſtricts, a ſmall province into fewer.

Each diſtrict to have a Truſtee appointed
out of its own reſident inhabitants, one who
is a freeholder that can give ſufficient ſecurity to the crown within the province. So
that

that the loan-office of the largeſt province will conſiſt of eight Truſtees, and the ſmaller in proporſion to their diſtricts, into which they are divided, ſome not having more than two.

The Truſtees to be appointed by act of aſſembly, and upon their appointment to qualify themſelves, by giving the ſecurity required to the crown, and taking the uſual oaths (or affirmation) and oath (or affirmation) of office.

Each Truſtee to have 100 *l. per annum.* out of the intereſt ariſing by the loans of the bills.

The principal acting Truſtee to reſide in the capital of the province where the office is to be kept, and to have 200 *l.* or leſs in ſome provinces, for his conſtant attendance, and the incidents of office, beſides his ſallary in common with the reſt.

The Truſtees to be appointed, only for the term of five years, at the expiration whereof, they are to account fully to the governor in council, aſſiſted by one of the inſpectors hereafter deſcribed, and deliver up all books, deeds, depoſited caſh, &c.

to

to their fucceffors, upon which they are to receive their quietus.

All the Truftees are to meet once a month at the office, to fign the bills to be iffued, to confider the applications for money, examine the goodnefs of the fecurity offered, and fix the fum to be lent on each fecurity, not lefs than a majority of the Truftees to order the loans, and not lefs than two to fign and date the bills to be iffued. They are alfo to take charge of, and keep in fome fafe place, the fecurity deeds mortgaged, and *they* are to chufe a perfon, fkilled in the law of titles, to be their *Sollicitor*, who is to be paid by the fees arifing in the office, viz. 20*s*. on every mortgage, for which he is to examine, and make extracts of the titles or fecurities offered, for the infpection of the *Chief Juftice* of the province, if referred to him, and of the Truftees; to prepare the mortgage and counterpart, with the bond and warrant of attorney, and to record the mortgage. He is alfo to keep a book of applications, noting them down in the order of time in which they are made, the fum defired, and the fecurity offered in mortgage. He is to get blank mortgages printed, of a prefcribed form. There are to be triplicates of each mort-

mortgage, the firſt is to be executed by the mortgager, and lodged in the office, the ſecond, an exact copy delivered to the mortgager for his direction, as it contains the times and proportions of payments, both of inſtallments and intereſt, the third to be kept in a bound book and there made the record.

The clerk is alſo to be appointed by the Truſtees. He keeps a book of allowances, ſo called, becauſe therein is put down what ſums the Truſtees think proper to allow or lend to each applyer, according to their opinion, of the ſecurity offered. He alſo computes the quotas or inſtallments and intereſt, making together, the ſum to be paid each year, by the mortgager, and gives a copy thereof to the Solicitor, to be by him, after the approbation of the Truſtees given to it, inſerted in the mortgage. He keeps alſo a day book, in which is noted,

The emiſſions and receipts of each day, viz.

The ſums lent in mortgage, and to whom.

The ſums received from each mortgager, diſtinguiſhing principal and intereſt.

The

The fums depofited in the office, for which 4 *per cent.* is to be allowed by the office.

The returning of fuch fums, with intereft paid.

The fums of new bills exchanged for old.

The drafts of government for intereft money, as paid by the Truftees.

The Truftees Salaries, when paid, and the allowance for incidents.

N. B. The perfon bringing any money bills to be depofited in the office, for the purpofe of receiving the 4 *per cent.* is to prepare two fchedules of faid bills, one to be figned by the acting Truftee, and delivered to him, the other to be figned by him and delivered into the office, to be kept by the Truftees. And no fum under 100 *l.* is to be depofited on the terms of receiving intereft, and *the intereft muft not commence till one month after the depofite made.*

The clerk is to keep a ledger, in which the day book accounts are to be pofted up, under their refpective heads.

The

The Truftees, from thefe books, &c. are to form monthly abftracts of the whole ftate of the currency, and the bufinefs of the office, and to fend the fame figned by a majority of the whole number, to the com-miffioner's office in England, in order that the commiffioners may form ftates from time to time, as the treafury fhall require, of the whole of the currency throughout the continent, as well as of the ftate of each office in the refpective Colonies.

Provifion for check and control of the exe-cution of the office in America.

1. The direction and inftructions of the commiffioners refiding in England.

2. Two *Infpectors* to be commiffioned by the treafury, to act under their inftructions, and the inftructions of the commiffioners, and to report to them. They are to vifit all the offices in America at leaft once a year, and to infpect the accounts, cafh, &c. as often as they fhall fee occafion, or fhall be directed by their fuperiors, and to join with the governor and council of each province in the auditing of the accounts of the office. And, if upon any of thefe infpections, an infpector fhall difcover any mifmanagement which requires immediate remedy, he is

not

not only to report to the commiffioners in
England, but to the governor of the province, and if it appears to the governor and
council neceffary, the governor to call together the affembly immediately, in order to
the appointing new Truftees, and to order,
by advice of council, the profecution of the
delinquent Truftees, to the forfeiture of
their fecurities, and fuch other penalties as
they may have incurred.

3. The governor and council (the infpector affifting) to audit the accounts of the
loan-office within each province annually.
The governor and council to be allowed
for their trouble.

N. B. In thofe provinces where the governor is not appointed by the crown, perhaps fome addition may be thought proper
to be made to this board for auditing.

4. A committee of the affembly to infpect the ftate of the office, for their own
fatisfaction and information, that in cafe
they difcover any mifmanagement or delin-
quency, they may apply to the governor, that
proper fteps may be taken to remedy the fame.

When the accounts are to be infpected
and fettled, the Truftees will be charged
with

with the loan money put into their hands,
and difcharge themfelves by producing
mortgages for the whole, or for part, and
the remainder in bills.

They will be charged with the new bills
put into their hands, to exchange fuch as by
wearing are become unfit for farther currency, and difcharge themfelves by producing fuch worn bills for part, and the
remainder in new bills unexchanged.

They will be charged by the account, of
intereft received, and difcharge themfelves
by their falaries, by government draughts
which they have paid, by intereft they have
paid on fums depofited, and by producing
the remainder in bills in their hands.

They will be charged with the parts of
the principal fums received yearly, as in-
ftalments, and difcharge themfelves by
mortgages on which the fame was remitted,
and the remainder in bills.

They will be charged with the fums depofited in their hands, to bear intereft, and
difcharge themfelves by producing receipts
for what they have returned, and for intereft paid, and bills in their hands for the
fums they have not returned.

Having

Having now gone through the consideration of every point of internal adminiſtration, let us next review thoſe external relations by which the intereſt of the American ſettlements ſtand connected with the Indian country and its inhabitants. Our Colonies muſt neceſſarily have connections both of trade and politicks with theſe people, of a nature different from any other, as they are are planted in countries inhabited by a race of people, who differ in their circumſtances and in their politicks from any other nation with whom there remains, either in hiſtory or on record, any example of alliance.

Perhaps it may not be unentertaining, I am ſure it is neceſſary to the true knowledge of Indian affairs, to take up this ſubject ſomewhat higher than has been uſual in the ordinary way of conſidering it.

The different manner in which this globe of earth is poſſeſſed, and occupied by the different ſpecies of the human race which inhabit it, muſt form the ſpecific difference in their intereſts and politicks.

The human race, which is at preſent found on this earth, may be preciſely divided into three families, generically, and in their eſſential properties, diſtinct and different each from

from the other. And, for aught I know, it is to this natural truth, that the heaven-directed pen of the author of the books of Mofes may refer, when he gives precifely and only three fons to Noah. Thefe three different fpecies, or race, are—The white race—the red—the black. It is not barely the colour of thefe two firft, which diftinguifhes them; the form of their fkull, and their hair, where there has been no mixture, is fpecifically different from each other; and a true Indian will not judge by any other diftinction: the black race has wool inftead of hair, as alfo a form of fkull different from each.

Thefe books, after having given a philofophical account, cloathed in drama, of the origin of things, feem to confine their real narrative to the hiftory of the white family, to that race of people who have been land-workers from the beginning, who, wherever they have fpread themfelves over the face of this globe, have carried with them the art of cultivating vines, and fruit trees—and the cultivation of bread corn; who, wherever they have extended themfelves, have become fettlers, and have conftantly carried with them the fheep, goat, oxen and horfe, domiciliated and fpecially applied to the ufes and labour of a fettlement.

7   Of

Of the black family I fay nothing in this place, as not concerned in the prefent confideration.

The red family, wherever found, are wanderers. The Tartars are in one part wandering herdfmen, and in other parts hunters and fifhermen. The American inhabitants, Indians, as we call them, from the word Anjô, or Ynguo, fignifying a man in their language, are the fame race of people from one end of the continent to the other; and are the fame race or family as the Tartars, precifely of the fame colour, of the fame form of fkull, of the fame fpecies of hair,—not to mention the language and their names.

America, in its natural ftate, is one great foreft of woods and lakes, ftocked not with fheep, oxen, or horfes; not with animals of labour, and fuch as may be domiciliated, but with wild beafts, game and fifh; vegetating not with bread-corn, but with a fpecies of pulfe, which we call maize, of which there is great doubt whether it be indigenous or not.—All therefore that this country afforded for food or raiment muft be hunted for. The inhabitants confequently would naturally be, as in fact they were, *not land-workers, but hunters ; not fettlers, but wanderers.*

derers. They would therefore, confequently, never have, as in fact they never had, any idea of property in land, of that property which arifes from a man's mixing his labour with it. They would confequently never have, as in fact they never had, any one communion of rights and actions as extended to fociety; any one civil union; and confequently they would not ever have any government. They know no fuch thing as adminiftrative or executive power, properly fo called: they allow the authority of advice, a kind of legiflative authority; but there is no civil coercion amongft them: they never had any one collective actuating power among the whole, nor any magiftrate or magiftrates to execute fuch power.

The race of white people migrating from Europe, ftill continue land-workers, and have made fettlements in parts of America which they occupy, and have tranfported thither bread-corn, fheep, oxen, horfes, and other ufually domeftic animals, that are domiciliate with thefe fettlers.

They are a community—they are a fociety——they live under government, and have a fixed property in their lands, have a fixed permanent intereft, which muft fubfift *under a continued feries of fecurity.* The locality

S

cality

cality of the labour of thefe fettlers, neceffarily produces a reciprocation of wants and
an intercommunion of fupply, by exchange
of mutual neceffaries. This alfo leads to an
intercourfe of commerce with others, who
are not immediately within their community—And hence arifes a commercial intereft
to thefe fettlers.

From the European defire of having the
furs and peltry of the Indian hunters, and
from the Indian defire of having the more
ufeful and neceffary tools and inftruments of
improved life, an artificial reciprocation of
wants has arifen between the European fettlers, and the original inhabitants of America, which hath gradually extended itfelf
to many articles not at firft called for——
And from this intercourfe of commerce has
arifen a neceffary relation of politicks between them.

The only true fpirit which ought to actuate thefe politicks, muft arife from a due
knowledge of the circumftances and interefts
of each, and from a conftant invariable attention to that compofite intereft which is
formed by their alliance.

The intereft of a community of fettlers
muft lye in *a permanent feries of fecurity* to
their

their cultured lands, as the making fettlements is by the fucceffive yearly application of repeated labour, and of its eventual future effect. Settlers and landworkers want but fmall tracts of land; but muft have a fixed and permanent local property therein. A nation of hunters require a much greater extent of country, in the proportion that the wide extended produce of a hunt, bears to the local bounded produce of a farm or fettlement; fo that the Indian property of country confifts of two forts, their dwelling lands and their hunt.

The intereft of a tribe of wanderers lyes in the protection and fupport of the aged, of the women and children—under the temporary locations of dwelling, which the feverity of the winter feafon, the occafion of the procuring pulfe in the feafon of vegetation, and the times of parturition, render neceffary even to wanderers.

As fixed regulations and protection of trade, muft be the effential fpirit of the politicks and the law of nations to a commercial nation *, fo an exact and ftrict obferv-

ance

* Hunting being but the amufement, the diverfion of a nation of fettlers, the rights and laws of it may not appear as national points—but to a nation of hunters

ance of the laws of sporting, the protection of the game, and the most rigid sanction
of the *hunt*, (better perhaps understood by
our sportsmen than our politicians) become
the *laws of nations* to an *hunting nation*.

From these principles let us carry our con-
siderations into facts.

The European landworkers, when they
came to settle in America, began trading
with the Indians; * obtained leave of the In-

ters these become the national interests and the laws of
nations.—A violation of these laws of nations; as sub-
sisting between nations of hunters, was the cause of the
war between the Five-nation confederacy, and the
Oïlinois. The Ohio hunt, to the south-east of lake
Erie, was common to these nations; the laws of the
hunt required, that at each beaver-pond, the Indians
should leave a certain number of males and females;
the Oïlinois, on some occasion of pique, destroyed all.
The Five-nations declared war against the Oïlinies.
The Indian war ends not but in the total reduction of
the one or the other. The Oïlinois were totally conquered. The conquered country, as well as the hunt,
became the right of the Five-nations, and were,
amongst the rest of their lands, put, by them, into
the hands of the English in trust.

* Perhaps New-England may be an exception:
The Indians began an unjust war against them; they
conquered these Indians, and their claim is best, as
well as justly, founded in conquest, which the Indians
acknowledge.

dians

dians to cultivate fmall tracts as fettlements or dwellings. The Indians having no other idea of property, than what was conformable to their tranfient temporary dwelling-places, eafily granted this. When they came to perceive the very different effect of fettlements of landworkers creating a permanent property always extending itfelf, they became very uneafy; but yet, in the true fpirit of juftice and honour, abided by the effects of conceffions which they had made, but which they would not have made, had they underftood beforehand the force of them.

From this moment the politics of the Indians were fixed on, and confined to, two points. The guarding their dwelling lands and their hunts from the encroachments of the European fettlers; and the perpetually labouring, to our utter fhame, in vain, to eftablifh fome equitable and fixed regulations in the trade carried on between them and the Europeans.

The European encroachments, not only by the extent of their fettlements, but by their prefuming to build forts in the Indian dwelling lands, and in the territories of their hunts, without leave, or by collufion; and the impofitions and frauds committed againft the Indians in trading with them, has been

S 3 the

the occafion of conftant complaint from the
Indians, and the invariable fource of Indian
hoftilities: and yet even thefe might have been
furmounted, were it not that we have conftantly added an aggravation to this injuftice,
by claiming a DOMINION in confequence of
a *landed poffeffion*. Againft this the free fpirit of an Indian will revolt, to the laft
drop of his blood: This will be perpetual,
unremitted caufe of war to them againft us.
Againft it, they have at all times, and upon
all occafions protefted, and they will never
give it up. As long as we keep up this ufelefs, faithlefs claim of dominion over them,
fo long fhall we be embroiled in war with
them. The European power may perhaps
finally extirpate them, but can never conquer them. The perpetually increafing gene-
rations of Europeans in America, may fupply numbers that muft, in the end, wear out
thefe poor Indian inhabitants from their own
country; but we fhall pay dear, both in
blood and treafure, in the mean while, for
our horrid injuftice. Our frontiers, from
the nature of advancing fettlements, difperfed along the branchings of the upper
parts of our rivers, and fcattered in the difunited vallies, amidft the mountains, muft
be always unguarded, and defencelefs againft
the incurfions of Indians. And were we
able, under an Indian war, to advance our
fettle-

settlements yet farther, they would be advanced up to the very dens of those savages. A settler wholly intent upon labouring on the soil, cannot stand to his arms, nor defend himself against, nor seek his enemy: Environed with woods and swamps, he knows nothing of the country beyond his farm: The Indian knows every spot for ambush or defence. The farmer, driven from his little cultured lot into the woods, is lost: the Indian in the woods, is every where at home; every bush, every thicket, is a camp to the Indian, from whence, at the very moment when he is sure of his blow, he can rush upon his prey. The farmer's cow, or his horse, cannot go into the woods, where alone they must subsist: his wife and children, if they shut themselves up in their poor wretched loghouse, will be burnt in it: and the husbandman in the field will be shot down while his hand holds the plough. An European settler can make but momentary efforts of war, in hopes to gain some point, that he may by it obtain a series of security, under which to work his lands in peace: The Indian's whole life is a warfare, and his operations never discontinued. In short, our frontier settlements must ever lie at the mercy of the savages: and a settler is the natural prey to an Indian, whose sole occupation is war and hunting. To countries circum-

stanced

ftanced as our Colonies are, an Indian is the moft dreadful of enemies. For, in a war with Indians, no force whatever can defend our frontiers from being a conftant wretched fcene of conflagrations, and of the moft fhocking murders. Whereas on the contrary, our temporary expeditions againft thefe Indians, even if fuccefsful, can do thefe wanderers little harm. Every article of their property is portable, which they always carry with them—And it is no great matter of diftrefs to an Indian to be driven from his dwelling ground, who finds a home in the firft place that he fits down upon. And of this formidable enemy, the numbers, by * the lateft accounts, are 23105 fighting men.

If we entertain an idea of conqueft, in fupport of this ambitious folly of dominion, we muft form fuch a feries of magazines and entrepôts for ftores, ammunition and provifions; we muft maintain in conftant employ fuch a numerous train of waggons for the roads, fuch multitudes of boats and veffels for the waters; we muft eftablifh fuch a train of fortified pofts; we muft fupport fuch a numerous army; we muft form and execute fuch an enlarged and comprehenfive fyftem of command, as fhall give us military poffeffion of the whole Indian coun-

* This refers to the year 1763.

try.

try. Let now any foldier or politician confider the enormous endlefs expence of all
this conduct, and then anfwer to what
profitable purpofe fuch meafure leads, which
may in a much better and jufter way be
obtained.

If our government confiders this well, and
will liften to thofe who are beft verfed in Indian affairs, it will be convinced that ho-
nefty is the beft policy ; and that our dominion in America, will be beft and fureft
founded in faith and juftice, toward the rem-
nant of thefe much injured natives of the
country.

In this hope, and with this view, I will
endeavour to ftate the Indian rights and our
duty toward them ; and to point out that line
of conduct, which leads to it—And firft of
the Kenunctioni, or the Five-nation confederacy.

The Indian lands are of two kinds——
Their dwelling land, where their caftles are,
and their hunting ground. The dwelling
lands of the Kenunctioni, or the Five-nation confederacy, is called Kenunctionîga,
and is at the top or higheft part of the continent, from whence the waters run every
way—By the waters of Canada into the
gulph

gulph of St. Laurence, by all the rivers of
the Englifh Colonies into the Atlantic ocean,
by the waters of the Miffiffippi into the gulph
of Mexico. They may, in a general manner,
be thus defcribed, by a line run from near
Albany, north-weftward, along the Mohawk
river on the north fide of it, north round
Oneida lake, to the north eaft corner of lake
Ontario, thence along the lakes to Cana-
hôga on lake Ofwego or Erie; thence fixty
miles directly back into the country; thence
to Shamôkin, on the Sufquehanna river;
thence along the Cufhïëtung mountains;
thence again to the lower Mohawk caftles.
The Indians themfelves defcribing, under
confidence, to a friend of mine at Onondaga, this their fituation, faid, " That it has
" many advantages fuperior to any other
" part of America. The endlefs moun-
" tains feparate them from the Englifh, all
" the way from Albany to Georgia. If
" they fhould have any defign againft the
" Englifh, they can fuddenly come down
" the Mohawk's river, the Delaware, the
" Sufquehanna, and Potomac, and that
" with the ftream. They have the fame
" advantage of invading the French, by
" the waters of the river St. Lawrence,
" Sorel, &c. If the French fhould pre-
" vail againft this country, they can, with
" their old men, wives and children, come
" down

" down the ſtreams to the Engliſh. If the
" Engliſh ſhould prevail in attacking their
" country, they have the ſame conveyance
" down to the French; and if both ſhould
" join againſt them, they can retire acroſs
" the lakes."

Their hunting lands are—*Firſt*, Couxſa-
chraga, a triangle, lying on the ſouth-eaſt
ſide of Canada, or St. Lawrence river,
bounded eaſtward by Saragtoga, and the
drowned lands; northward, by a line from
Regiôchne point (on lake Champlain, or, as
the Indians call it, Caniaderiguarûnte, the
lake that is the gate of the country) through
the Cloven rock, on the ſame lake, to Oſ-
wegatchie, or la Galette; ſouth-weſtward
by the dwelling lands of the Mohawks,
Oneidas, and Tuſcaroraos.

Secondly, Ohio, all that fine country (and
therefore called Ohio) lying on the ſouth
and eaſt ſides of lake Erie, ſouth-eaſt of their
dwelling lands.

Thirdly, Tieuckſouckrondtie; all that
tract of country lying between the lakes Erie
and Oilinois.

Fourthly, 'Scaniaderiada, or the country
beyond the lake; all that tract of country
lying

lying on the north of lake Erie, and north-
weft of lake Ontario, and between the lakes
Ontario and Hurons.

The right of the Five-nation confederacy
to their dwelling lands and the hunting
ground of Couxfachrága, and even down to
the bottom of lake Champlain, was never
difputed. The lands to the northward of
Regiôchne, and la Galette, have long fince
been ceded to the Canada Indians as an
hunting ground.

In the year 1684, the Five nations finding
themfelves hard preffed by the French and
their Indians, did, by a treaty at Albany,
put the lands and caftles of the Mohawks
and Oneidas *under the protection of the Englifh government*: and the Englifh accordingly undertook *the truft* to guarantee them
to thefe Indians. And as the external mark,
by which this act and deed fhould be anoun-
ced, the Indians defired that the duke of
York's arms might be affixed to their
caftles.

The right of the Five-nation confederacy
to the hunting lands of Ohio, Tieûck-
fouchrondite and 'Scaniaderiada, by the conqueft they had made in fubduing the Shaö-
anaes, Delawares, (as we call them) Twic-
twes

twes and Oïlinois, may be fairly proved as they ſtood poſſeſſed thereof, at the pace of Reſwick, in 1697.

In the year 1701, they put all their hunting lands under the protection of the Engliſh, as appears by the records, and by the recital and confirmation thereof in the following deed.

In the year 1726, the Seneccas, Cayougaes and Ononda-agaes acceded to the ſame terms of alliance, in which the Mohaws and Oneidas were already———So that the whole of the dwelling and hunting lands of the Five-nation confederacy were put under the protection of the Engliſh, and held by them IN TRUST, for and to the USE of theſe Indians and their poſterity.

Copy of Agreement with the Sachems of the Five Nations.

TO all people to whom this preſent inſtrument of writing ſhall come, Whereas the Sachems of the Five Nations did, on the nineteenth day of July, One thouſand ſeven hundred and one, in a conference held at Albany, between John Nanfan, Eſq; late lieutenant-governor of new-York, give and render up all their land where the beaver-
hunting

hunting is, which they won with the fword, then 80 years ago, to Coorakhoo *, our great King, praying that he might be their protector and defender there, for which they defired that their fecretary might then draw an inftrument for them, to fign and feal, that it might be carried to the King, as by the minutes thereof, now in the cuftody of the fecretary for Indian affairs at Albany, may fully, and at large appear.

WE, Kanakarighton and Shanintfaronwe, Sinneke Sachems; Ottfoghkoree Dekanifo-ree and Aenjeueratt, Cayouge Sachems; Raclyakadorodon and Sadageenaghtie, O-nondaga Sachems, of our own accord, free and voluntary will, do hereby ratify, con-firm, fubmit and grant; and by thefe pre-fents do (for ourfelves, our heirs and fuccef-fors, and in behalf of the whole Nations of Sinnekes, Cayouges and Onondages) ratify, confirm, fubmit and grant unto our moft Sovereign Lord George, by the Grace of God, King of Great Britain, France, and Ireland, Defender of the Faith, &c. his heirs and fucceffors for ever, all the faid land and beaver-hunting, *to be protected and defended by his faid majefty*, his heirs and fuc-

---

* It is by this name that they mean the King of England.

ceffors,

ceſſors, *to and for the* USE *of us, our heirs and ſucceſſors, and the ſaid three Nations;* and we do alſo of our own accord, free and voluntary will, give, render, ſubmit and grant, and by theſe preſents do, for ourſelves, our heirs and ſucceſſors, give, render, ſubmit, and grant unto our ſaid Sovereign Lord King George, his heirs and ſucceſſors for ever, all that land lying and being ſixty miles diſtance taken directly from the water, into the country, beginning from a Creek called Canahôge, on the lake Oſwego, all along the ſaid lake, and all along the narrow paſſage from the ſaid lake to the falls of Oniâgara, called Canaquaraghe, and all along the river of Oniâgara, and all along the lake Cataraqui to the creek called Sodons, belonging to the Sinnekes, and from Sodons to the hill called Tegechunckſerôde, belonging to the Cayouges, and from Tegechunckſerôde to the creek called Cayhunghâge, belonging to the Onondages; all the ſaid lands being of the breadth of ſixty Engliſh miles as aforeſaid, all the way from the aforeſaid lakes or rivers, directly into the country, and thereby including all the caſtles of the aforeſaid three Nations, with all the rivers, creeks and lakes, within the ſaid limits, *to be protected and defended by his ſaid majeſty, his heirs and ſucceſſors for ever, to and for our*

USE,

4

USE, *our heirs and fucceffors, and the faid three nations.——*

In teftimony whereof, we have hereunto fet our marks and affixed our feals, in the city of Albany, this fourteenth day of September, in the thirteenth year of his majefty's reign, *Annoque Domini* 1726.

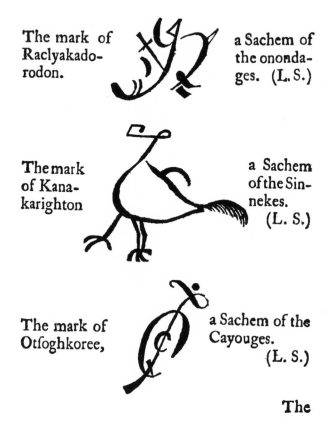

The mark of Raclyakado-rodon.

a Sachem of the ononda-ges. (L. S.)

The mark of Kana-karighton

a Sachem of the Sinnekes. (L. S.)

The mark of Otfoghkoree,

a Sachem of the Cayouges. (L. S.)

The

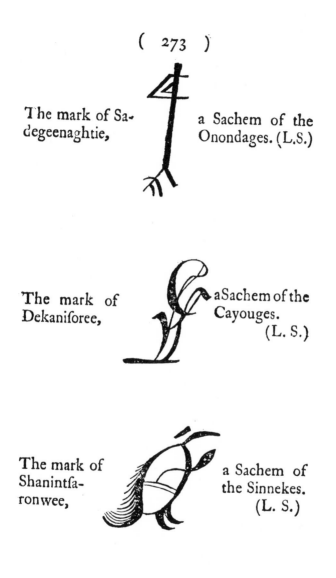

The mark of Sa-degeenaghtie,

a Sachem of the Onondages. (L.S.)

The mark of Dekaniforee,

a Sachem of the Cayouges. (L. S.)

The mark of Shanintfa-ronwee,

a Sachem of the Sinnekes. (L. S.)

T

The

The mark of Aenjeweratt, a Sachem of the Cayouges. (L. S.)

Signed, fealed, and delivered,
in the Prefence of us

Philip Livingfton,   Mynderft Schuyler,
Peter Vanbrugh,   Lawrence Claufen.

Secretary's Office, New-York. The preceding is a true copy of the Record in Lib.
Patents, Numb. 9. p. 253, 254. Examined
and compared therewith by
GEO. BANYER, Deputy Secretary.

Inftead of executing *this truft* faithfully and
with honour, by extending to the Indians
our civil protection againft the frauds of the
Englifh, and our military protection againft
the attempts of the French, we have ufed
this truft only as a pretence to *affume a dominion* over them—We have fuffered the Englifh fettlers to profit of every bad occafion
to defraud them of their lands—We have
never

never made any effectual regulations to prevent their being defrauded in their trade;
and until our own intereſt appeared to be
affected, we abandoned them to their own
chance and force, oppoſed to the ſtrength of
a powerful enemy. Nay, when at laſt we
thought neceſſary for the ſake, not of national faith and honour, for the ſake, not of
theſe our faithful allies, but for the ſake of
our own ſafety and intereſt to interfere, in
oppoſing the French encroachments, we took
it up as diſputing the empire of America
with the French; not as protecting and
guarding the Indian lands and intereſt to
their uſe, agreeable to the ſacred truſt by
which we were bound.—And thus theſe ſavages (as we to our own ſhame call them)
repeatedly told us, " That both we and the
" French ſought to amuſe them with *fine*
" *tales* of our ſeveral upright intentions;
" that both parties told them, that they
" made war for the protection of the Indian
" rights, but that *our actions* plainly diſco-
" vered that the war was only a conteſt
" who ſhould become maſters of the coun-
" try, which was the property neither of
" the one nor the other." Since we have
driven the French government from America, we have confirmed this charge of the
Indians againſt us, by aſſuming that dominion which in faith and juſtice we cannot

T 2   ſay

say we have gained over the Indians, which, in fact, we have not gained, and which, be it remembered, will cost more blood and treasure before we do gain it, than it is for the honour and interest of Great-Britain to expend in so bad and useless a cause. While these poor tribes of hunters remain, it will be our own fault if they do not remain in perfect harmony and good alliance with us. As hunters, their interest can never interfere with ours, as settlers; but, on the contrary, will become the source of the natural and most profitable trade to us as traders. They are continually wearing away, and as they diminish or retire, they cede their lands to us in peace; which we, thus in time as fast as we can really want them, may possess in right and justice, untainted with the impeachment of having been gained by murder and fraud. While therefore we do remain a great and just nation, as we pride ourselves Great-Britain is, we should abhor the black base thought of using the power which providence hath given us, to the ruin and destruction of these brave and free people; of these people who gave us our first settlement in this country, and have lived with us, except under some temporary interruptions, in a series of faithful alliance.

If

If thefe confiderations, taken up in the courfe of that general review of the Colonies, and of the adminiftration of their affairs, which I now publifh, were intended as an exprefs treatife on Indian affairs, I fhould think it right to examine all the complaints and feveral claims of juftice which the Five-nations have made, and have repea ed for many years, which I would found firft on extracts from the records of Indian affairs, and fecondly, on the hiftory of the landed patents, and thirdly, on the occafions taken to erect, without their leave, forts on the Indian lands, which meafure the Indians always confider as an act of dominion. In this general view I fhall only point out that fhameful patent of Ka-y-adarofferos above Albany : that pretence of claim by the corporation of Albany for the Mohawk-flats, the very refidence of the Mohawks, and f me others on the carrying place, at the head of the Mohawk river———all which ought to be taken into immediate confideration, that juftice may be done both to the Indian and European claimants; and that the matter may not remain perpetual caufe of umbrage, and perhaps the fource of war. Government ought alfo very ferioufly to revife the principles on which they are now endeavouring to take poffeffion of the Indian country by forts and

T 3 garifons;

garifons; built many within the Indian dwelling lands, and many within their hunting
lands, and on the paffes and communications of thefe. It is undoubtedly right to
maintain the command of that country; but
there is a way to do it with fafety and juftice.
The meafures we are taking by force will
be found to have neither the one nor the
other in them; nor do I fee how common
prudence can adopt the enormous charge to
which fuch meafures muft lead.

We have feen that Sir William Johnfon,
although he took Niagara *from the French*
by force of arms, never confidered this as a
conqueft of thefe lands *from Indians*; but
has, agreeably to his ufual prudence and his
perfect knowledge of Indian affairs, obtained
by formal treaty, a ceffion of thefe lands
from the Indians to the crown of Great-
Britain. The wifdom, as well as the fuccefs of this example, ought to lead our politicks to the fame conduct in every other
cafe, where we have built or obtained forts
within their lands, efpecially as many of
them were built under exprefs promife of
their being difmantled as foon as the war
fhould ceafe: and as the Indians were exprefsly and folemnly promifed to have a fatisfaction given to them for the ufe of thefe
lands.

The

The Shawänefe and Delawares are more immediately connected with the province of Penfylvania; and although, as fubdued, they are under obedience to the confederacy of the Five-nations; yet, under tutelage and protection of the confederacy, they poffefs their rights to their own country. Was this, as I have faid, a particular treatife on Indian affairs, I might here point out " *the caufes of the alienation of the Delawares and Sha-wänefe Indians from the Britiſh intereſt, by extraEts from the public treaties, and other authentic papers relating to the tranfaEtions between the government of Penfylvania and the faid Indians for near forty years paſt,*" as fet forth in a memoir which I have had by me for many years. I could alfo from a feries * of letters for ten years, from Monfieur de Vaudreüil, while governor of Louifiana, to his court, point out thefe neglects and errors, as alfo the manner in which the French profited of thofe our errors, by which we loft the Cherokees, and other fouthern tribes.

After what has been explained, it will be fufficient here to fay, that, 1ft, Doing juftice

---

* Thefe letters in manufcript are authentic; but I am not at liberty to fay how they came into my poffef-fion.

to

to our faith and honour, by treating the Indians according to the real fpirit of our alliances with them ; 2dly, That doing the Indians juftice in their lands, and 3dly, giving up that idle, ufelefs claim of dominion over them, are points abfolutely and indifpenfibly neceffary to be adopted into our politicks, unlefs we have ferioufly taken the refolution to force our way by war. Until thefe points are adopted, we never fhall have peace——And it deferves thorough and mature deliberation how we engage to fettle and poffefs America by war.

Thefe meafures of found policy once fixed upon, the next ftep is to eftablifh an Adminiftration for the conducting Indian affairs——This part of the plan which I propofed is in part adopted, by dividing the management of Indian affairs into two Intendencies—one for the northern, the other for the fouthern nations, but, as every thing which I could fay further on this head hath been fome years paft ftated in the memorial annexed to thefe papers, I will here refer the reader to that memorial on thefe points. The meafures recommended therein I have by an opportunity of comparing them with the events of eight ‡ years, found to be fuch as I do moft fincerely wifh may be carried into execution. And if a

‡ This refers to the year 1755.

private

private perfon might prefume to obtrude advice, which has not formerly been neglected,
when the affairs of the plantations were full
as happily adminiftered, as they have been
of late. I would now venture to recommend the confideration of thefe meafures to
thofe whofe duty it is to act upon thefe matters. When thefe matters fhall be fettled
as they ought to be, then it may be time to
take up the confideration of proper regulations for the Indian trade; and when that
time comes, if a plan, which I have accidentally feen, be carried into execution, I
would venture to fay, that every thing which
can or ought to be done in Indian affairs will
be effected.

If with the fame fpirit, guided by the
fame principles *, a revifion was made of
the laws of trade, fo far as they refpect the
Colonies, it would anfwer more wife ends
of government, and more the intereft of the
governed, both here as well as in the Colonies, than any endeavour, even though fuccefsful, to carry the prefent laws into execution.

The principles on which the act of navigation is founded are juft, and of found po-

* This hath been in part done by the late American revenue act.

licy ;

licy; but the application of them, by the modes prescribed, as the laws now stand, to the present state of the Colony trade, is neither founded in justice or prudence. Any spirit that would force this application, would injure the principles themselves, and prove injurious to that commercial interest, which those very acts of trade mean to secure to Great Britain: whereas, upon a due revision of those laws, it would appear that there are means of producing this same end consistent with the particular interest of the Colonies, and what would carry the general commercial interest of the mother country to the utmost extent that it is capable of.

The laws of trade respecting America were framed and enacted for the regulating *mere plantations,* tracts of foreign country, employed in raising certain specified and enumerated commodities, solely for the use of the trade and manufactures of the mother-country—the purchase of which, the mother-country appropriated to itself. These laws considered these plantations as a kind of farms, which the mother country had caused to be worked and cultured for its own use. But the spirit of commerce, operating on the nature and situation of these external dominions, beyond what the mother country or the Colonists themselves ever

thought

thought of, planned, or even hoped for, has *wrought up thefe plantations to become objects of trade*; has enlarged and combined the intercourfe of the barter and exchange of their various produce, into a very complex and extenfive commercial interest : The operation of this fpirit, has, in every fource of interest and power, raifed and eftablifhed the *Britifh government on a grand commercial bafis*, has by the fame power to the true purpofes of the fame interest, extended the Britifh dominions through every part of the Atlantic Ocean, to the actually forming A GRAND MARINE EMPIRE, if the adminiftration of our government, will do their part, by extending the Britifh government to wherefoever the Britifh dominions do extend. If, on the contrary, we are predetermined to carry into ftrict and literal execution, the navigation act, and other laws refpecting the plantation trade—without reviewing and confidering what the very different circumftances of the Colonies now are, from what they were when they were firft fettled, merely as plantations, and when thefe laws were firft made,—we muft determine to reduce our Colonies again to fuch mere plantations : We muft either narrow the bottom of our commercial interest, to the model of our plantation laws, or we muft enlarge the

fp rit

fpirit of our commercial laws, to that lati-
tude to which our commercial intereft does
actually extend. Thus ftands the fact. This
is the truth. There is no other alternative.
But if we would profit of them in thofe
great commercial benefits, to thofe great
political purpofes, which they are capable
to produce; which they lead to; which the
whole ftrain of our politics have, for many
years, taught us to value ourfelves upon;
and which have really been the fource of all
our wealth and power; we muft examine
thoroughly the ftate of this commercial intereft, we muft make a fincere, unpreju-
diced and candid review of thefe laws of
trade,—and by true and more enlarged principles, model them on the ideas of regulating the conduct and the intereft, of various and widely extended parts of a one
great commercial dominion.

I will firft defcribe the circuit of the
North American commerce, and then fuggeft fome fuch meafures as may tend to
produce a happy eftablifhment of our trading intereft, on true commercial principles.
As the matters contained in the following
reprefentation, are fairly ftated, according
to the truth and fact, and the confequences
thence deduced, are fuch as actual experience

ence fhows to be in exiftence, I am fure I cannot give a more clear, diftinct, or better ftate
of the American commerce than it contains.

† This reprefentation ftates, that it is the
fingular difadvantage of the Northern Britifh Colonies, that, while they ftand in need
of vaft quantities of the manufactures of
Great Britain, the country is productive of
very little which affords a direct remittance
thither in payment; and that from neceffity
therefore, the inhabitants have been driven
to feek a market for their produce, where it
could be vended, and, by a courfe of traffick,
to acquire either money or fuch merchandize as would anfwer the purpofe of a remittance, and enable them to fuftain their
credit with the mother country; that the
prodigious balance arifing in her favour is a
fact too well known to the merchants of
Great Britain trading to thofe parts to need
any elucidation; but, as the nature of the
petitioners commerce when free from re-
ftraints, *which they think of fatal effect, and
deftructive to it*, ought to be underftood,
they beg leave to obferve that their produce
then fent to our own and the foreign iflands,
was chiefly bartered for fugar, rum, melaffes, cotton, and indigo; that the fugar,
cotton, and indigo, ferved as remittance to

† New-York petition.

Great

Great Britain; but the * rum and melaffes conftituted effential branches of the petitioners commerce, and enabled them to barter with our own Colonies for fifh and rice; and by that means to purfue a valuable trade with *Spain, Portugal,* and *Italy,* where they chiefly obtained money or bills of exchange in return ; and likewife qualified them for adventures to Africa, where they had the advantage of putting off great quantities of Britifh manufactures, and of receiving in exchange gold, ivory, and flaves, which laft, difpofed of in the Weft India iflands,

---

* This rum and melaffes became, to the Carolinas and other fouthern Colonies, not only a matter of aid in their own confumption, but alfo an article in their Indian commerce ; became to the inhabitants of New England and New Scotland, an aid in their internal confumption, but alfo a confiderable aid to the confumption in their fifhery. The avowed and chief articles of commerce between North America and the parts of Europe to the fouthward of Cape Finiftre are, fifh and rice. Rice is the produce of Carolina, and the fifhery is the more peculiar bufinefs of New England and Nova Scotia. Each of thefe countries produces and manufactures, the one more rice, the other more fifh than they confume in their own fubfiftance and in their own foreign trade, and fo each exchanges that furplufage for the rum, or rather the melaffes which the New Yorkers fetch from the Weft Indies. By which the New Yorkers, like the Dutch in Father-land, chiefly carriers, are enabled to make out adventures to the Streights and to Africa.

com-

commanded money or bills : Rum was in-
difpenfable in their Indian trade ; and, with
Britifh manufactures, procured furs and fkins,
which ferved for confiderable returns to
Great Britain, and encreafed the revenue
thereof ; that the trade to the bay of Hon-
duras was alfo very material to their commerce, being managed with fmall cargoes of
provifions, rum, and Britifh manufactures,
which, while they were at liberty to fend
foreign logwood to the different ports in Europe, furnifhed them with another valuable
branch of remittance ; that, from this view,
it is evident that fugar, rum, melaffes, and
logwood, with cotton and indigo, are the
effentials of their return-cargoes, and the
chief fources from which, in a courfe of
trade, that they have extended their ufeful-
nefs to, and maintained their credit with
Great Britain.

That confidering the prodigious confumption of Weft India produce in Great Britain,
Ireland, and the continental Colonies, the
rapid increafe of thofe Colonies, their inhabitants already exceeding † two millions,
the vaft acceffion of fubjects by the late con-
quefts, befides the innumerable tribes of In-

† Including the Blacks.

dians

dians in the extensive countries annexed to
the British crown, the utter incapacity of
our own islands to supply so great a demand,
must be out of all question: on the other
hand, the lumber produced from clearing
this immense territory, * and provisions ex-
tracted from the fertile soil, which most of
the inhabitants are employed in cultivating,
must raise a supply for exportation, with
which the consumption of our own islands
can bear no sort of proportion; ‡ that it seems
therefore consistent with sound policy to indulge those Colonies in a free and unre-
strained exportation of all the lumber and
produce they raise and can spare, and an

* This includes bread, corn, biscuit, flour, beef,
pork, horses, and the smaller articles of live stock.
‡ If we, by artificial restraints, endeavour to cut off
from between the foreign West India islands, and our
North American Colonies, that intercourse and exchange of supplies which is now necessary to them, or
to clogg it in a manner that renders it detrimental or
impracticable to those islands,——may we not force
them into what should seem their natural course of
commerce, an intercourse with their own Colonies,
in the southern latitudes; whence they may be supplied with all those articles of lumber and live stock
and bread, corn, &c. which at present, by a lucky,
rather than a natural or necessary course of trade,
create almost a monopoly to the Northern American
Colonies of the West India supply.——

2

ample

ample importation of fugar, rum, and melaffes, to fupply the various branches of their
trade, to which they appear fo neceffary;
that, without the one, the clearing of new
lands, which is extremely laborious and ex-
penfive, will be difcouraged; and provifions,
for want of vent, become of little profit to
the farmer; without the other, the petitioners muft be plunged into a total incapacity of making good their payments for Britifh debts; their credit muft fink, and their
imports from Great Britain gradually dimi-
nifh, till they are *contracted to the narrow
compafs of remittances, barely in articles of
their own produce*; and that, how little foever their intereft of commerce could be promoted, the Colonies, thus checked, muft,
from inevitable neceffity, betake themfelves
to manufactures of their own, which will be
attended with confequences very detrimental
to thofe of Great Britain. The petitioners,
having thus reprefented the nature of their
commerce, proceed to point out the feveral
grievances, which it labours under, from
the regulations prefcribed by the laws of
trade; and which, if not remedied, they
conceive muft have a direct tendency to prevent the cultivation, and ruin the trade, of
the Colonies, and prove highly pernicious

U

to

to both the landed and trading interest of
Great Britain *

That the heavy embaraffments, which
attend the article of fugar, is a capital fubject of complaint ; and, befides the abfolute
neceffity of a great importation to fuftain
their trade, it is a well known truth, that it
often happens, at the foreign iflands with
which they have intercourfe, that a fufficient
return-cargo, independent of fugar, cannot
be procured, which alone muft render trade
precarious and difcouraging ; but the high
duty of five fhillings fterling a hundred is
proved, by experience, to be exceffive, and
has induced the fair trader to decline that
branch of bufinefs, while it prefents an irre-
fiftable incentive to fmuggling, to people
lefs fcrupulous ; that it anfwers not the purpofes of the government, or of the nation,
fince it cannot be duly collected, and, if it
could, would have a neceffary tendency to
contract remittances for Britifh debts, while,

* Whether the Britifh merchant will attend to this
or not—it is neverthelefs true. The views of merchants feldom, in courfe of trade, go beyond themfelves and the prefent profit,——but the ftatefman,
whether we look to him in adminiftration or in parliament, ought thoroughly to weigh the truth and confequence of this afferted fact, as it may affect the Britifh commerce in general.

at

at the fame time, it is moſt miſchievous to
the Colonies, by cutting off one of the grand
ſprings of their traffic; and, that the preſ-
ſure of this duty is not aggravated, the petitioners appeal to the officers of the cuſtoms
of their port, that the petitioners therefore
moſt humbly intreat, that a moderate duty
be laid on foreign ſugars, which, they are
aſſured, would not only greatly conduce to
the proſperity of thoſe Colonies, and their
utility to the mother country, but encreaſe
the royal revenue far beyond what can be
expected under the preſent reſtraints.

† That the compelling merchants to land
and ſtore foreign ſugars in Great Britain, before they can be exported to other parts of
Europe, is another moſt expenſive and dila-
tory reſtriction, without being of any material advantage to the revenue of Great Britain; for it effectually puts it out of the
petitioners power, to meet foreigners at
market upon an equal footing, is a great and
heavy burden in times of peace and ſecurity,
but in war will expoſe the trader to ſuch

† That the New Yorkers, only carriers, ſhould
regard this regulation with uneaſineſs, is natural, but
ſurely it is a wiſe and prudent regulation, for the benefit of the Britiſh Iſles, to create and give a preference to the Britiſh produce and manufacture of the
ſubjects of thoſe Iſlands.

peril

peril and hazard, as muſt wholly extinguiſh this uſeful branch of remittance ; that Britiſh plantation ſugar exported from North America, ſhould be declared French on being landed in England, the petitioners conceive may juſtly be claſſed among the number of hardſhips, inflicted by thoſe regulations, as in effect it deprives them of making a remittance in that article, by expoſing them to the payment of the foreign duty in Great Britain, which appears the more ſevere, as their fellow ſubjects of the iſlands are left at liberty to export thoſe ſugars for what they really are, and a diſtinction is thus created in their favour, which the petitioners cannot but regard with uneaſineſs.

That foreign rum, French excepted, is the next article which the petitioners moſt humbly propoſe for conſideration, as the importation thereof, on a moderate duty, would add conſiderably to the revenue, prevent ſmuggling, promote the petitioners navigation, encreaſe the vent of their own produce with Britiſh manufactures, and enable them to bring back the full value of their cargoes, more eſpecially from the Daniſh iſlands of St. Thomas and St. Croix, from whence they can now only receive half the value in ſugar and cotton, conſequently rum alone can be expected for the other half, thoſe

thofe iflands affording nothing elfe for returns, and having no fpecie but of a bafe
kind.

That the exportation of foreign logwood
to foreign markets, has already been diftinguifhed as one of the principal means, by
which thofe Colonies have been enabled to
fuftain the weight of their debts for Britifh
manufactures, and it is with the greateft
concern, the petitioners obferve it to be
ranked by the late act among the enumerated articles; and confequently made fubject
to the delay, the hazard, and expence, of
being landed in Great Britain; the low price
of logwood, its bulk, and the duty with
which it is now burthened, muft totally deftroy that valuable branch of the petitioners
commerce, and throw it into the hands of
foreigners, unfettered with thofe heavy embarraffments.

That their lumber and pot-afh even when
fhipped for Ireland, where they are fo neceffary, the latter particularly for the progrefs
of their linen manufacture, and provifions
themfelves, though intended to relieve that
kingdom from a famine, are fubject to
the fame diftreffing impediments; nor is
flax-feed, on the timely importation of which
the very exiftence of the linen manufacture

U 3   of

of Ireland immediately depends, exempted, although it is a fact capable of the moſt ſatisfactory proof, that, without the delay now created, it has been with difficulty tranſported from that Colony, to be there in proper ſeaſon for ſowing; that what renders ſo injurious an obſtruction the more affecting is the reflection, that, while it deprives the petitioners of the benefits ariſing from flax-ſeed, lumber, and pot-aſh, theſe articles may all be imported into Ireland directly from the Baltic, where they are purchaſed from foreigners, under the national diſadvantage of being paid for with money inſtead of manufactures; and the petitioners therefore humbly beg leave to expreſs their hopes, that an evil in ſo high a degree pernicious to them, to the ſtaple of Ireland, and to the trade and manufactures of Great Britain, and which in times of war muſt fall on all with a redoubled weight, will not fail of obtaining the attention of the houſe, and an immediate and effectual redreſs.

That they beg leave further to repreſent, that the wines from the iſlands, in exchange for wheat, flour, fiſh, and lumber, would confiderably augment the important article of remittance, was the American duty withdrawn, on exportation to Great Britain: and that it is therefore humbly ſubmitted,

whether

whether fuch an expedient, calculated at
once to attach them to hufbandry by ex-
panding the confumption of American produce, to encourage Britifh manufactures by
enabling the petitioners to make good their
payments, and to encreafe the royal revenue
by an additional import of wines into Great
Britain, will not be confiftent with the united
interefts both of the mother country and her
Colonies.

That the petitioners conceive the North
American fifhery to be an object of the
higheft national importance; that nothing
is fo effential for the fupport of navigation,
fince by employing annually fo great a
number of fhipping, it conftitutes a refpect-
able nurfery for feamen, and is fo clearly
advantageous for remittances, in payment
for Britifh manufactures; that the petitioners
therefore humbly prefume, that it will be
cherifhed by the houfe with every poffible
mark of indulgence, and every impediment
be removed, which tends to check its progrefs.

That the enlarging the jurifdiction of the
admiralty, is another part of the ftatute of
the fourth of his prefent majefty, very grie-
vous to the trade and navigation of the Colonies, and oppreffive to the fubject, the property

perty of the trader being open to the invaſion of every informer, and the means of juſtice ſo remote as to be ſcarcely attainable.

That the petitioners beg leave to expreſs the warmeſt ſentiments of gratitude, for the advantages intended by parliament, to America in general, in the opening free ports at the iſlands of Jamaica and Dominica; yet, at the ſame time, they cannot but lament, that it is their unhappineſs to be in no condition to reap the benefits which, as it was imagined, would flow from ſo wiſe a policy; that the collecting great quantities of the produce of Martinico, Guadaloupe, &c. at the iſland of Dominica, will be the natural conſequence of opening that port, and would prove of real importance to thoſe Colonies, were they at liberty to bring them back, in return for their lumber and proviſions; but, as they are now prohibited from taking any thing, except melaſſes, and, it is juſtly apprehended, there cannot be a ſufficient quantity of that commodity to ſupport any conſiderable trade, the petitioners think it evident, that no ſubſtantial advantage can be derived to them under ſuch a reſtraint; that they are, at the ſame time, at a loſs to diſcern the principle on which the prohibition is founded; for, ſince ſugar may be imported direct from the foreign iſlands, it

ſeems

feems much more reafonable, to fuffer it
from a free port belonging to Great Britain;
that the petitioners therefore humbly hope,
that it will be thought equitable to adapt
this trade to their circumftances, by granting them liberty to import into the Colonies
all Weft India productions, in exchange for
their commodities. That upon the whole,
although, at the laft feffion, the neceffity of
relieving the trade of thofe Colonies feems
to have been univerfally admitted, and the
tender regard of parliament for their happinefs highly diftinguifhed, neverthelefs, experience has evinced, that the commercial
regulations, then enacted, inftead of remedying, have encreafed the heavy burthen
under which it already laboured.

* " In this furvey one thing muft be
" taken notice of as peculiar to this country,
" which is, that as in the nature of its
" government, fo in the very improvement
" of its trade and riches, it ought to be
" confidered not only in its own proper
" intereft, but likewife in its relation to

* Letter of Sir William Temple to Lord Effex, in
July 22, 1673, concerning the ftate of Ireland,
wherein the reader will fee the furvey taken of the
trade of that country, at that time fo appofite to the
ftate of the trade of the Colonies at this feafon, it will
be impoffible not to apply it.

" Eng-

" England, to which it is fubordinate, and
" upon whofe weal in the main, that of this
" kingdom depends, and therefore a regard
" muſt be had to thofe points wherein the
" trade of Ireland comes to interfere with
" any main branches of the trade of Eng-
" land, in which cafe the encouragement
" of fuch trade ought to be either declined
" or moderated, and fo give way to the
" intereſt of trade in England. Upon the
" health and vigour whereof the ſtrength,
" riches and glory of his majefty's crown
" feem chiefly to depend. But on the
" other fide, *fome fuch branches of trade*
" *ought not wholly to be fuppreffed*, but ra-
" ther fo far admitted as may ferve the
" general confumption of the kingdom, *left*
" *by too great an importation of commodities,*
" *though out of England itself, the money of*
" *this kingdom happen to be drawn away in*
" *fuch a degree, as not to leave a ftock fuffi-*
" *cient for turning the trade at home.*"

If many of thefe regulations above propofed and fubmitted to confideration, cannot
be admitted, while the Colonies are, by the
laws of trade, confidered as *mere plantations:*
And if the improved commerce of the Colonies cannot any longer fubfift as a branch of
the commercial intereſt of Great Britain, if
they are not admitted, Great Britain is reduced

duced to the dangerous alternative of either giving up the fubordination of the trade of its plantations, or of giving up its commerce, as it hath been extended and improved by its Colonies becoming commercial ftates; from which, otherwife inevitable danger, nothing but the general plan of union, as repeatedly above recommended, can preferve it.

The general principle of the laws of trade regulating the Colony trade, is, that the Colonies fhall not, on one hand, be fupplied with any thing but from a Britifh market, nor export their produce any where but to a Britifh market. In the application of this principle, the prefent laws direct, except in fome fpecial particulars, that the Colonies fhall import all their fupplies *from Britain,* and carry all their produce *to Britain.*

If now, inftead of confining this market for the Colonies to Britain only, which is a partial and defective application of the general principle whereon the act of navigation is founded; this Colony trade was made, amidft other courfes of trade, an occafion of eftablifhing *Britifh markets even in other countries,* the true ufe would be derived to the general intereft from thefe advantageous circumftances, while in particular the Colonies and the mother country would be mutually

tually accommodated. In the firft cafe, the general intereft, perverted to partial purpofes, becomes fo far forth obftructed; in the fecond, it would be carried by the genuine fpirit of it to its utmoft extent.—If, under certain reftrictions, fecuring alfo thofe duties which the produce of the Colonies, carried to market, ought to pay to the mother country, the Colonies were permitted to export their produce (fuch as are the bafis or materials of any Britifh manufacture excepted) directly to foreign countries, if fo be they fold it to any *Britifh houfe* eftablifhed in fuch place, and were alfo permitted, if they bought their fupplies from a *Britifh houfe* eftablifhed in thofe parts, to fupply themfelves with the natural fruits and produce of that country (all manufactures that any way interfere with the Britifh manufactures excepted) paying there to fome Britifh officer, or upon their arrival in the Colonies, the fame duties as they would have paid by purchafing the fame commodities in England, every end propofed by the principal of the act of navigation would be anfwered; the exports of the Colonies would be encouraged; and *the Britifh market* greatly extended.

The Colonies would not only trade to, and be fupplied by, a *Britifh market*, but would

would become an occafion of eftablifhing
the Britifh market in foreign countries. The
fame reafons of commerce, which, in a narrower view, became the grounds for eftablifhing factories at Peterfburgh, Riga, Hamborough, Lifbon, Cadiz, &c. would on a
more general and extenfive bafis become the
foundation for eftablifhing and building up
thefe Britifh markets in every region to which
our trade extended itfelf; for while it neceffarily enlarged the fpecial intereft of the Colonies, it would enlarge it only at Britifh
markets, and to the final profit of the Britifh general commerce. The profits of fuch
market finally centering in Great Britain.
If this maxim be not true, that the profits
of the factories fettled in foreign ports finally
center in Great Britain, the meafure of eftablifhing fuch is falfe in policy; if the maxim
be true, the permitting our Colony exports
to go directly to the ports where fuch factories are eftablifhed, is not contrary to the
principle on which the act of navigation
arofe, but becomes coincident with, and
aiding to it, in extending the Britifh navigation and Britifh markets, and fecuring the
final profits thereof to Britain only.

If this method of reafoning be found not
contrary to the principle of the act of navigation; if this meafure at the fame time

that

that it encourages the trade of our Colonies, is found to do it in a way fubfervient to the general commerce of Great Britain, extending the Britifh markets, and fecuring the final balance of profit to Britain only; if this fpirit of adminiftration, fo far as government has a right to direct the courfe of trade, be adopted in this part of it, the great points which it has to fecure, are firft, that the Colony exports to, and the fupplies purchafed by them from thofe foreign ports, *be fold and bought at a Britifh market only.*—— The government has a right to extend its laws to thefe Colony traders, and to the factories eftablifhed in foreign ports.——It can therefore, partly by fuch laws as it finds proper to enact, for the regulation of this factory trade, and partly by obliging thefe Colony traders to give bond before their departure from the Colonies, fecure and confine all thefe tranfactions of that commerce, which is permitted at any fuch port, to a Britifh market only, the laws that eftablifhed thefe being a favour extended to the Colonies, and promoting the intereft of thefe factories, would, as all laws of trade fhould do, execute themfelves; and by giving the requifite powers to a conful or naval officer refident there, would be eafily adminiftered by fuch officer.

The

The next point to be guarded, would be the fecuring thofe duties which this trade ought to pay to the government of Great-Britain : If the fame duties were paid, or fecurity for them taken in thefe foreign ports, as would be or fhould be paid by the Colony trade, if the traders were ftill obliged to come to Britain, every end would be anfwered to the government revenue, and thefe charges might be fufficiently fecured, by obliging all ˑhefe traders to fail under bond. The arrangements to be taken in fuch cafe ought to be that of adding to the office of conful, fuch powers as in the Colonies, before the eftablifhment of fpecial revenue officers there, were given to the naval officer, or to eftablifh a naval officer. The conful or naval officer, in this branch of his adminiftration, fhould be fubordinate to the commiffioners of the cuftoms and the lords of the treafury. If the duties were collected by him, in the ports of his diftrict, he fhould account and give fecurity for the fame ; if bonds only, as fecurity for the payment at fuch Britifh or plantation ports, were given, he fhould keep the regifter of the ˑfame, and correfpond with the commiffioners of the cuftoms, and fuch officers as they direct, as to the fulfilling, cancelling, or profecuting to effect faid bonds. Thefe general arrangements, taken, together with fuch further

7   fpecial

fpecial regulations, as the experience of the commiffioners of the cuftoms fhould fuggeft, the revenue of the Colony and factory trade, under this mode of adminiftration, would be well fecured, chearfully paid, and eafily collected.

Under the adminiftration of fuch meafures, there does not appear any reafon why all the produce of the Britifh Colonies, which are not the bafis of, or do not interfere with the Britifh manufactures, might not be carried directly to a Britifh market at a foreign port, —and why the carrying of rice to foreign ports might not be extended, under thefe laws, to all fuch foreign ports whereat a Britifh factory is eftablifhed.—Nor under this mode of commerce can any fufficient reafon upon earth fubfift, why the Colony traders fhould not be permitted to load at thefe ports, the fruits, wine, oil, pickles, the produce of that country, and alfo fuch raw unmanu-factured produce, as would not interfere with the manufacture of Great Britain, in-ftead of being obliged to come to Britain to buy or reload here, after the expence of an unneceffary voyage, thofe very commodities which they might have bought in a *Britifh market*, at the port which they left. Why not any of thefe as well as falt, as well as wines from the Madeiras and weftern ifles?

In

In the fame manner, by the fame law, why may not our Colony traders be permitted to carry fugar, ginger, tobacco, rice, &c. to fuch ports in the rivers Wefer and Elbe, in the Sound and in Ruffia, whereat a Britifh factory is, or may be eftablifhed? It can never be right policy to fuffer labour in vain in a community: it is juft fo much loft to the community: and yet this coming round by England is labour in vain: If the fubordinacy of the Colony-trade, and the duties arifing thereon, can be by any other means fecured, it is fo much labour loft. The two points of a *Britifh market*, and the revenue of the duties being fecured, why may not thefe traders be permitted to load at thefe ports directly for the Colonies, hemp, yarn, and fuch coarfe linens, as do no way interfere with the Britifh manufactories? Thefe meafures taken, which would prove to be the true means of encouraging the Colonytrade, the beft method to put a ftop to the contraband trade carried on in this branch of bufinefs, and the true grounds whereon to eftablifh the general commercial interefts of Great Britain, government could not be too ftrict in enforcing the execution of the laws of trade, nor too fevere in punifhing the breach of them.——Wherever they found thefe traders endeavouring to carry from thefe ports to the Colonies raw filk, filks, velvets,

X   foreign

foreign cloths, laces, iron, fteel, arms, ammunition, fails or rigging, or any manufactures whatever, that interfere with the manufacture of Great Britain: whenever they found thefe traders endeavouring to carry from the Colonies to thofe ports, any dying-wood whatever, indigo, cotton, filk, bees or myrtle-wax, flax-feed, naval ftores, furs, fkins or peltry, hides, provifion, grain, flour, bread or bifcuit; whale-oil, blubber, bone, or any other fifh-oil, or tallow, or candles, with an exception perhaps to myrtle and fpermaceti candles, government could not be too ftrict and watchful to reftrain them. Under proper regulations, the rum of the northern Colonies fhould be carried to Africa, and the fale of it to the French on the banks of Newfoundland encouraged, if fuch vent could be procured, as we fhould thereby reap at leaft fome fhare even of the profit of the French fifhery.

In the above revifion of, and the propofed regulations for the Colony trade, as connected with that of Europe, it will be feen that all mention of Eaft India goods is purpofely omitted. I think a fpecial meafure might be contrived of fupplying the Colonies with Eaft-India goods, in a way that would effectually put to a ftop to that contraband trade, by which it is complained they are at pre-

fent

fent fupplied, in a way by which one of the greateſt marts in the world, with every attendant advantage to the Britiſh general commerce, and the ſpecial intereſt of the Eaſt-India trade, might be eſtabliſhed.

If meaſures were at this juncture taken, between the government and the Eaſt-India company, ſo that an Eaſt-India ſhip might annually ſtop at ſome iſland in the Weſt-Indies, the traders, not only of the Weſt-Indies, but of North America, would ſupply themſelves with every advantage at ſuch mart, not only for their own proper conſumption, but alſo for a trade of the greateſt extent; and this mart, in return, would be to the Eaſt-India company, the collector of all the ſurplus ſilver of America, and perhaps even of ſome of the gold and ivory of Africa alſo. The extenſive advantages of this meaſure cannot but be ſeen; nor would this any way interfere with that ſupply with which the Eaſt-India trade, by way of the Manilla's, furniſhes the Spaniſh Weſt-Indies, ſo far as our Eaſt-India company may be ſuppoſed to be concerned, but would, in other reſpects, open a better channel of trade between the Eaſt and Weſt-Indies, which our company muſt command. The difficulties in the execution lie in ſecuring to government the revenue that ſhould ariſe

X 2 from

from the duties duly paid by this trade, and
in fecuring the company againft the perverfion of this trade to the profit of their officers
and fervants.——

In the fame manner, fome revifion of the
ftate of the trade of the Colonies of the feveral maritime powers amongft each other
will be neceffary.——The laws and ordonnances of thefe do in general prohibit all
trade of foreign Colonies with their own;——
and yet, without fome fuch trade as fupplies
the Spanifh provinces with Britifh goods and
provifions, as fupplies the Britifh Colonies
with Spanifh filver, as fupplies the French
iflands with Britifh lumber, fifh, provifions,
horfes, and live ftock, as fupplies the Britifh Colonies with French mellaffes, the
trade and culture of thefe Colonies would be
greatly obftructed and impaired; and yet
notwithftanding this fact, our laws of trade,
by an impracticable duty, extend to the prohibiting the importation of French mellaffes
into our Colonies.—If the government, under this law, could prevent effectually this
importation, not only into the northern Colonies, *but into the Britifh ifles alfo*, the re-
ward of that pains would be the deftruction
of a beneficial branch of trade, perhaps of
driving the Britifh American diftillery into
the

the French, Dutch, or Danifh ifles, or of
forcing the French, contrary to their own
falfe policy, into a profitable manufacture of
that produce which they now fell as refufe
materials. I need not point out here the
very effential change that this would make
in the Colony trade.——On the contrary, it
is the duty of government to permit, nay
even to encourage, under proper regulations,
thefe branches of trade; in the firft place,
in order to extract out of the foreign Colonies, to the benefit of the Britifh commerce,
as much as poffible the profits of thefe Colonies, and which is more material, in order
to create a neceffary dependence in the trade
and culture of thofe Colonies for their fupplies on the Britifh commerce.——When it is
remembered that the law, which lays a duty
equal to a prohibition, on the importation
of French mellaffes in the Britifh Colonies,
was obtained at the folicitation of the Britifh ifles, it will be feen, that the obtaining
this law is not fo much meant to prohibit
totally the introduction of French mellaffes
into the Britifh trade, as to determine a
ftruggle between the Weft-India and North
American traders, who fhould have the profits of it. And thus, from the predominant
intereft of thefe partial views, has government been led to embarrafs the general
courfes of its trade.——But as the Weft

X 3 India

India traders fee that this law has not, never had, and never will have the effect propofed, they will be better reconciled to its ceafing; and as government muft now, after the experiment, fee the falfe policy of it, * there is no doubt but that it will ceafe, fo far as to reduce the duty to a moderate and practicable charge, fuch as will be paid, and fuch as will raife to the crown a very confiderable revenue thus paid.

I fpeak not this by guefs; but, from a comparifon of the quantity of fugars and mellaffes brought to account in the cuftomhoufe books of the *King's revenue*, with the quantity of the fame article, in the fame ports, brought to account in the impoft-books of the *Colony revenue*, for fix years together, could, with fome precifion, mark the extent of it. I own I did always apprehend that two-pence *per* gallon on foreign mellaffes imported into any Britifh plantation, and fo in proportion of fugars, was the beft rate at which to fix this duty; that being thus *moderate*, it might be eafier and with lefs alarm and oppofition collected, and might therefore the fooner introduce the practice of fair trade, and the fooner become

* This meafure hath, fince the writing of the above, taken place by 6 Geo. 3. c. 52.

an

an *effective revenue*: But when I fee a
groundlefs clamour raifed, which reprefents
the rate fixed by the late revenue-act as deftructive of the American diftillery, as ruinous to the American fifhery, as a prohibition
of the returns made from the foreign iflands
for the North American fifh; I muft own
that I have never feen any fact ftated, or
calculation fairly made on which fuch affer-
tions found themfelves.

The French ifles, fince the furrender of
Canada and Louifiana, muft depend entirely
for their fupplies of lumber, ftaves, heads,
provifions, live ftock, horfes, &c. on the
Britifh Colonies, immediately exported from
thence to thofe ifles, unlefs by fome means
fupplied from markets created at New Orleans and the ifland of St. Peter, as from
another Ifle of Man; it will therefore be the
duty of government to keep a watchful eye
to the formation and extent of thefe markets;—fo at leaft, if they be permitted, as
to have the command of them, and fo as
to prevent their being, to the French traders,
the means of fupplying the Spanifh markets
alfo, as well as their own.

Since the writing of what the paragraph
above contains, very proper regulations have
been by the late American revenue-act provided;

vided; and if proportionate care be taken in the execution of it, this danger is for the prefent guarded againft.

Some revifion alfo will be neceffary in the laws about naval ftores, efpecially that refpecting the mafts. The prefent law, under an idea of preferving the White Pine or maft trees, directs, That no White Pines fhall be cut or felled within the limits of any townfhip, if not actually private property.— This part of the law arifes from a miftaken apprehenfion of a townfhip, there being no lands within fuch but what are private property.—2*dly*, That no pines out of a townfhip, of the dimenfions of 24 inches and upwards, diameter, at the heighth of 20 inches from the ground, fhall be felled.— This part of the law is *felo de fe*.—Thofe who find their profits in cutting down thefe trees for logs or making fhingles, &c. or who know the embarraffments which would arife to their property, if they fhould ever apply for a grant of thefe lands, by letting fuch Pine-trees, the property of the crown, grow there, never (if they have not other means to evade this law) will permit thefe Pines to come to *this dimenfion* which makes them royal property. The falfe policy of this law, and the defects in the eftablifhment of an office of furveyor-general of his

Majefty's

Majefty's woods, will foon, if not obviated,
be felt in the fcarcity and price of mafts,
which will be the effect of it. The neceffity of their going a great diftance from the
rivers for the mafts has already taken effect,
and the cafe of there being none within any
practicable diftance will foon follow. The
navy-office finding that their maft-fhips do
come regularly hitherto to England, cannot
entertain any fear of fuch want, and it will
be the intereft of others to fupprefs and con-
tradict this fact; yet it is a fact, and will be
foon known in its effects. On the contrary,
if it is confidered how difproportionate a
value the price of the Pine-tree growing
bears to the price of the maft when brought
in the middle of winter, over the fnow, with
70 or 80 yoke of oxen to the water-fide;
if, inftead of aiming to make thefe trees,
thus growing, *royal exclufive property*, the
crown was not only to permit a free mafting
in lands not granted, and to make the maft-
trees of all dimenfions, *private property* on
lands actually granted, but alfo (as it is done
in other cafes of naval ftores) to give a
bounty befides the price, to the perfon who
fhould bring down any fuch mafts to the
water-fide, it would have an immediate
effect in fupplying the crown with mafts
at a cheaper rate, and in the prefervation
of

of thefe trees, thus become a branch of trade.

I would wifh here alfo to recommend the giving fome advantages and encouragement to the importation of American timber into Great Britain.

I have not gone into the thorough examination of thefe fubjects above-mentioned, nor have I pointed out, in all their confequences, the effects that this or that ftate of them would have. I have only pointed them out as worthy the attention of government; and, I am fure, whenever government takes them under confideration, they will be better underftood than any explanation of mine can make them.

Were fome fuch arrangements taken for a revifion and further eftabliihment of the laws of trade, upon the principle of extending the Britifh general commerce, by encouraging the trade of the Colonies, in fubordination to, and in coincidence therewith, the trade of the Colonies would be adminiftered by that true fpirit from whence it rofe, and by which it acts; and the true application of the benefits which arife to a mother country from its Colonies would be made. Under this fpirit of adminiftration, the government,

as

as I faid above, could not be too watchful
to carry its laws of trade into effectual execution.—But under the prefent ftate of thofe
laws, and that trade, there is great danger
that any feverity of execution, which fhould
prove effectual in the cafes of the importation into the Colonies of foreign European
and Eaft-India goods, might force the Americans to trade for their imports, upon terms,
on which the trade could not fupport itfelf,
and therefore become in the event a means
to bring on the neceffity of thefe Americans
manufacturing for themfelves. Nothing does
at prefent, with that active and acute people,
prevent their going into manufactures, except the proportionate dearnefs of labour,
as referred to the terms on which they can
import; but encreafe the price of their imports to a certain degree, let the extent of
their fettlements, either by policy from home
or invafion of Indians abroad, be confined,
and let their foreign trade and navigation be,
in fome meafure fuppreffed;————their paper-currency limited within too narrow
bounds, and the exclufion of that trade
which hath ufually fupplied them with fil-
ver-money too feverely infifted upon;————
this proportion of the price of labour will
much fooner ceafe to be an object of objection to manufacturing there, than is com-
monly apprehended. The winters in that
climate

climate are long and fevere; during which
feafon no labour can be done without doors.
That application therefore of their fervants
·labour, to manufactures for home confumption, which under any other circumftances
would be too dear for the product created
by it, becomes, under thefe circumftances,
all clear gains. And if the Colonifts cannot on one hand purchafe foreign manufactures at any reafonable price, or have not
money to purchafe with, and there are, on
the other, many hands idle which ufed to
be employed in navigation, and all thefe,
as well as the hufbandmen, want employment; thefe circumftances will foon overbalance the difference of the rate of labour
in Europe and in America. And if the Colonies, under any future ftate of adminiftration, which they fee unequal to the management of their affairs, *once come to feel
their own ftrength in this way*, their inde-
pendence on government, at leaft on the adminiftration of government, will not be an
event fo remote as our leaders may think,
which yet nothing but fuch falfe policy can
bring on. For, on the contrary, put their
governments and laws on a true and conftitutional bafis, regulate their money, their
revenue, and their trade, and do not check
their fettlements, they muft ever depend on
the

the trade of the mother country for their supplies, they will never eftablifh manufactures,
their hands being elfewhere employed, and
the merchants being always able to import
fuch on * terms that muft ruin the manufac-
turer. Unable to fubfift without, or to unite
againft the mother country, they muft always remain fubordinate to it, in all the
tranfactions of their commerce, in all the
operation of their laws, in every act of their
government:——The feveral Colonies, no
longer confidered as demefnes of the crown,
mere appendages to the realm, will thus become united therein, members and parts of

* This is a fact too well known and underftood to
need any particular proof—but if need were, the writer
of thefe papers could demonftrate this from the prices of
wool, hemp, and flax, and the labour of carding, dreff-
ing, fpinning, weaving, &c. in North America, compared with the prices of the fame articles of produce
and labour in Britain. It is therefore an idle vaunt in
the Americans, when they talk of fetting up manufactures *for trade* ; but it would be equally injudicious in
government here to force any meafure that may render
the manufacturing for *home confumption* an object of
prudence, or even of pique in the Americans. And
yet after all, fhould any thing of this fort extend itfelf
to a degree that interfered with the exports of Great
Britain to the Colonies——the fame duties of an excife
which lie upon the manufactures of Great Britain, levied upon thofe of America, would foon reftore the
balance. This confideration, one might imagine,
would induce thofe who are prudent in America, to
advife the reft to moderation in their oppofition.

the

the realm, as essential parts of a one organized whole, *the commercial dominion of Great Britain.* THE TAKING LEADING MEASURES TO THE FORMING OF WHICH, OUGHT, AT THIS JUNCTURE, TO BE THE GREAT OBJECT OF GOVERNMENT.

The END.

APPENDIX.

SECTION I.

ALTHOUGH the following papers, at the time in which they were written, had reference to the ſtate of the ſervice as oppoſed to the French meaſures and power in America: Although they are parts of another work intended to be publiſhed at ſome future time, yet they are here annexed to *the Adminiſtration of the Colonies*, as they treat of matters very worthy preſent conſideration; and as in general they contain ideas of police, which reſpect the poſſeſſion, preſervation, and improvement of thoſe acquiſitions which our conqueſts have put into our hands,—and the forming them into ſome ſyſtem of Empire that ſhall be the Empire of Great Britain.

The firſt paper, which had for its object the forming of the Britiſh poſſeſſions, together with thoſe of our allies the Indians, into a ſyſtem of barrier againſt the French, was written at a time when the ſubject was entirely new, ſcarce ever brought forward to conſideration here in England, and when authentic accounts of the true ſtate of the country as poſſeſſed by the Engliſh and French, were with great difficulty, if at all, to
be

be obtained; and I may venture to fay, utterly unknown to our military.

The latter of thefe papers, was written after it became neceffary to change the object of the war; and the only thing which I wifh to fay of the ideas that it contained, is, that they were literally juftified by the events.

A MEMORIAL:

STATING the NATURE of the SERVICE in NORTH AMERICA, and propofing a GENERAL PLAN of OPERATIONS, as founded thereon.

Drawn up by Order of, and prefented to, his Royal Highnefs the Duke of Cumberland, 1756. By T. POWNALL.

HIS Majefty has now united the fervice in North America into one power of action, and under one direction, by appointing a commander in chief over all North America, with powers to direct, and with force to carry on this fervice as a one whole. The next and neceffary point therefore is, that there fhould be fome *one general plan of operations* fixed, which may be carried on, not only by the general forces employed in the general and military part of this plan, but by every particular province and colony, within its own private councils, and own

private

private operations, coincident with the whole. When ſuch plan is fixed, every ſum of money that is raiſed for this ſervice, will be applied to what ſhall be of real ſervice and permanent uſe ; and every the moſt minute operation that is undertaken, will become as part of ſuch plan, Ἔργον εἰς ἀεὶ ;———and every (the moſt otherwiſe inſignificant) meaſure would become of more importance, and more ſervice, than twenty the moſt expenſive and buſtling operations, that ariſe from momentary and partial ſtarts of whim, vanity, or intereſt : There could not even a logg houſe be built, nor ſcarce a piquet ſtuck down in any part of the country, but what would be a neceſſary meaſure, and whoſe uſe (however trifling the thing in itſelf)would extend to the grand ſervice of the whole : There would not be a pound, ſcarce a penny raiſed, but would have its ſhare in this grand ſervice. On the contrary, while private perſons, or particular independent bodies of people, have conſulted only the momentary partial ſtarts of whim, vanity, party, or intereſt, under the influence of ſuch motives, without any general ſcheme to the defence of the country, the *taking poſſeſſion* of it, or the command of it, without any reference to any general idea, forts have been built up and down the country, that could never have been of uſe, have never been uſed, have never been ſupported, have been left to go to ruin, have been abandoned to the enemy ; or, if they have been kept up at all, have been a private ſtanding job to all concerned in them : While thus large ſums of money have been ſquandered away to no uſe, or bad ones ; while thus fruitleſs detached meaſures, that have

Y   been

been of no ufe, but a perverfion of, and incumbrance to the general fervice, and interfering amongft each other, have been purfued by vague, random fits and ftarts, the public fervice has not only been ruined, but the people have loft all opinion and confidence in military operations, have been difcouraged and alienated from engaging in any active meafures, and always fufpicious, that whatever fums they give to fuch, are either thrown away, or put into the private pocket of fome job. On the contrary, were there fome one general plan of operations formed, upon the practicability and really intended execution of which they might confide, the affemblies might be perfuaded, the people would be willing, and I verily believe, would be perfuaded to give amply and chearfully : So that it is not only neceffary to the gaining the end propofed, but alfo abfolutely neceffary to the gaining the means, that fome fuch general plan fhould be fixed.

In order to which, the following paper propofes to confider,

1ft, The fite of the country :

2dly, The interefts of the poffeffions and fettlements :
As the bafis of

3dly, The ftate of the fervice in America.

It becomes neceffary to a right underftanding of thefe propofed objects, to recur and run up to the firft principles on which they were founded,

not

not only becaufe the fubject is *new*, but becaufe
it has been mifconceived, and mifreprefented.

1*ft*, Prior to any obfervations on the fettlers
and fettlements, it will be neceffary to take fome
notice of the peculiar ftate and fite of the countries, in which they are fettled : For it is the fite
and circumftances (I mean thofe that are unchangeable) of a country, which give the cha-
racteriftic form to the ftate and nature of the
people who inhabit it.

The confideration of the continent of America
may be properly divided into two parts, from
the two very different and diftinct ideas that the
face of the country prefents, but more efpecially
from the two diftinct effects which muft neceffarily, and have actually arifen, from the two very
different forts of circumftances to be found in
each tract of country.

All the continent of North America, as far
as known to the Europeans, is to the weftward
of the endlefs mountains, a high level plane : All
to the fouth-eaft of thefe mountains, flopes away
fouth-eafterly down to the Atlantic Ocean. By
a level plane, I muft not be underftood, as if I
thought there were no hills, or vallies, or mountains in it ; but that the plane of a fection, parallel to the main face of the country, would be
nearly an horizontal plane, as the plane of a like
fection of this other part would be inclined to the
horizon, with a large flope to the Atlantic Ocean.
The line that divides thefe two tracts, that is
the fouth eaft edge of thefe planes, or the higheft

part

part of this slope, may in general be said, to run
from Onondaga, along the westernmost Allege-
hani ridge of the endless mountains, to Apa-
latche in the gulph of Mexico.

2*dly*, In considering first the main continent,
this high plain, it may be observed, with very
few exceptions in comparison to the whole, that
the multitude of waters found in it is properly
speaking but of two masses: The one composed
of the waters of the lakes and their suite, which
disembogue by the river St. Lawrence; the other
that multitude of waters which all lead into the
Missisippi, and from thence to the ocean; the
former into the gulph of St. Lawrence, the latter
into the gulph of Mexico.

There are in all the waters of Missisippi, at least
as far as we know, but two falls; the one at a
place called by the French St. Antoine, high up
on the west or main branch of Missisippi; the
other on the east branch called Ohio. Except
these, and the temporary rapidity arising from
the freshes of spring, and the rainy seasons; all
the waters of the Missisippi run to the ocean,
with a still, easy and gentle current.

As to all the waters of the five great lakes,
and the many large rivers that empty themselves
into them, the waters of the great Otawawa river, the waters of the lake Champlain, of Trois
Rivieres, and the many others that run into the
river St. Lawrence above Quebec, they may all
be considered in one mass, as a *stagnation* or lake
of a wilderness of waters, spreading over the
country

country by an infinite number and variety of branchings, bays, ftraits, &c. for although at particular places of their communications, and at the mouths of their ftreams, they feem to pour out fuch an immenfe ocean of waters, yet when they are all collected and affembled together, as at a general rendezvous where they all difembogue themfelves into the river St. Lawrence, the whole embouchure of this multitude of waters is not larger than the * Seine at Paris; the waters of each refpective mafs not only the leffer ftreams, but the main general body of each going through this continent in every courfe and direction, have, by their approach to each other, by their inter-locking with each other, by their communication to every quarter and in every direction, an alliance and unity, and form one mafs, a one whole.

Let any one raife in his mind the idea of fome low country incapable of being travelled, except on the roads, caufeways, dykes, &c. that have been made through it, and that thefe roads have throughout the whole country a communication which connects and forms them into a one fyftem of defign, a one whole: Such perfon will readily conceive how eafily and with what few numbers a General may take poffeffion and hold the com-

---

* About 12 French leagues above Quebec, over againft a place called la Loubiniere, the river St. Lawrence appears to be of a very confiderable bread'h; but when the tide, which runs up much higher than that place, has at its ebb entirely retired, that breadth which one would have judged to have been that of the St. Lawrence river, remains all dry, except a fmall channel in the middle, which does not appear to be much larger than the Seine at Paris, nor the waters of it that pafs there to have a greater current.

Y 3

mand

mand of this country; and when once poffeffed,
how eafily he may defend it, by fortifying with
redoubts and fuch works, the ftrong holds and
paffes in it, and at what an almoft infurmountable difadvantage any one who aims to recover
it muft act, even with twenty times the numbers.
If thefe roads and lines have thus a communication forming a one whole, they are the foundation or bafis of a command throughout the whole
country; and whoever becomes poffeffed of them
has the command of that country.

Now let any one behold and confider the continent of America, as it really is, a wildernefs of
woods and mountains, incapable of land carriage
in its prefent natural unwrought form, and not
even to be travelled on foot, unlefs by the good
will of the inhabitants, as fuch travelling in thofe
woods and mountains is perpetually and unavoidably liable to ambufcades, and to the having the
communication from the one part to the other cut
off. Let fuch perfon alfo know, that the waters for
thefe reafons have ever been the only roads that
the inhabitants ufe, and until art and force make
others, are the only roads that any body of people
can in general take. Compare this ftate of country with what is above defcribed, and the fame
conclufion, *mutatis mutandis,* will be found to be
derived from it.

Seeing this, as fact and experience fhews it to
be, let fuch perfon then recollect what is faid
above of the communication and alliance amongft
the feveral waters of this continent—of the unity,
one mafs, and one whole, which they form;—
he

he will fee in a ftrong light how the watry element claims and holds dominion over this extent
of land ; that the great lakes which lie upon its
bofom on one hand, and the great river Miffifippi and the multitude of waters which run into
it, form there a communication,—an alliance or
dominion of the watry element, that commands
throughout the whole ; that thefe great lakes appear to be *the throne*, the *centre of a dominion*,
whofe influence, by an infinite number of rivers,
creeks and ftreams, extends itfelf through all and
every part of the continent, fupported by the
communication of, and alliance with, the waters
of Miffifippi.

If we give attention to the nature of this country, and the one united command and dominion
which the waters hold throughout it, we fhall
not be furprized to find the French (though fo
few in number) in poffeffion of a power which
commands this country; nor on the other hand,
when we come to confider the nature of this
eaftern part of America, on which the Englifh
are fettled, if we give any degree of attention to
the facts, fhall we be furprifed to find them,
though fo numerous, to have fo little and languid
a power of command even within the country
where they are actually fettled. I fay a very ftrong
reafon for this fact arifes out of the different nature of the country, prior to any confideration of
the difference arifing from the nature of their government, and their method of taking poffeffion
of this country.

This

This country, by a communication of waters which are extended throughout, and by an alliance of all thefe into a one whole, is capable of being and is naturally a foundation of a one fyftem of command: Accordingly, fuch a fyftem would, and has actually taken root in it under the French. Their various *poffeffions* throughout this country have an order, a connection and communication, an unity, a fyftem, forming faft into a one government, as will be feen by and by: Whereas the Englifh fettlements have naturally, neither order, connection, communication, unity, nor fyftem. The waters of the tract on which the Englifh are fettled, are a number of rivers and bays, unconnected with, and independent of each other, either in intereft or natural communication within land. The vague diffipated random fettlements therefore, fcattered up and down thefe, will have no more communication or connection amongft themfelves, than there is amongft the various independent ftreams they are fettled upon.—— This country, inftead of being united and ftrengthened by the alliance of the waters which run in it, is divided by thefe feveral various ftreams, detached from, and independent of each other, into many feparate detached tracts, that do naturally and have actually become the foundation of as many feparate and independent interefts.

As far as the communion of the waters of any river, or the communion there may be between any two rivers extends, fo far extended will arife a communication of fyftem, of intereft and command; the fettlements therefore on this tract of country, would be naturally, as they are actually, divided

divided into numbers of little weak, unconnected, independent governments—Were I to point out the natural divifion of thefe tracts and interefts, it would point out a new divifion of the governments of the colonies, which is not the purport of this paper.——

The confideration of this country, fo far as it is connected with, or has any effect upon the interefts and politicks of the Englifh fettlements, prefents itfelf to view divided in two ideas. 1*ft*, The country between the fea and the mountains: 2*dly*, The mountains themfelves. The firft part is almoft throughout the whole capable of culture, and is entirely fettled: The fecond, a wildernefs, in which is found here and there in fmall portions, in comparifon of the whole, folitary detached fpots of ground fit for fettlements: the reft is nothing but cover for vermine and rapine, a den for wild beafts, and the more wild favages who wander in it.

Thus far of the fite of the country, as it becomes the foundation of a natural difference between the Englifh and French poffeffions in America. The next point that prefents itfelf to confideration is, the manner in which the Englifh and French have taken poffeffion of, and fettled in this country: And,

1*ft*, Of the French.

The French in their firft attempts to fettle themfelves in thefe parts, endeavoured to penetrate by force of arms, to fix their poffeffions by military

military expeditions, till through the perpetual and conſtant abortion of theſe meaſures, and the certain diſappointment and ſure loſs that attended them, they through a kind of deſpair gave over all thoughts of ſuch attempts.

Whether the dear-bought experience that they learnt from hence, or whether deſpair leaving their colony to make its own way, or whether rather, the right good ſenſe of Mr. Frontenac and Mr. Calliers led them to it, is neither eaſy nor material to determine; but ſo it was, they fell afterwards into that only path, in which the real ſpirit and nature of the ſervice led.

The native inhabitants (the Indians) of this country are all hunters; all the laws of nations they know or acknowledge, are the laws of ſporting, and the chief idea which they have of landed poſſeſſions, is that of a *hunt*. The French ſettlers of Canada univerſally commenced hunters, and ſo inſinuated themſelves into a connection with theſe natives.

While the French kept themſelves thus allied with the Indians as hunters, and communicated with them in, and ſtrictly maintained all the laws and rights of ſporting, the Indians did eaſily and readily admit them to a local landed poſſeſſion; a grant which rightly acquired and applied, they are always ready to make, as none of the rights or intereſts of their nation are hurt by it: While on the contrary, they experience and receive great uſe, benefit, and profit, from the commerce which the Europeans therein eſtabliſh with them.

Whereas

Whereas on the contrary, the Englifh with an infatiable thirft after landed poffeffions, have gotten deeds and other fraudulent pretences grounded on the abufe of treaties, and by thefe deeds claim poffeffion even to the exclufion of the Indians, not only from many parts of their hunting grounds, (which with them is a right of great confequence) but even from their houfe and home, as by particular inftances from one end of the continent to the other might be made appear. Upon thefe pretences they have driven the Indians off their lands.—The Indians unable to bear it any longer, told Sir William Johnfon, *that they believed foon they fhould not be able to hunt a bear into a hole in a tree, but fome Englifhman would claim a right to the property of it as being his tree:*—And whatever the great proprietors, patentees, and land jobbers, may affirm or affect to prove, or however angry they may be with thofe who declare this truth ; this is the *fole ground* of the lofs and alienation of the Indians from the Englifh intereft, and this is the ground the French work upon.—On the contrary, the French poffeffions interfere not with the Indians rights, but aid and affift their intereft, and become a means of their fupport.—This will more clearly and better appear, by a more minute and particular attention to the French meafures in thefe matters.

1*ft*, No Canadian is fuffered to trade with the Indians, but by licence from the government, and under fuch regulations as that licence ordains. The main police of which is this. The government divides the Indian countries into fo many hunts,

hunts, according as they are divided by the Indians themselves. To thefe feveral hunts there are licences refpectively adapted, with regulations refpecting the fpirit of the nation whofe hunt it is ; refpecting the commerce and intereft of that nation ; refpecting the nature of that hunt.

The Canadian having fuch licence, ought not to trade and hunt within the limits of fuch hunt, but according to the above regulations ; and he is hereby abfolutely excluded under fevere penalties to trade or hunt beyond thefe limits, on any account whatever.

It were needlefs to point out the many good and beneficial effects arifing from this police, which gave thus a right attention to the intereft of the Indians, which obferved the true fpirit of the alliance in putting the trade upon a fair foundation, and which maintained all the rights and laws of the hunt, that the Indians moft indifpenfably exact.

But the confequence of the moft important fervice which arifes out of this police, is a regular, definite, precife, affured knowledge of the country.

A man whofe intereft and commerce are circumfcribed within a certain department, will pry into, and fcrutinize every hole and corner of that diftrict : When fuch a hunt is by thefe means as full of thefe coureurs des boix, as the commerce of it will bear, whoever applies for a licence muft betake himfelf to fome new tract or

Hunt,

hunt, by which again begins an opening to new
difcoveries and frefh acquifitions.

When the French have by thefe means eftablifhed a hunt, a commerce, alliance and influence amongft the Indians of that tract, and have
by thefe means acquired a knowledge of all the
waters, paffes, portages, and pofts, that may
hold the command of that country, in fhort, *a
military knowledge* of the ground, then, and not
before, *they afk and obtain leave* of the Indians to
ftrengthen their trading houfe, to make it a fort,
to put a garrifon in it.

In this manner, by becoming hunters and creating alliances with the Indians as brother-fportf-
men, by founding that alliance upon, and maintaining it (according to the true fpirit of the Indian law of nations) in a right communication and
exercife of the true intereft of the hunt, they have
infinuated themfelves into an influence over the
Indians, have been admitted into a landed poffeffion, and by locating and fixing thofe poffeffions in alliance with, and by the friendly guidance
of the waters, whofe influence extends throughout
the whole, they are become poffeffed of a real
intereft in, and real command over the country.
They have thus throughout the country fixty or
feventy forts, and almoft as many fettlements,
which take the lead in the command of the country, *not even one of which forts, without the above
true fpirit of policy, could they fupport, with all the
expence and force of Canada :* Not all the power of
France could ; 'tis the Indian intereft alone, that
does maintain thefe pofts.

Having

Having thus got poffeffion in any certain tract, and having one principal fort, they get leave to build other trading houfes and entrepôts, at length to ftrengthen fuch, and in fine to take poffeffion of more and more advanced pofts, and to fortify and garrifon them, as little fubordinate forts under the command of the principal one.

Though thefe principal forts have fubordinate forts dependent on them, they are yet independent of each other, and only under the command of the governor general ; there is a routine of duty fettled for thefe, and the officers and commanders are removed to better and better commands : What the particulars of this are, and of the diftribution of the troops, I have not yet learned as to Canada ; but in general the prefent eftablifhment for this fervice is three thoufand men, of which there are generally two thoufand three or four hundred effective.

I have not been able to get an exact lift of the forts in Canada, but the following is fufficient to fketch out the manner in which they conduct this fervice.

It will be neceffary firft to defcribe the line which now divides Canada and Louifiana in the Illinois country. It begins from the Oubafch at the mouth of Vermillon river, thence to the poft called Le Rocher on the river Pæorias, and from thence to the peninfula formed at the confluence of Rocky river and the Miffifippi.

Forts

Forts in CANADA.

ST. FREDERICK, { St. John.
{ Carillon or Ticonderôga.

FRONTENAC, { L' Prefentation.
{ Les Coudres.
{ Quintez.

NIAGARA, { Torento.
{ One other.

MISSILIMAKINAC, and its Dependencies.

DU QUESNE, { Prefq' Ifle.
{ Riviere au Bœuf.
{ One other.

LE DETROIT, TWO { 'Twas propofed to the Court
{ in the year 1752, to erect
{ this into a Lieutenancy du
{ Roy.

The Poſt MIAMIS
and SIOUX.

NIPIGON, { Two or three.
{ One on the River Michi-
{ pocoton.
{ One other on the Long
{ River.

ST. JOSEPH, and one other
LE PETIT PARIS.
ALIBI.
SAGUENAY.
ST. JOHNS, in Nova-Scotia.
In all about fixty.

Moſt of theſe forts have fine fettlements round
them, and they do entirely fupport themfelves ;

it

it being ufual for both officers and men to defer
receiving their pay till the garrifon is relieved,
which is generally in fix years ; and fcarce any
thing is fent to thefe garrifons, but dry goods and
ammunition.

There is a fine fettlement at Detroit, of near
two hundred families ; a better ftill at St. Jofeph,
of above two hundred ; a fine one at St. Antoine, many fine ones about Petit Paris. But the
French government does not encourage thefe,
and has, by a pofitive ordonance, abfolutely forbid any one to make a fettlement without fpecial
licence ; which meafure they found neceffary to
take, in order to reftrain the Canadians from
totally abandoning Canada.

The eftablifhments, pofts, and fettlements of
Louifiana, are as follow :

Thirty feven companies of fifty men each, and
two Swiffe companies of feventy five men each.

1. The garrifon of New Orleans :

French   - 900 ⎱
Swiffe - -   75 ⎰   - - - - - - - 975

Out of which are garrifoned the outpofts
of Báliffe, and other fmall pofts.

Detour Anglois : The garrifon of this
confifts of four companies, which have their
tour of duty with the Mobile, Illinois, &c.

Mobile,

Brought over 975

Mobile, eight French companies, and one
    Swiffe - - - - - 475

" It is neceffary to fix this number here,
" on account of the proximity of Panfa-
" cola, on one part, and of the Englifh
" on the other; as alfo to influence the In-
" dians, as there are at our meetings and
" treaties, held here annually with the In-
" dians, fometimes 2, fometimes 3,000
" Indians prefent *."

Tombechbé, } One company each, a de-
Alibamous, } tachment from the garri-
             } fon of Mobile.

Four companies of this garrifon relieved
every year.

The Illinois, fix companies   =   =   300

The pofts were, { Cafkafias.
   in 1752,   { Fort de Chartres.
                { Village de St. Philip.
                { Praire de Rocher.
                { Cohôkias.
                { Village de St. Jeune
                {   Veuve.

The Akanfas, a lefs principal poft, one
    company - - - - 50
The Natches, one company - - - 50
                                   ‾‾‾‾
                                   1850

* Mr. Vaudreuil to the court.
                Z   The

Brought over 1850

The Nachitoches, one company   - · -   50
for the prefent on account of their not
being able to prevent defertions to the
Adages, a Spanifh poft within 7 leagues
of it.   They propofe, when they fhall
be able to fettle a cartel with the Spanifh
governor, and his Majefty approves of
it, to fix two companies there, it being
a frontier poft.

The Point Coupe, one company   -   -   50
The German Settlement, one company   -   50

Total   2,000

The fettlements of Louifiana in general, produce Indigo equal to the Guatimalo, which admit three cuttings or crops annually; rice in great
abundance, and cotton, but they find great difficulty
in cleanfing it from the feeds that accompany its
growth here ; tobacco, pitch, tar ; they have a
trade to their own iflands with flour, peas, beans,
falted or corned wild beef, and pork, hams of
hogs and bears, tallow, greafe, oil, hides, lumber, planks ; they have alfo myrtle wax, which
they export to France ; they do alfo, in fmall
quantities, manufacture the buffalo wool.   From
the abundance and natural growth of mulberry trees,
they have their thoughts turned to filk ; they have
iron, lead, copper, and coals in abundance ; befides
the fkins and coarfe furs, arifing from the Indian
trade and hunt ; they had, fo long ago as in the
year 1744, feveral veffels at their port, which
came from Florida and Havanna, and the bay of
Campeachy, to trade for boards, lumber, pitch,

7   dry

dry goods, and live ftock, to the value of 150,000
pieces of eight. They had a fettled treaty of
commerce with the Royal Company of Havanna,
by the terms of which, the French were to deliver them at Louifiana, pitch at two piaftres a barrel, tar at three piaftres a barrel, boards at two
reals each. Their fettlements towards the mouth
of Miffifippi, are almoft deferted and ruined, the
fettlers not being able to fupport the expence of
banking againft the inundations of the fea and
land floods. Mr. Vaudreuil fays, in a letter to
the court, September 28, 1752, he thinks it
would be much better, to defer for fome years
attempting fettlements here, till the ground be
more raifed and elevated by the accretion of foil,
as it has been three feet in fifteen years laft paft.

I mention nothing here of the pofts of New
Orleans, Detour Anglois, and Balife, nor of
Mobile; becaufe, being marine pofts, the confideration of them does not come within the
fcope of this paper. I will obferve, that they require our particular attention : They are become
the ports to which all the men and ftores, with
which the country of the Ohio is furnifhed, are
fent annually and conftantly ; as from New Orleans to this country, the way is much fhorter
than through Canada, the diftance being at the
moft, where they are obliged at low water to
follow all the windings of the river, not more
than 340 French leagues; but at the ufual times
that they fend their convoys, not more than 300,
and to which they can go up with decked floops,
nine or ten months in the year. The trade comes
down from the Illinois, about the latter end of

De-

December, and goes up towards the latter end of January, or the beginning of February.

I shall describe the post of Tombechbé, from Mr. Vaudreuil's letters.

April 20, 1751. This post restrains the Alibamóus, Talapouches, Abekas, and Cowêtas, preserves the communication between the waters of Mobile, Alibamous river and the Missisippi; 'tis necessary for us in order to keep up amongst the Chactaws, the spirit of warring against the Chickasaws; tis also necessary as an entrepôt in our expeditions against the Chickasaws and English. From hence we can go within seven or eight leagues of the villages of the Chickasaws with periaugues, by the river Tombechbé, over which, seven or eight leagues of land carriage, we can easily go by land, and carry cohorns and light field pieces: from hence also it is, that we must send out our parties against the Carolinians; yet this fort being a heavy expence, and with great difficulty supplied, and being so situated as to be of no use to hinder the English from going to the Chactaws, when that nation is inclined to receive them, as they may conduct their convoys a little above, or a little below the fort, without our being able to oppose them. This being the case, were the Chactaws entirely secured in our interest, were the Chickasaws destroyed, and had the English lost and given up all hopes of strengthening themselves in that quarter, as we hope to effect, I then think it would be no longer necessary to keep up this post; yet till this be effected, it must be kept up, and more especially as by sup-

pressing

January 6, 1746.

October 28, 1746.

March 6, 1749.

September 24, 1751.

January 12, 1751.

preffing it now, the Chactaws would think themfelves abandoned. This poft, as well as Aliba- May 30, 1751.
môus, fhould always be victualled for a year,
left by any revolution in Indian affairs, the road
to it fhould be obftructed.

As to the pofts in the Illinois country, I am
not able to defcribe them particularly ; but what
appears to be of more confequence, I collect from
Mr. Vaudreuil's letters, (from 1743, to 1752)
the general idea upon which the fortifying and
fecuring that country is founded.

The firft fort of their plan, in fortifying the July 18, 1743.
Illinois country, was on the peninfula, in lat. 41. Auguft 30,
30. This was a check upon, and barrier againft 1744.
the feveral nations of Sioux (not then in confederacy with them.) The next poft in this plan
was on the river Dorias, (fo called after the
junction of the Illinois river and Theakiki) which
would be of more efpecial ufe, if fituated on the
north of the lake on that river, whence the roads
divide, that lead to Maffilimakinac and St. Jofeph: This he defcribes as the key to the Illin is
country from Canada.

The next is the garrifoning and fortifying the
country, from the mouth of Miffouris to Kafkafias, where there are five pofts. Mr. Vaudreuil May 15,
thinks that Kafkafias is the principal, as it is the 1751.
pafs and inlet of the convoys of Louifiana, as alfo
of thofe of Canada, and of the traders and hunters
of the poft Detroit, and that of the greateft part
of the favage nations.

Z 3   There

There is alfo at this poft, a river where the
floops which come from New Orleans, may be
fafely laid up in winter.

Mr. M'Car-
tey to Mr.
Vaudruile,
January 20,
1752. But Mr. M'Carty, who was on the fpot, thinks
the environs of Chartres a far better fituation to
place this poft in, provided there were more inhabitants. He vifited fort Chartres, found it
very good, only wanting a few repairs, and
thinks it ought to be kept up.

The next poft (I take them in order of place,
not of time) which comes into this plan, is on
the Ohio, over againft the mouth of the Cherokee
November
4, 1745. river: This, he fays, would be the key of
the colony of Louifiana, would be a fufficient
Auguft 30,
1744.
May 15,
1751. barrier againft the Englifh, and reftrain their incroachments, and would obftruct their defigns in
alienating the Indians of the Ohio; it would reftrain the incurfions of the Cherokees, on the river Ouabafh, and river Miffifippi; it would alfo
check the Chichafaws, and would by thefe means
fecure the navigation of the Miffifippi, and the
November
4, 1745. communication with our pofts. He here expreffes the greateft uneafinefs, (as the French
court did not care to engage in the meafure at
that time) left the Englifh fhould build a fort
here, in which cafe, fays he, we muft give up
all communication with the Illinois; for the Englifh would become mafters of all the navigation
of that country.

April 8,
1752. Mr. Jonquiere propofes another fort at the
mouth of Rocky river, (this is in the government

ment of Canada) which, he says, would secure the tranquillity of the south of Canada. This, says Mr. Vaudreuil, together with the post of the Illinois, would restrain and become a barrier against the English, and cover all our Indian allies to the west, from our enemies, the English, the Cherokees, Catawbas, and others.

By these posts above, and the posts of the Miamis, this whole country is secured and fortified. This country, says Charlevoix, (in 1721) will become the granary of Louisiana, and in 1746 we find it actually becoming so; for in that year it sent down to New Orleans fifty ton of flour; in 1747, we find it well furnished with provisions, and having fine crops; and in a letter of Mr. Vaudreuil's 1748, we have an account of its produce and exports—flour, corn, bacon, hams, both of bears and hogs, corned pork and wild beef, myrtle wax, cotton, tallow, leather, tobacco, lead, copper, some small quantity of buffalo wool, venison, poultry, bearsgrease, oil, skins, and some coarse furs; and we find a regular communication settled with New Orleans, by convoys which come down annually the latter end of December, and return at latest by the middle of February.

Thus the French do not only *settle* the country, but also *take possession of it*; and by the form, site, and police of such possessions, (led on and established by the guidance of, and in alliance with the waters,) a natural foundation of a one command, have they acquired, and become possessed of *the command of this country*.

By

By thefe means, I repeat it, have they created an alliance, an intereft with all the Indians on the continent; by thefe means have they acquired an influence, a command throughout the country: They know too well the fpirit of Indian politicks, to affect a fuperiority, a government, over the Indians; yet they have in reality and truth of more folid effect, an influence, *an afcendency* *, in all the councils of all the Indians on the continent, and lead and direct their meafures, not even our own allies, the Five nations, excepted; unlefs in that remains of our intereft, which, partly the good effects of our trading houfe at Ofwego, and partly General Johnfon, has preferved to the Englifh, by the great efteem and high opinion the Indians have of his fpirit, truth, and honour.

* I mention nothing here of the influence of the Jefuit miffionaries, becaufe nothing is meant lefs than religion by them.

EAST.

In the French Interest.

Esquimaux.
St. John's.
Micmacs.
Penobscots.
Noridgwalks.
Abenakais.
St. Francis Indians.
Cachnewage.
Scaatecoke.
Ofwegatchie.

Senekes.
Onondagas.
Cayuges.
Oneides.
Tufkaroras.
} Supposed to be in the British Interest, but greatly debauched by the French.

Mohawks.
Mehikanders.
} Wholly in the British Interest.

Delawares.
Shawenese.
} Loft to the English, except a few on Sufquehanah.

Catawbas.
Cherokees.
Chickafaws.
} Supposed in the English Interest, but much debauched by the French.

WEST.

French

Sioux.
Nadonefferies.

Illinois.
Tawigtwaes.
Miamis.
Piankefshanaes.
Wawyactaes.
Picques.
Kafkufkies.
Cawetas.
Abekas.
Talaponches.
Alibamôus.
} The four Nations of the Creeks, as above.

NORTH.

Wholly French.

Affinipoeles.
Adirondacks.
Algonkins.
Outawawaes.
Chononderdes or Hurons.
Meffifagues.
} Skaniadere-roenues.

Outagamies.
Mifcontiris.
Sakis.
Chriftanaux.
Almipogins.
Nipifenes.

SOUTH.

Ofagaes.
Akanfaes.
Chactaws.
Panimaes.
Adages.
} Wholly French.

The English American provinces are as fine *settlements* as any in the world ; but can scarce be called *possessions*, because they are so settled, as to have no possession of the country : They are settled as farmers, millers, fishermen, upon bays and rivers, that have no communication or connection of interest, consequently, the settlers belonging to these rivers, bays, &c. have no natural connection.

But

But further, the settlers upon any one river or set of waters, which waters having a connection, might become the natural seat of a one interest, are yet so settled, that they have no connection nor union amongst each other, scarce of comunion, much less of defence.

Their settlements are vague without design, scattered, independent; they are so settled, that from their situation, 'tis not easy for them to unite in a system of mutual defence, nor does their interest lead them to such system, and even if both did, yet through the want of a *police* to form them into a community of alliance, unity, and activity amongst themselves, they are helpless and defenceless; and thus may the English be considered as having, for many hundred miles, a long *indefensible line of frontiers*, prior to the confideration of the nature of the enemy they may be engaged with.

3*dly*, The state of the service as arising from the above facts.

It appears from the first cast of the eye, that the English, without some *preparative measures*, will not be able to carry into execution any military expeditions against the French in the upper part of America; because from any post where they can form an army, and lay in all its stores, ammunition and provision, they must undertake for many hundred miles, a long, dangerous, and tiresome march, by roads the most harrassing, and of almost insuperable difficulty, through a wilderness of woods and mountains, without maga-

zines

zines of forage, &c. or any other affiftance; through a country liable to ambufcades, and all the ftrokes of war; through a country whereof the French are poffeffed of the command, or if through any part where their perfonal command does not actually exift, yet where Indians, (the moft dangerous enemies in fuch a wildernefs) where the Indians, I fay, are mafters, and poffeffed of every hold and pafs.

To put this matter in a ftill ftronger light, let any one confider, whence arifes the danger of marching through a fortified country; whence the danger of a general's leaving behind him any enemy's fort or garrifon, not taken.—It is that the enemy, who has poffeffion of thefe, has the command of the whole country, except the fole confined fpot, where the ftronger army is prefent, can forbid and reftrain the inhabitants from furnifhing you with fuch affiftance as the country is otherwife capable of affording; can, by failies from thefe pofts, cut off and intercept all your parties and convoys, all your intelligence; can cut off all communication with your magazines, and your own pofts; can perpetually harrafs and obftruct your march, and return within cover, before any fuperior party, fent out from the main body, can reach them; you are alfo always liable to furprize, even within your camp.

A march from any poft where the Englifh can *at prefent* form any army, and collect its ftores, ammunition, provifions, carriages, &c. through the country, as at this day above circumftanced,

is,

is, literally and precifely in its effect, the fame
thing as the march here defcribed.

While the Indians, whofe chief art of war is
that of forming ambufcades, who have acquired,
from practice and art, a peculiar method of fe-
cretly traverfing the woods and lying concealed in
them ;—while the Indians, whofe military fkill
of fighting either fingle or in parties amidft thefe
woods, renders the fituation to them equivalent
to fighting under cover ;—while the Indians thus
trained, and incredibly expert in the art, can at
any time fally out from the holds, faftneffes,
lurking places, and ambufhes, in which the
country abounds, (and all which they know)
nay, even from the cover of the woods, and drive
in all your fmall out parties, prevent fuch fo-
raging as the country will afford, intercept and
obftruct your convoys, cut off your communication of intelligence, provifions and fuccours,
and retire again within cover, out of danger of
any purfuit, and continue thus conftantly to harrafs, and, perhaps, furprize your army : while
they can do this, and (believe it) all this they
can do and will do, your army is to all intents
and purpofes, (as to the war with the Indians)
marching through a country of forts and for-
treffes. Let any one here, compare this ftate of
the cafe with the caufe and reafons of the failure
of the feveral military expeditions on this continent, and its truth will be ftill more evinced.

As then no general would think of making a
campaign in any country, to reach which, he
muft march through an enemy's fortified country,
                                    ....-hout

without fome *previous meafures* to maintain his
march and fecure his retreat through fuch : fo
here (I repeat it) there are fome *previous meafures neceffary.*

The *firft* of thefe meafures is, the fettling the
police of our alliance with the [Kenunctioni] or
Five-nation confederacy, upon a permanent, folid,
and effectual bafis, fo as to reftore and re-eftablifh
our intereft with them.

The *fecond* is, taking poffeffion of, and fortifying a fyftem of advanced pofts, entrepô's, *viz.*
magazines whereat to collect ftores and provifions, camps from whence (within a reafonable
diftance and by a practicable way) to make our
fortis.

Thirdly, The fecuring the dominion of lake
Ontario for the prefent, and laying a foundation
for the like dominion on lakes Erie, Huron, and
Michigan.

Let now any one confider the above ftating of
the form of the country that the Englifh inhabit, and in which the operations of our arms
muft lie : Let him raife in his mind ferioufly, the
precife idea of the native inhabitants who poffefs
this country, and of the kind of operations by
which we are, and fhall be attacked, and by
which we may be able to defend ourfelves : Let
any one, I fay, by a ferious attention to the
above facts, form to himfelf that idea, which an
actual and practical knowledge of the country
would give him : Let him then be told a melancholy

láncholy truth, that almoſt all thoſe Indians, whoſe friendſhip and alliance were once our beſt and ſecureſt barrier, are now by the French debauched and alienated from us, nay even turned againſt us, and become the ſervile inſtruments of the French robberies, maſſacres, and treacherous incroachments: Let then his eye be turned upon the ſtate of our back inhabitants, ſettled in a vague, unconnected, defenceleſs manner, up to the mountains, to the very mouth of the dens of theſe ſavages.——Any one attentively conſidering the above facts, will ſee the Engliſh colonies in not only a weak defenceleſs ſtate, but expoſed to, and almoſt at the mercy of a very powerful enemy: Conſidering this, and the above facts, he would ſee how ſuperficial, wild, and falſe an idea of the ſervice that is, which would create a barrier by a line of forts; a barrier that might as well pretend to cut off the bears, wolves, and foxes from coming within it, as the Indians; a barrier that would have no more effect than ſo many ſcarecrows, unleſs you could actually build another Chineſe wall, and ſo another, ſtill advancing your wall-fence, as you advanced your ſettlements; a barrier that would take more troops to man it, than the country incloſed within it would take people to cultivate it; a line of 13 or 14 hundred miles, that is at laſt no line at all; he would, I ſay, ſee this meaſure not only impracticable, but ineffectual: Nay, were it practicable, and could it take effect, yet the inſupportable expence of it, would render it impoſſible to be engaged in. Any one reaſoning on the ideas as above ſtated, and knowing them to be what they really are, *facts,* would turn his
thoughts

thoughts on thofe objects which experience, fact, and reafon point out to be one part of our barrier: Namely, a real and ftable alliance with the Indians, formed on fuch articles as fhould give us the fame kind of poffeffion and command in the Indian country, the fame influence in Indian affairs, as the French have. And,

Firft, As to that part of our barrier, and the fervice which is connected with, and depends on our alliance and intereft with the Kenunctioni, the confederacy of the Five nations, I can only repeat what I have faid formerly on this fubject.

* " The original natural form under which the Indian country lay being that of a foreft, ftocked not with fheep, or oxen, or horfes, not with beafts of labour and domeftic animals, but only with wild beafts and game, all that the country afforded for food or raiment muft be hunted for: The Indians, therefore, would conftantly be, as they were in fact, not land-workers, but hunters; not fettlers, but wanderers; they would therefore, confequently never have, as in fact they never had, any idea of property in land; they would confequently never have, as in fact they never had, any one common fixed intereft, any one communion of rights and actions, one civil union, and confequently not any government;

* This propofal, amongft others, was contained in a paper, delivered by the author of this memoir, to the commiffioners of all the Colonies, affembled at Albany in 1754. and tranfmitted to government with their minutes.

they

they know no fuch thing as an adminiftrative or executive power, properly fo called. They allow the authority of advice, a kind of legiflative authority, but there is no civil coercion; they never had any one collective, actuating power of the whole, nor any magiftrate or magiftrates to execute fuch power.

But the country now appearing under a very different form, and they, the Indians, being under very different circumftances, arifing from trade, treaties and war, begin to feel rather than fee, to find by experience rather than reafon, the neceffity of a civil union of power and action; and that thefe circumftances have in fact, for many years been formed, and have at length formed to them fuch a collective power: Thefe people are precifely in that point of circumftances, where a community, that was before only a community of fociety, is becoming that of government.

In all their actions, therefore, of late years, whether of treaty or war, they have recurred to *fome agent* to actuate this power: They are not only become capable of fuch a general leading, but their circumftances require it. The circumftances with which they are connected, had formed them into a ftate, but from the circumftances of the fociety under which they live, they can never have amongft themfelves a *ftateholder*; their circumftances require and look out for fome fuch; fome fuch they muft have, and if we do not find fuch for them, the French will, and are, actually attempting it. Further, as they know not, nor

acknow-

acknowledge any leading power, but that of authority, there can be no nominal, visible appointment of such leader; they will never appoint such within themselves, nor will they ever submit to any one appointed from without. This was the mistake of the governor of Canada, which had like to have lost him all the Cachnuagas two years ago.

Therefore such person or persons only, as can acquire, or actually are, in possession of this leading power, this authority with them, can be *this agent, this leader, this* STATEHOLDER."

For this manager, this stateholder, the government hath appointed Sir William Johnson; a person not only the proper one, but precisely the very and only person that the above circumstances and nature of things pointed out; the person whose knowledge of Indians, whose influence, by the opinion the Indians have of him, whose very uncommon zeal for the interest of his country, whose integrity and bravery, will, by such measures as the Indians can really and indeed trust in, if properly supported, restore this branch of our affairs to its salutary effect.

He has, in his papers, communicated by me, mentioned every thing necessary, as to the management of this Indian administration: I cannot but add, as a collateral measure, that would

* This paper was drawn up, in the year 1754, not only to suggest the necessity of the office, but to recommend Colonel, since Sir William Johnson, to be the officer. It succeeded accordingly.

strengthen

strengthen and finally confirm such our interest amongst the Indians, the making little settlements at Ofwego, Niarondaquat, and Niagara *, and at our other forts, by leave of the Indians.

Secondly, We should then, according to good faith and truth, leave the Indians in full and free poffeffion of their dwelling country and hunting grounds, which the English have, in the most so- lemn manner, confirmed to them by treaty, and of which, by the same treaty, we have under- taken the protection: We should guaranty and protect such to them, to their use, and also all their hunting-grounds.—This part of the general scheme also, is in some degree carried into exe- cution, by the instructions given by general Braddock to general Johnson, for his direction in his late treaty with the Indians; which instructions were, at the desire of general Braddock and go- vernor Shirley, drawn up by your memorialist, having been first proposed by him. This mea- sure will be absolutely necessary to preserve these Indians to our alliance, as may be seen in almost every treaty held with them since the first surren- der of those lands; it is also necessary to support ourselves against the western French Indians: This proposed measure will be so far from being an impediment or hurt to our interest, that the greatest advantages may be made of it, both in the means towards executing the general plan, and in the final execution of it. The uses that

* If we had done this, or would now do it, we need ne- ver suffer ourselves to think of abandoning our several distant posts, on account of the very enormous expence of maintain- ing them.

may

may be made of this meafure towards the executing of this plan, are, That while we are under-
taking the protection of the Indian country and
hunting grounds, we are actually becoming poffeffed of the command of the country. Of which,
in the whole, when we are poffeffed of the command and protection (by means of a very few
forts neceffary to be erected, which I do not here
mention) upon which, in part, according to the
propofed colonies and fettlements, when we are
fettled, the Indians will be preferved and protected to their fatisfaction, and yet cannot move
to war, nor even to hunt, nor fubfift, but as
they maintain their alliance with the Englifh;
and yet in conjunction with us, their whole force
by thefe means being become infinitely greater,
may be directed at any time into the heart of the
enemy's country.

Thirdly, As to the adminiftration of * Indian
affairs to the fouthward, the firft ftep neceffary to

* Thefe Indians are the Catawbaes, Cherokees, Chickafaws, and Creeks. The Creeks are in part debauched and
alienated from us by the French, and attend the French treaties conftantly at the Mobile, efpecially the Alibamôus,
Cowëtaes, Talapôuches, and Abekaes, and are in great meafure held under fubjection by the French forts at Alibamôus,
and tombeckbá.

The Chickafaws are greatly weakened, and almoft ruined
by the intrigues of the French within them, and by the wars
with the Chactaws, and other French Indians, being unfup-
ported by us.

The Cherokees and Catawbaes; but ill fupported by us,
are conftantly harraffed and warred upon by the Five Nations,
at the inftance of the French influence among that people.

A a 2   be

be taken is, that there be an abfolute ftop put to all provincial adminiftration ; that there be no more agents, commiffaries, or interpreters, appointed by, and acting under the private orders of a particular province or proprietories, from whence arifes interferings and confufion, and oppofition in our Indian affairs, always to the obftructing, often to the utter ruin, of the Britifh general intereft.

Inftead of thefe, there fhould be one only principal commiffary (who underftands the language and intereft, and is acquainted with the people of that nation) appointed feverally to each nation : This perfon fhould have under him feveral ftore-keepers and fmiths.

All thefe principal commiffaries fhould be fubordinate to a one general agent or fuperintendent *, who fhould be under the orders of the commander in chief only,—acting by his orders and inftructions, form'd on a *one general idea* of the Englifh and Indian intereft, of our alliance, and of the meafures to be conftantly and uniformly purfued.

As the being fupplied with European goods, is to the Indians the firft effential intereft of their politicks, is the fole and actual object of their alliance with us, and the only real and permanent motive of their attachment to us ; and as, according to the cuftom of thefe people, all pub-

---

* *N. B.* There has been one fince appointed, Mr. Stewart, a very active, intelligent, and able man.

lic

lic tranfactions are executed by exchange of prefents, all public friendſhip preferved and animated
by public hofpitality and liberality, the firſt
and fundamental object of the Engliſh meafures
ſhould be to provide for thefe, in a regular and
ſufficient manner. The being able to do this, is
our peculiar advantage and fuperiority over the
French in thefe affairs; their meafures are perpetually impeded and diſtreſſed, through their
being unable to do this; it is the only difficulty
that they have not furmounted, and cannot fur-
mount; it is this that makes our alliance, if we
did conduct it as we ought, the true and natural
intereſt, the true and natural politicks of the
Indians.

There ought therefore to be concluded with
thefe fouthern nations, a general alliance of
friendſhip and mutual defence and affiſtance,
founded on the Britiſh general intereſt, not any
provincial private one, upon a one general, uniform plan: The 1ſt article of which ſhould be,
To do juſtice to all their claims, to redrefs all
their wrongs.

2dly, To maintain with them all public hoſpi-
tality and friendſhip, by public, annual, and occafional prefents, by entertaining them, and by
all other ufual affiſtance, to eſtabliſh a fair and
juſt trade with them, and fettle ſtores within
their countries, or wherever is moſt convenient
for them, with a conſtant fupply of goods at a
fettled and cheaper rate than the French do fupply them.

3dly,

3*dly*, Mutually to affist each other againft all attempts of the French or their Indians, or any hoftile attempt whatfoever upon either; conftantly and faithfully to give all intelligence to each other, to mend their guns when they have occafion to go to war, to fupply them at fuch times with ammunition, and always to fend fome of our people along with them if they require it, except againft Indians in alliance with the Englifh; and whenever the Englifh call upon them, to go out with them to war, that the Englifh fupply fuch as want them, with arms, and *all* with provifions and ammunition, and defend and maintain their wives and children in the mean time.

This being done, a fund capable of anfwering the above engagements, and of conftantly and faithfully executing them, and alfo capable of fupporting an adminiftration of Indian affairs, that may work effectually to the preferving and maintaining the Britifh intereft in fuch meafures, fhould be fettled on a general and permanent foundation; which may be as follows:

That the feveral colonies who have hitherto conftantly raifed monies for Indian affairs, as a private provincial fervice, fhould for the future appropriate fuch monies to this general fund.

That fuch colonies as have never raifed any monies for thefe fervices, fhould, for the future, raife and appropriate to this fund, fuch fums under a quota, in proportion to the benefit received, or the harm avoided, by the barrier arifing from
this

this general alliance and adminiftration of Indian affairs; and it becomes worthy of confideration, whether the iflands in the Weft Indies, their intereft being infeparably connected with that of the continent, fhould not bear a certain proportion of taxes towards the charge of the war.

Matters within ourfelves being thus prepared and provided for :

The firft ftep of our meafure in this branch fhould be, eftablifhing, by the advice of people of the beft authorities, and moft knowledge of the affairs of each nation refpectively, at proper places, general magazines for this fervice, at the moft convenient entrepôts between *marine and inland navigation* of carriage, whence leffer ftores, refpectively fubordinate to thefe, might be beft fupplied within the Indian countries, or where is moft convenient for the Indians: As for inftance, one at Schenectady, or rather at Mount Johnfon;——one either at William's ferry on the Potomac, or at Fort Cumberland on Will's creek;——one other fomewhere on the Roanoak, or James river;——one other at fort Augufta, on the Savanah.

From thefe general magazines, the feveral national or tribe-ftores fhould be conftantly fupplied: Thefe ftores fhould be alfo public truckhoufes, and the ftore keeper be alfo a public truck mafter: Thefe to be fixed in each particular nation, in fuch places, and in fuch number as hath been ufual, or will be beft for the good of the fervice, at each of which there fhould alfo be

a fmith. The commiffary appointed to the affairs
of each nation, to command and fuperintend all
the ftore keepers, truck mafters, fmiths, and all
the ftores, and to be conftantly circuiting through
thefe, living always at fome one of them, and
attending refpectively at any of them, wherefoever he is commanded by the general agent, or
the good of the fervice requires: Alfo at all
times (unlefs in matters of a more public general
import, when the general agent is to attend) to
negotiate and tranfact all matters of bufinefs
which fuch nation may have to do with any other,
or with any colony, and to interpret between the
Indians of the nation he is appointed commiffary
to; and in general, within the powers of his inftructions, to do all thofe matters and things as
have ufually been done by provincial agents or
interpreters; that the ftore keepers and fmiths do
keep conftant journals, and make report to the
commiffary; that the commiffaries keep a regular journal of thefe reports, and of their own
tranfactions, and report to the general agent, and
he likewife to keep a journal and record, and report to the commander in chief.

The order then of the public prefents, the
public hofpitality and liberality being fettled,
according to the nature of thofe Indians and our
alliance with them:

The method and laws of the trade with them
being alfo fettled:

The next ftep to be obferved, I take entirely
from the French; and it is a meafure, according
to

to my idea, abfolutely neceffary. Obferving the want of fubordination among the Indians, the French make a number of fachems, to whom they give medals and appoint them to prefide a's chiefs, leaders, counfellors, fpeakers, &c. fome over eight, fome over ten villages, and fo on as their influence extends; being eafily, by prefents and money, poffeffed of thefe medal-chiefs, they thus eafily acquire a more uniform and ftable management of their Indians, than the Indians even know of amongft themfelves.

Let it be a ftanding inftruction, faithfully in all and every matter, to execute and fulfil, according to the true fpirit and intent, the above treaty and alliance, both as to the true intereft of the Indians, and as to the forming their alliance into a firm barrier againft the French, and enemy Indians.

The feveral people employed in Indian affairs to have conftantly in view, the fcheme *of uniting the feveral nations into a confederacy* like that of the Five Nations. In order to this, that there be found out and fixed upon fome one place in the back country, whereat the general agent fhould hold all his general treaties and parlies with thefe Indians, as the French do at the Mobil; which place, upon the fuccefs of this fcheme, to be the council place,—as Onondaga is to the Five Nations. Let any one confider how a little republick, formed by the Welinis on the river Ouäbafch, by fome free and independent Indians, did greatly embarafs, and had well nigh ruined the French affairs there.

This

This third branch (according to my idea of our barrier) being thus or in some such way provided for and administered;

The fourth, is, that of *a system of magazines and fortified camps* as entrepôts, whereat either to collect for defence, or from whence, within a reasonable distance and by a practicable way, to make our fortis. This branch is in part provided for ; for by removing and advancing these stores, and at length, when a proper place is found to fix them on, that would defend and command the country, getting leave to fortify them, and so erect them into forts, the Indians are defended, are at the same time held within proper terms, and we have within a friend's country, advanced posts or entrepôts,——that would answer all the purposes of defensive or offensive operations against the enemy ; and all that could be in this place said on that head, I have very minutely entered into in that part, where I explain the nature and state of the country and its inhabitants. I will only add their opinion of one post, which we once had, and of another that they feared we were about to make.

Mr. Vaudreuil, governor of Canada, in his letter to the court, May 1C, 1744, mentioning the leave which the English had got to build a fortified trading house at Ockfusques, amongst the Creeks, says, " If the measure of which this might be a foundation, should be properly carried into execution, it would oblige the French to retire from their fort of Alibamóus down to the Mobile."

And again in another letter, September 17, 1744, he mentions this ſtore-houſe having opened a traffick with the Chactaws,—yet this the Engliſh abandoned; and the French have now a fort on each main branch of the river Mobile; one at Tombechbé, and fort Touloufe at Alibamóus.

In another letter of November, 1748, he ſays, it would be very eaſy for the Engliſh, by means of the river Ohio, to form an entrepôt at Prudehomme to ſerve them as a retreat, having the nations of the Shawoänaes, Cherokees, and Chickaſaws, on their back to ſupport them. From this entrepôt, it would not be difficult for them to penetrate to the Ackanſas, Panis, Oſà-ges, Padouces, and Miſouris, and all the other nations of that country, if the poſts and ſettle-ments of the Illinois were broke up, as they would certainly be, did the Engliſh ſettle and fortify at Prudehomme; not only the inhabitants of the Illinois would be loſt to us, but alſo the inhabitants near New Orleans, would be ſo greatly diſtreſſed for the want of the ſuccours and proviſions of this country, the granary to it, by loſs of the benefit of the trade with that poſt, it would be difficult for them to ſubſiſt, it would be impoſſible to maintain the expence they muſt live at without it, and they muſt be obliged to abandon the colony: But ſhould not matters be ſo bad as this, yet, were the poſt of

the

the Illinois taken away, the colony would not be able to extend itfelf at furtheft, beyond the poft of the Natches, without a very ftrong garrifon at the poft of the Ackanfas, and at beft that poft would be too low to cover the hunting country.

When fuch forts are erected, the commanding officer at each fort fhould be a kind of comptroller on the commiffary or ftore keepers for that divifion, and fhould be furnifhed with provifions and neceffary ftores to make prefents to, and to entertain the Indians when they come to him, and to fupply their neceffities: He fhould, for this reafon, have a right to make an order on the magazine of his divifion for this purpofe.

Fifthly, In other parts of our frontier, that are not the immediate refidence and country of Indians, fome other fpecies of barrier fhould be thought of, of which nothing can be more effectual than a barrier colony; but even this cannot be carried, as is hereafter explained, into execution and effect, without this previous meafure of a fyftem of entrepôts in the country between us and the enemy. *The nature of this* fyftem, muft depend on the nature of the ground, which can only be determined by a particular view, and will then immediately be beft known to military men; but all mankind muft know that no body of men, whether as an army, or as an emigration of colonifts, can march from one country to another, through an inhofpitable wildernefs, without

maga-

magazines, nor with any fafety without pofts, communicating amongft each other by practicable roads, to which to retire in cafe of accidents, repulfe, or delay.

It is a fact which experience evinces the truth of, that we have always been able to outfettle the French, and have driven the Indians out of the country more by fettling than fighting ; and that wherever our fettlements have been wifely and completely made, the French neither by themfelves, nor their dogs of war, the Indians, have been able to remove us. It is upon this fact that I found the propriety of the meafure of fettling a barrier colony in thofe parts of our frontiers, *which are not the immediate refidence or hunting grounds of our Indians.* This is a meafure that will be effectual, and will not only in time pay its expence, but make as great returns as any of our prefent colonies do ; will give a ftrength and unity to our dominions in North America, and give us *poffeffion* of the country as well as *fettlements* in it. But above all this, the ftate and circumftances of our fettlements renders fuch a meafure not only proper and eligible, but abfolutely neceffary. The Englifh fettlements, as they are at prefent circumftanced, are abfolutely at a ftand ; they are fettled up to the mountains, and in the mountains there is no where together, land fufficient for a fettlement large enough to fubfift by itfelf and to defend itfelf, and preferve a communication with the prefent fettlements.

If

If the English would advance one step further, or cover themselves where they are, it must
be at once, by one large step over the mountains, with a numerous and military colony.
Where such should be settled, I do not now take
upon me to say; at present I shall only point out
the measure and the nature of it, by inserting
two schemes, one of Mr. Franklin's; the other
of your memorialist; and if I might indulge my-
self with scheming, I should imagine that two
such were sufficient, and only requisite and proper; one at the back of Virginia, filling up the
vacant space between the Five Nations and
southern confederacy, and connecting, into a
one system, our barrier: The other somewhere
in the Cohass on Connecticut river, or wherever
best adapted to cover the four New England
colonies. These, with the little settlements
mentioned above, in the Indian countries, compleats my idea of this branch.

The dominion then of the lakes being maintained
by a *British navy* of armed vessels, suited to the
nature of the service, according to a plan proposed by your memorialist, in June 1754, to the
commissioners met at Albany; which part of the
general frontier is, according to that proposal,
by order from England, and at the expence of
the crown, now carried into execution, compleats
the whole of my idea of this frontier.

These matters being thus proposed, I do not
at all enter into that point of their execution
which is the duty of the military, as it is a mat-

9   ter

ter in which the judgment of a civil man may not have its weight, nor into the manner of removing the French from their encroachments; yet I cannot but in general obferve, that as the prefent military object of his Majefty's fervice in this country, is either to erect forts, or to demolifh thofe erected by the French on his Majefty's lands; and as the way to all fuch lies through woods and wildernefles, there is a proper fphere of action peculiar to each, both for his Majefty's regular troops, and for the provincial troops of the country. The provincial forces of thefe countries, as irregulars or light troops, can, the beft of any forces in the world, efcort his Majefty's troops through thefe woods, to where their proper fcene of action lies; they can alfo in the fame manner hand up all their convoys, and would, I am perfuaded, fhould any occafion call for their fervice, act with bravery and fpirit: They are alfo fit for what may be properly called an expedition, fome excurfion a la brufque of ten or twenty days continuance: They fhould therefore be employed either as a covering army, or kept with the regular army, in companies of light infantry, for efcorts, fcouring and fcouting parties; while the regular troops, as a main body, marching by thefe means without being harraffed, fuftain them; while his Majefty's troops alone are fit for the various duties and fervices of a continued regular campaign, and for the fatigues and perfeverance, and fkill, neceffary in a fiege.

I muft

I muſt alſo obſerve, that this is not propoſed as à ſcheme to be executed all at once; but, as a general plan of operations, to be preſerved and attended to in the whole ; to which every part of our meaſures, as they ſhall ariſe into action and come upon the field, are to be referred ; to which, in all ſeaſons and at all occaſions, as from time to time ſuch ſhall offer or ſerve, our meaſures muſt be directed ; and to which every individual, and every part, muſt conſpire and co-operate to form a whole.

T. POWNALL.

S E C-

SECTION II.

THE ideas of the fervice contained in the paper above, lead by fair confequence to the following propofition, that after the Englifh had been repeatedly difappointed in their attempts to penetrate the country, by the way of Crown-point and lake Champlain, and had loft Ofwego and the command of the lake Ontario, confider-ing the reafon there was alfo to expect the de-fection of the Indians in confequence of it, there remained no other alternative, but either to make peace, *or to change the object of the war*, by making a direct attack, up the river St. Lawrence, upon Quebec itfelf, urged to a total deftruction of Ca-nada. The writer of thefe papers came over to England in the latter end of the year 1756, to propofe and ftate thefe meafures, nearly in the fame form as was afterwards repeated by the paper that follows, particularly marking the ne-ceffity of two fleets, and two armies: One army deftined for the attack; the other under orders to inveft Canada, by taking poft fomewhere between Albany and Montreal, fo as to cover the Englifh colonies: One fleet to efcort and convoy the army up the river St. Lawrence; and the other to cover and protect the fea-line of the colonies. The ob-ject was adopted. Why nothing was done in the year 1757, and why no more was done in the

B b   year

year 1758, than the taking of Louïsbourg, will be explained on a future occasion; the ideas contained in the following paper lead to the rest.——

IDEA of the SERVICE in AMERICA, for the year 1759.

BOSTON, December 5th, 1758.

IF the point difputed between us and the French, be determinately and precifely underftood, the manner of conducting it may be foon fixed: If we are ftill, as we were at the firft breaking out of the war, difputing about a boundary line, and for the poffeffion of fuch pofts, communications and paffes, as may be *a foundation* to our poffeffions *of a future dominion* in America, we are ftill engaged in a petty fkirmifhing war: from the ftate of which it was always plain, and experience now proves it, that we fhall ever be inferior, and beaten by the French; for the French have long ago, by a continued fyftem of meafures, been taking poffeffion of fuch pofts as hath given them that foundation: They have already eftablifhed that which we muft fight to eftablifh, inch by inch.

If we have changed the point, and brought it to its true iffue, its natural crifis, whether we, as provinces of Great Britain, or Canada as the province of France, fhall be fuperior in America; then the fervice to be done, is *a general invafion of of Canada, in conjunction with the European troops and fleet*; then is our natural strength employed, and we muft confequently be as naturally fupe-rior.

This being fixed, the next point is, where the real attack muft be made : the fame reafons that fhow the neceffity of fuch a general attack, fhow that it will *never effectually be carried on over land* ; for, if it could, Canada might as effectually be deftroyed, by the petty fkirmifhing war, for pofts, paffes, &c. as by a general invafion. But experience has now fhown, what reafon might have feen fome time ago, that as the ftate of the fervice is circumftanced between us and the French, that cannot be ; the poffeffion which the enemy has of the pofts of ftrength, the carrying places, paffes, water communications, and roads, by forts, redoubts, and their Indians, would render the paffage to Canada by land, the work of a campaign, even with fuccefs ; but finally alfo, the fuccefs doubtful. The road to Quebec, up St. Lawrence river, we poffefs by *the fuperiority of our marine navigation.* There is neither danger nor difficulty, nor do I fee how there can be any oppofition, to hinder the fleet getting up to the ifland of Orleans ; and a fupe-rior army in poffeffion of that, may, by proper meafures, command the reft of the way to Que-bec. If our army can once fet down before Quebec, it muft take it : If Quebec be taken, the capitulation may at leaft ftrip Canada of all the regulars, after which the inhabitants might poffibly be induced to furrender.

If

If this attack be determined, the fleet of tranſports will be eſcorted up the river by the frigates, bombs, and other ſmall veſſels of war: *But while our forces are all up the river, a very ſtrong ſquadron ſeems neceſſary to cover the maritime parts of our own colonies.*

I am told, that many French veſſels proceed early in ſpring, to the bay of Gaſpee, before the river St. Lawrence is navigable, and lie there till the river breaks up, then ſlip up without danger, when for ſome time it would be almoſt impoſſible to croſs the gulph; for as ſoon as the ice breaks up in the river, it is preſently clear; but the ice embayed in the gulph, ſwims about for a long time, and renders the navigation of that gulph extreamly dangerous, long after the river may be navigated with ſafety. If this fact be true, it ſeems neceſſary, that two or three of the ſhips of war ſhould proceed to Gaſpee, before the river St. Lawrence breaks up, in order to prevent any ſuccours being ſent up the river in ſpring.

But although this attempt on Quebec, by way of St. Lawrence river, may be the only real, and will be the only effectual attack on Canada; yet one other, if not two falſe attacks will be neceſſary, one by way of lake Champlain; the other by way of lake Ontario. That by way of lake Champlain may, as far as Crown-point, be offenſive, and ſhould then change into a defenſive meaſure, by taking ſtrong poſt there, with a garriſon which will effectually check the enemy at that gate of the country, and from whence

9   con-

continual fcouting parties, to harrafs the fettlements, and beat up the quarters of the enemy,
fhould be fent down the lake. As there are now
fo many regiments at Albany, Sckenectady, fort
Edward, and the pofts on the river, the taking
fort Carillon, at Ticonderôga, and of confequence fort St. Frederick at Crown-point, might
be effected with thefe, together with fuch provincials as fhall be thought neceffary, (if not in
winter) yet, before the time for embarking for
St. Lawrence river approaches: and this time
appears the more proper, as it may poffibly be
before the French can fufficiently relieve it. The
reafon that makes me think that this fhould be
attempted is, that the poffeffion of this poft is an
effectual invefting of Canada in that quarter:
The reafon why I think no more fhould be attempted is, that it *would prove unfuccefsful,*
and that all the labour and expence that is employed in the attempt, is loft as foon as it is
given over.

As we have now fo good an entrepôt towards
lake Ontario, as the fort at the Oneida carrying place, it is now in our power to attempt acting on that lake; the want of this rendered all
attempts there before, abortive and unfupport-
able. An appearance of an attack on Canada by
that way, muft greatly alarm the enemy at
Montreal; and, though I do verily believe we
fhall never fucceed to make an effectual irruption
that way, *until Quebec be taken,* yet as whatever
fhall be done on that lake towards fuch an attempt,
viz. taking poft at fome part on the lake, and
building veffels, will have a collateral effect; even

B b 3   fup-

fuppofing the firft to prove abortive, that will prove a moft effential point of fervice, namely, the gaining dominion of the navigation of the lake. So that fhould nothing elfe be done, yet what is done, and what is fpent, will not be thrown away; but remain a chief corner-ftone in the foundation of the Britifh dominion in America :—Befides, if we remain, during the campaign, fuperior in the lake, the enemies communication with their fouthern pofts is cut off, their connection with the Indians of the Five Nations interrupted; and we may, in the courfe of chances, poffibly take Niagara. This amphibious kind of fervice feems adapted to the provincials, efpecially thofe of New York and Rhode Ifland, accuftomed to privateering and batteauing : but thefe fhould be fupported by good garrifons of regulars, in fuch pofts as may be found neceffary to be taken at the entrepôt on the Oneida carrying place, and at the port it fhall be found neceffary to poffefs on the lake.

As to the number of regular troops neceffary for the attack on Quebec, I have not prefumed to fpeak, for I am no judge ; but a number of provincials will certainly be neceffary, and thefe fuch as are ufed to the water, and marine navigation, for fuch will be of the moft effential fervice in the paffage of the army from the lower end of the Ifle of Orleans to Quebec, where moft of the difficulty and danger will lie. Now for this fervice, none can be fo well adapted as the people of the province of Maffachufetts Bay, as they are all, in the fouthern parts, whalers and fifhermen. After the troops are landed near Quebec, numbers will
be

be wanted, such as are used to carrying heavy lumber and timber, &c. through the woods. Now for this service, none can be so well adapted as the inhabitants of New Hampshire, and the county of York, in the province of Massachusetts Bay, who are so perfectly accustomed to the masting service, that is, fetching the great masts down from the woods; besides, the people of Massachusetts in the counties of Hampshire, Worcester and York, are the best wood hunters in America; and would therefore, disposed in proper out-posts, be the best adapted to the keeping the camp before Quebec quiet from the enemies partizans and Indians, or perhaps in breaking up the enemies settlements in the country, while the regulars were taking their towns. For this purpose also, I should think, if about a hundred thorough wood hunters, properly officered, could be obtained in the county of York, a scout of such might make an attempt upon the settlements by way of Chaudier river. Such a scout, to the purposes of alarming and keeping the enemy in abeyance there, or perhaps breaking up the settlements, is practicable; and, I think, with early notice, such a scout may be obtained.

These are the services our people are fitted for; and therefore, as far as relate to the people of the province his Majesty has committed to my care, I can be positive, that if his Majesty's General would have a real and effectual service from them, they must be employed in such. Take those who live inland and carry them to sea, or those who have lived by the sea, and march them through the woods, they will be useless and sickly.

Employ

Employ each in their proper element; let thofe who are naturally connected with Hudfon's river, and acquainted with inland navigation, be employed up in the back country, and lakes to the weftward; and thofe who border on the fea, and are ufed to marine navigation, be employed in the fervice that goes by fea to the eaftward; and then for every ten men on paper, there will be ten men's real fervice.

I have in this paper confined my idea to the invafion of Canada, and the attacks on that country, and fo have faid nothing of that very neceffary fervice, the erecting a fort at Penobfcot river, which on different occafions I have before repeatedly expreffed.

I have confined my idea to Canada, and have therefore faid nothing of fort Du Quefne; but if I had extended my idea to that part, I fhould have endeavoured to confider how far, or not, it might be practicable to break up the enemies fettlements on the Ohio, and the Illinois country, founded on this opinion of Mr. Vaudreuil himfelf, in his letter to his court, when governor of Louifiana, November 1748.——" It would be very eafy
" for the Englifh, by means of the river Ohio,
" to form an entrepôt at Prudehomme, to ferve
" them as a retreat, having the nations of the
" Shawöanefe, Cherokees and Chickafaws on their
" back and to fupport them. From this entre-
" pôt it would not be difficult to penetrate to the
" Akanfaes, Panis, Ofagaes, Padouces, and
" Miffouris, and all the Ohio nations of that
" country, if the pofts and fettlements of the
" Illi-

" Illinois were broken up, as they would cer-
" tainly be, did the Englifh fettle and fortify
" at Prudehomme; not only the inhabitants of
" the Illinois would be loft to us, but alfo the
" inhabitants near New Orleans would be fo
" greatly diftreff d for want of the fuccours and
" provifions of this country, *the granary to it,*
" by the 'ofs of the trade with that poft, that it
" would be difficult for them to fubfift, it would
" be impoffible to maintain the expence they
" muft live at without it, and they muft be
" obliged to abandon the colony: But fhould
" not matters be fo bad as this, yet, were the
" pofts of the Illinois taken away, the colony
" would not be able to extend itfelf at furtheft
" beyond the poft of the Natches, without a
" very ftrong garrifon at the poft of Akanfaes,
" and at beft that poft would be too low to *cover*
" *the hunting ground.*"

I fhould have extended my idea to an attempt
by a Weft India fquadron, with troops raifed in
the iflands on Mobile, for nothing would more
embarrafs the enemy's Indian affairs in Louifiana,
than the taking this place, the grand rendezvous
at all their treaties. For they fupport a garrifon
here; amongft other reafons, for this alfo, (as
Mr. Vaudreuil, in one of his letters to the court,
fays) " to influence the Indians, as there are
" at our meetings and treaties, held here annu-
" ally with the Indians, fometimes 2, fometimes
" 3,000 Indians prefent."

I fhould alfo have recommended the taking
poft at Ockfufqué amongft the Creeks, becaufe,
fays

says Mr. Vaudreuil, " If the meafures of which
" this might be a foundation, fhould be properly
" carried into execution by the Englifh, it would
" oblige the French to retire from their fort at
" Alibamôus down to the Mobile."

T. POWNALL.

To the Right Honourable
Mr. Secretary Pitt.

The reader is here defired to refer to the events
of the year 1759 in America.

Quebec was taken by general Townfhend, the
moment that the army was enabled to fet down
before it, by the greatly hazarded, and glorioufly
fuccefsful ftroke of general Wolf.

The operations of the army under general
Amherft, could not, by all the fkill and determined perfeverance of that excellent officer, be
pufhed further than Crown-point, and there became defenfive by fortifying that point.

The operations up the Mohawks river, and
on lake Ontario, were carried juft to that effect
which opened the way for the next campaign,
1760, when general Amherft went that way to
take poffeffion of Canada.

Amidft thefe objects, I mention the taking poffeffion of the Penobfcot country, and the building
a fort there by the governor of the Maffachufetts
province, merely as it was propofed in the paper
above,

above, and as the propofal and execution of it was approved by the King and his minifters at that time.

The whole fleet was taken up the river St. Lawrence, where, as general Wolf exprefly declares, it was a part of the force leaft adapted to the object: The fea-line of the colonies was left uncovered and open. If the French had had fenfe enough to have fent two fhips of the line, with a frigate or two, and one or two bomb-ketches, they might have burnt Halifax, Bofton, New York, or Philadelphia, without interruption; or even if fuch meafure had not been carried to that degree of fuccefs, they might have raifed fuch an alarm as fhould have broken up fome of our active, offenfive operations, in order to come to the defence of this fea-line; and, perhaps, thus the whole of the operations of 1759 have been difconcerted and defeated. To enquire why this was done, would at this time become a mere criticifm, for as, by good luck, no fuch accident happened, it is right that fuccefs fhould juftify every meafure.

To give reafons why nothing was attempted towards the quarters of Louifiana at that time, will be the folution of fome future difcuffion.

S E C-

SECTION III.

The following inftructions, referr'd to in page 36, Appendix, drawn up by T. Pownall, and recommended to General Braddock, were, by that Officer, fent to Col. Johnson.

YOU are to produce to the Indians of the Six Nations, a deed which will be delivered to you by Col. Shirly, and in my name, to recite to them as follows.

Whereas it appears, by a treaty of the Five Nations, made at Albany on the nineteenth day of July 1701, with John Nanfan Efq; Lt. Governor of New York, That the faid Five Nations did put all their Beaver Hunt, which they won with the fword, then eighty years ago, *under the protection of the King of England,* to be guarantied to them and their ufe. And it alfo appearing, by a deed executed in the year 1726, between the Three Nations Cayouges, Senecaes, and Onondagaes, and the then Governor of New York, that the faid Three Nations did then furrender all the lands lying and being, fixty miles

miles diſtance, taken directly from the waters
into the country, beginning from a creek called
Canahoqué on the lake Oeſwego, extending
along the ſaid lake to the falls of O'niagära, and
along the lake Cataraquis to Sodons creek, and
from Sodons creek, to the hill called Tegechunckſerôde, and from thence to the creek
called Cayhunghâge, as is particularly deſcribed
in ſaid deed, including all the caſtles of the
aforeſaid Three Nations, with all the rivers,
creeks, and lakes within the ſaid limits, to *be
protected and defended* by the King of Great Britain his heirs and ſucceſſors for ever, to and for
the uſe of them the ſaid Indians, their heirs and
ſucceſſors for ever.

And it appearing that the French have, from
time to time, by fraud and violence, built ſtrong
forts within the limits of the ſaid lands, contrary
to the covenant-chain of the ſaid deed and treaties : You are in my name, to aſſure the ſaid
Nations, that I am come, by his Majeſty's order,
to deſtroy all the ſaid forts, and to build ſuch
others *as ſhall protect and ſecure* the ſaid lands to
them, their heirs and ſucceſſors for ever, according to the intent and ſpirit of the ſaid treaty, and
do therefore call upon them to take up the
hatchet, and come and take poſſeſſion of their
own lands.———

SECTION IV.

The following is referr'd to in page 47.

Pro Johanne Caboto &. filiis suis super terrâ
incognitâ investigandâ.

Rex omnibus, ad quos &c.   Salutem.

A.D. 1496.
A. 11. H. 7. NOTUM sit et manifestum, quod dedimus & concessimus, ac per præsentes
damus & concedimus, pro noblis & hæredibus
nostris, dilectis nobis Johanni Cabotto, civi Ve-
netiarum, ac Lodovico, Sebastiano, & Sancto,
filiis dicti Johannis, & eorum ac cujuslibet eorum
hæredibus & deputatis, plenam ac liberam aucto-
ritatem, facultatem & potestatem navigandi ad
omnes, partes, regiones, & sinus maris orien-
talis, occidentalis, & septentrionalis, sub ban-
neris, vexillis & insigniis nostris, cum quinque
nabibus five navigiis, cujuscumque portituræ
& qualitatis existant, & cum tot & tantis nautis
& hominibus, quot & quantis indictis navibus
secum ducere voluerint, *suis & eorum propriis
sumptibus & expensis*;

Ad

Ad inveniendum, difcooperiendum & invefti-
gandum quafcúmque infulas, patrias, regiones,
five provincias gentilium & infidelium, in qua-
cumque parte mundi pofitas, quæ Chriftianis
omnibus ante hæc tempora fuerunt incognitæ.

Conceffimus etiam eifdem & eorum cuilibet,
eorumque & cujuflibet eorum hæredibus & deputatis, ac *licentiam dedimus affigendi prædictas
banneras noftras & infignia in quacúmque villâ,
oppido, caftro, infulâ feu terrâ firmâ à fe noviter
inventis.*

Et quod prænominati Johannes & filii ejuf-
dem, feu hæredes & eorum deputati quafcúmque
hujufmodi. villas, caftra, oppida & infulas à fe
inventas, quæ fubjugari, occupari, & poffideri
poffint, fubjugare, occupare & poffidere valeant,
tanquam vafalli noftri, & gubernatores, loca-
tenentes & deputati eorumdem, dominium, titu-
lum & jurifdictionem eorumdem villarum,
caftrorum, oppidorum, infularum, ac terræ firmæ
fic inventarum, nobis acquirendo;

Ita tamen at ex omnibus fructubus, proficuis,
emolumentis, commodis, lucris & obventioni-
bus, ex hujus modi navigatione provenientibus,
præfati Johannes & filii, ac hæredes & eorum
deputati teneantur & fint obligati nobis, pro
omni viagio fuo, totiens quotiens ad portum
noftrum briftolliæ applicuerint, ad quem omnino
applicare teneantur, & fint aftricti, deductis
omnibus fumptibus & impenfis neceffariis per
eofdem factis, *quintam partem totius capitalis*
lucri

lucri fui facti five in mercibus five in pecuniis perfolvere;

Dantes nos & concedentes eifdem fuifque hæredibus & deputatis, ut ab omni folutione cuftumarum omnium & fingulorum bonorum ac mercium, quas fecum reportârint ab illis locis fic noviter inventis, liberi fint & immunes.

Et infuper dedimus & conceffimus eifdem ac fuis hæredibus & deputatis, quod terræ omnes firmæ, infulæ, villæ, oppida, caftra, & loca quæcúmque, a fe inventa, quotquot ab eis inveniri contigerit, non poffint ab aliis quibufvis noftris fubditis frequentari feu vifitari, abfque licentia prædictorum Johannis & ejus filiorum fuorumque deputatorum, fub pæna amiffionis tam navium five navigiorum, quam bonorum omnium quorumcumque ad ea loca fic inventa navigare præfumentium;

Volentes & ftictiffimè mandantes omnibus & fingulis noftris fubditis tam in terra quam in mare conftitutis, ut præfato Johanni & ejus filiis ac deputatis bonam affiftentiam faciant, & tam in armandis navibus feu navigiis, quam in provifione commeatûs & victualium pro fua pecunia emendorum, atque aliarum rerum fibi providendarum, fuos omnes favores & auxilia impartiantur.

In cujus &c.

Tefte rege weftmonafterium quinto die Martii,

Per ipfum Regem.

SECTION V.

This Commiffion—erecting and eftablifhing a board, for the purpofe of governing the Plantations, is referr'd to in page 62.

De Commiffione fpeciali domino archiepif-copo Cantuarienfi et aliis.

REX &c. reverendiffimo in Chrifto patri et A. D. 1636, perquam fideli confiliario noftro, Willielmo providentiâ divinâ Cantuarienfi archiepifcopo, totius anglie primati et metropolitano.

Ac perdilecto & perquam fideli confiliario noftro Thome domino Coventrie magni figilli noftri Anglie cuftodi.

Ac etiam reverendiffimo in Chrifto patri ac. perdilecto & perquam fideli confiliario noftro Ricardo providentiâ divinâ Eborum Archiepifcopo, Anglie primati & metropolitano.

Necnon reverendo in Chrifto patri & perdilecto & perquam fideli confiliario noftro, Willielmo

C c

lielmo episcopo London, summo thesaurario nostro Anglie;

Perdilectisque & perquam fidelibus consanguineis & consiliariis nostris,

Henrico comiti Manchester privati sigilli nostri custodi,

Thome Comiti Arundell & Surr', comiti marescallo Anglie;

Edwardo Comiti Dorchestrie, camerario perchariffime consortis nostre regine;

Ac perdilectis & fidelibus consiliariis nostris,

Francisco Domino Cottington, Cancellario & subthesaurario scaccarii nostri ac magistro Curie nostre Wardorum & Liberationum,

Thome Edmonds militi, thesaurario hospitii nostri,

Henrico Vane Militi Controrotulatori Hospitii Nostri,

Johanni Coke militi, secretariorum nostrorum primariorum uni, et

Francisco Windebanke militi, secretariorum nostrorum primariorum alteri, salutem.

Cum

Cùm ſubditorum noſtrorum et nuper patris noſtri domini Jacobi nuper regis anglie, memorie recolende, nonulli, regiâ licentiâ mediante, imperii noſtri territoria, non tantum dilatandi ſtudio, ſed precipuè ex pio & religioſo domini noſtri Jeſu Chriſti evangelium propagandi affectu & deſiderio, copioſas gentis Anglicane Colonias, ſumma induſtria & magnis expenſis in diverſas mundi plagas incultas penitus & incolis vacuas, vel a barbaris nullam divini numinis notitiam habentibus occupatas, deduci fecerunt; nos eorum tranquillitati proſpicere volentes gratioſè & quieti, veſtrumque fide, prudentiâ juſtitia, et provida circumſpectione plenius confidentes, conſtituimus vos predictos,

Archiepiſcopum Cantuarienſem, dominum cuſtodem magni ſigilli noſtri Anglie,

Eboracenſem archiepiſcopum, dominum theſaurarium noſtrum Anglie, dominum cuſtodem privati ſigilli noſtri, comitem mareſcallum Anglie,

Edwardum Comitem Dorcheſtrie, Franciſcum Dominum Cottington, Thomam Edmonds Militem, Henricum Vane Militem, Johannem Coke Militem, et Franciſcum Windebank Militem, & quoſlibet quinque vel plures veſtrum commiſſionarios noſtros & vobis & quibuſlibet quinque vel pluribus veſtrum damus & committimus poteſtatem ad regimen & tutamen dictarum coloniarum deductarum vel que gentis Anglicane inpoſterum fuerint in partibus hujuſmodi deducte, leges, conſtitutiones et ordinationes, ſeu

ad

ad publicum coloniarum illarum ftatum, feu ad
privatam, fingulorum utilitatem pertinentes,
eorumque terras, bona, debita & fucceffionem
in eifdem partibus concernentes, ac qualiter
invicem & erga principes exteros eorumque po-
pulum; nos etiam & fubditos noftros tam in
partibus exteris quibus cunque; quam in mari in
partes illas vel retrò navigando, fe gerant, vel
que ad fuftentationem cleri, regimen vel curam
animarum populi in partibus illis degentis, exer-
centis, congruas portiones in decimis, oblationi-
bus, aliifque proventibus defignando fpectant,
juxta fanas difcretiones veftras in politicis & civilibus, & habito confilio duorum vel trium epif-
coporum, quos ad' vos convocandos duxeritis
neceffarios in ecclefiafticis, & clero portiones de-
fignandi, condendi, faciendi, & edendi, ac in
legum, conftitutionum & ordinationum illarum
violatores, penas & mulctas, impofitionem, in-
carcerationem & aliam quamlibet coertionem,
etiam fi oporteat & delicti qualitas exigerit per
membri vel vite privationem inflingendas pro-
videre; cum poteftate etiam (noftro adhibito
affenfu) gubernatores & prefectos coloniarum
illarum a locis fuis amovere ex caufis que vobis
legitime vife fuerint aliofque eorum loco confti-
tuere, ac de eis rationem prefecture & regiminis
fuorum exigere, & quos culpabiles inveneritis vel a
loci privatione, mulcte impofitione de bonis
eorum in partibus illis levando, vel abdicatione
à provinciis illis quibus prefuerint, vel aliter fecundum quantitatem delicti caftigare, judicefque
& magiftratus politicos & civiles ad caufas civiles,
& cum poteftate & fub formâ, quâ vobis quinque vel pluribus veftrum videbitur expedire, ac
judices,

judices, magiftratus & dignitates ad caufas
ecclefiafticas, & fub poteftate & formâ que vobis
quinque vel pluribus veftrum epifcopis fuffra-
ganeais (archiepifcopo Cantuarienfi protempore
exiftenti confulto,) videbitur expedire, confti-
tuere & ordinare; curiafque, pretoria, & tri-
bunalia tam ecclefiaftica quam civilia, judiciorum
formas & procedendi modos in eifdem, & ab eis
appellandi in caufis & negotiis tam criminalibus
quam civilibus, perfonalibus, realibus & mixtis
pretoriis, feu de equo & bono, conftituendi, &
que crimina, delicta vel exceffus, contractus vel
injurias ad forum ecclefiafticum, et que ad Forum civile & pretorium fpectare debeant, deter-
minare;

Provifo tamen, quod leges, ordinationes, &
conftitutiones hujufmodi executioni non manden-
tur, quo ufque affenfus nofter eifdem adhibeatur
regius in fcriptis fub fignetto noftro fignatis, ad
minus & hujufmodi affenfu adhibito, eifque pub-
lice promulgatis in provinciis in quibus fint
exequende, leges, ordinationes, & conftitutiones
illas plenarie Juris firmitatem adipifci, & ab
omnibus quorum intereffe poterit inviolabiliter
obfervari, volumus & mandamus; liceat tamen
vobis quinque vel pluribus veftrum, ut predictum
eft, leges, conftitutiones & ordinationes fic eden-
das, licet promulgate fuerint, affenfu noftro
regio, mutare, revocare & abrogare, aliafque
novas in forma predicta de tempore in tempus
facere & edere, ut predictum eft, novifque
emergentibus malis vel periculis nova apponere
remedia, prout decet, toties quoties expediens
vobis videbitur et neceffarium;

Sciatis

Sciatis ulterius, quod conftituimus vos &
quoflibet quinque & plures veftrum, prefatos
Willielmum archiepifcopum Cantuarienfem,
Thomam : dominum Coventrie——, maghi
figilli noftri Anglie cuftodem. Ricardum Ebo-
racenfem archiepifcopum, dominum thefaura-
rium, Henricum comitem Manchefter, Thomam
comitem Arundelle & Sutrie, Edward comiterh
Dorcheftrie, Francifcum dominum Cottington,
· Thomam Edmonds militem, Henricum Vane
militem, Johannem Cooke militem, et Francifcum Windebanke militem, commiffionarios nof:
tros, ad audiendum & terminandum, juxta fanas
difcretiones veftras, omnimodas querelas five
contra colonias ipfas feu eorum prefectos vel
gubernatores ad inftantiam partis gravate, vel
ad delationem de injuriis hinc vel inde inter
ipfas vel ipforum membra aliquod illatis moven-
das, partifque coram vobis evocare, ac partibus
vel ecrum procuratoribus hinc et inde auditis,
plenum juftirie complementum exhibendum;
d 3 vobis & quibuflibet quinque vel pluribus
t .trum, quod fi quas coloniarum predictarum
vel aliquem prefectorum eorum ditiones alienas
injufte poffidendo, vel ufurpando vel invicem
feipfos gravando, feu nobis rebelles a fide noftra
fubtrahendo, aut mandatis noftris non obtempe-
rantes inveneritis, nobis prius in hac parte con-
fultis, colonias hujufmodi & prefectos eorum ob
caufas predictas, vel aliis juftis de caufis, vel in
Angliam redire, aut ad alia loca defignanda
diver'ere mandare, prout fecundum fanas difcretiones veftras equum, juftum vel neceffarium
videbitur;

Damus